IGOR SIKORSKY
The Russian Years

IGOR SIKORSKY

THE RUSSIAN YEARS

K. N. FINNE

Carl J. Bobrow and Von Hardesty, Editors

Translated and adapted by Von Hardesty

Airlife

England

Copyright © 1987 by
Carl J. Bobrow

03327546

ISBN 1 85310 012 9

British Library Cataloguing-in-
Publication information available

Published 1988 by Airlife Publishing
Ltd. with the permission of the
Smithsonian Institution

First published in the United States of
America in 1987 by the
Smithsonian Institution Press

Printed in the United States of America

Airlife Publishing Ltd.
7 St. John's Hill, Shrewsbury, England

∞ The paper used in this publication
meets the minimum requirements of the
American National Standard for
Permanence of Paper for Printed Library
Materials Z39.48–1984.

CONTENTS

PREFACE

In October 1983 the National Air and Space Museum conducted a six-day seminar on World War I aviation. Nearly every significant aspect of World War I aviation was covered by some of the finest scholars in the area of military aviation. Von Hardesty, curator in the Department of Aeronautics, gave a lecture on the Imperial Russian Air Force. His lecture covered the remarkable history of the Il'ya Muromets, the world's first four-engine bomber, designed by Igor Sikorsky, and the men who flew it. My interest in Russian aviation and the Il'ya Muromets had been sparked, and afterward I spoke at length with Dr. Hardesty. He supplied me with some articles on the Murometsy (plural of Il'ya Muromets), which were in turn a catalyst to further study.

I soon discovered that little had been published in English on this subject. I searched the extensive library at the National Air and Space Museum (NASM), and with the help of Larry Wilson, a member of the library staff, I obtained a few more pieces of information. That same afternoon I visited the office of Peter Grosz, then the Verville Fellow at NASM, who advised me to get in touch with Harry Woodman in London, England. Mr. Woodman has emerged during the past decade as the leading authority on the Il'ya Muromets, and he provided me with a solid introduction to the Il'ya Muromets and its history.

My continued research on the Il'ya Muromets ran like a detective's inquiry, with many leads to follow, some rewarding, others just dead ends. The New York Public Library revealed some fascinating, hitherto forgotten data. Soon I had located most of the existing articles and contemporary accounts of Sikorsky's work in Russia, but these references alone did not provide a substantial amount of information or support serious research. In fact, they raised as many questions as they answered.

Then two significant breaks occurred. A translation by W. H. Schoenmaker of V. B. Shavrov's *Istoriya konstruktsii samoletov v SSSR* [History of aircraft design in the USSR], an authoritative reference work, became available in serial form through the Russian Aviation Research Group of Air-Britain. At the same time, I learned of the existence of K. N. Finne's *Russkiye vozdushnyye bogatyri I. I. Sikorskogo* [Russian air warriors of Igor Sikorsky], which had been published in Belgrade, Yugoslavia, in 1930. Finne, a flight surgeon attached to the squadron of Il'ya Muromets bombers in World War I, had written the most complete account of Sikorsky's unique aircraft during the war years.

These two sources provided detailed information on the Il'ya Muromets and the men associated with its development and combat history. I felt that the technical data contained in the Shavrov book could be supplemented by Finne's history of the Murometsy in World War I. Accordingly, I commissioned a translation of the Finne book for my personal study. This preliminary translation revealed a considerable amount of historical detail that was not contained in Igor Sikorsky's autobiography, *The Story of the Winged "S,"* or in other English-language accounts of Sikorsky's aviation career. After Von Hardesty, Harry Woodman, and I had carefully reviewed the Finne book, it was agreed that the publication of an English translation would make a substantial contribution to the historical literature on early flight.

The prospect of bringing Finne's *Russkiye vozdushnyye bogatyri I. I. Sikorskogo* to a Western audience also provided a way to shed light on the aviation scene in Imperial Russia and on Igor Sikorsky's work as a young aircraft designer in that historical setting. Russia on the eve of the 1917 Revolution was a complicated society in which most of the people were peasants and the sound of the airplane was little known. Yet this same society gave birth to the Il'ya Muromets and was the testing ground for Igor Sikorsky, truly one of the pioneering geniuses of aviation. It was also a time of heroic deeds by the men who flew in the Murometsy and a tragic era of war and revolution.

With Von Hardesty as coeditor, we launched a major undertaking to bring the Finne book out of historical obscurity. Together we began a thorough program of historical research on every aspect of the history of the Il'ya Muromets. The goal was to uncover Russian- and English-language textual materials, photographs, and any surviving bits of information among Russian émigrés and others who were associated with the Il'ya Muromets. We visited the Archives of the United Technologies Corporation and the New York Public Library and worked at NASM, where substantial archives of Russian aviation had been assembled. To my surprise, a large number of photographs, many of excellent quality, were available to us.

Harry Woodman assisted me by preparing detailed and precise sketches of the technical aspects of the Il'ya Muromets. His drawings of the Russkiy vityaz (the Grand), the prototype for the Murometsy series, and of the Il'ya Muromets represent the most accurate renderings of Sikorsky's historic four-engine aircraft. The same drawings, which represent years of research, have been incorporated into the present volume.

To supplement these important drawings we have assembled an appendix section, which includes significant data on all the Murometsy aircraft and the personnel of the *Eskadra vozdushnykh korablei (EVK)*, the Squadron of Flying Ships. We have also assembled a comprehensive bibliography on the subject of early Russian aviation, which contains information on the Il'ya Muromets and other related aspects of aviation history of that period. For its subject area, the bibliography is the most comprehensive and authoritative yet assembled, including both English and Russian language titles.

Von Hardesty assumed the formidable task of preparing a new English-language translation. Finne was not a professional historian or writer. His account was written from the perspective of a man who had participated in the events he described and knew at first hand many of the personalities associated with the Il'ya Muromets. Finne's writing style is often cumbersome and opaque, supplying detail on some topics and leaving other important themes undeveloped. His organization is roughly chronological, but his text is rambling at times. His viewpoint, as a Russian émigré, is frequently bitter and accusatory toward those who, in his opinion, betrayed Russia's national cause in World War I. Rather than publish a literal translation of Finne's original Russian narrative, we decided to present Finne's story in abbreviated and adapted form. Von Hardesty has labored to keep the narrative as close to the original as possible, but on occasion he has adapted certain portions for the sake of clarity. In addition, he has made an effort to eliminate redundant sections.

One problem was how best to describe the confusing sequence of the frequent changes of design and field modifications of Murometsy aircraft. We decided to adopt an abbreviated aircraft nomenclature for the narrative. When each variant of the Il'ya Muromets first appears in the narrative, a note is provided to establish a precise designation for reference and clarity. The appendix section contains a complete list of known Il'ya Muromets aircraft, together with their specifications.

Wherever they were appropriate, K. N. Finne's original notes have been included. Many obscure events, names, and unfamiliar terms punctuate Finne's narrative. As editors, Von Hardesty and I have added another set of notes, running parallel to Finne's notations, to define or amplify certain historical points.

The editorial notes, along with a selection of inserts, are designed to enhance the reader's understanding of the narrative. Finne included long combat reports in his original history. These cumbersome sections have been abbreviated to make the narrative readable and more coherent; the complete reports have been translated and placed in the appendix section.

For this translation we have used the transliteration system of the United States Board on Geographic Names (BGN), except for names that have acquired a familiar transliterated form—Sikorsky, for example, instead of Sikorskiy. All dates have been converted from the Julian calendar to the Gregorian. Before the 1917 Revolution, Russia followed the Julian calendar, which in the twentieth century was thirteen days behind the Gregorian or Western calendar. Similarly, we have converted the old Russian system of measurement of weights and distance to the metric system, giving approximate figures whenever they are needed.

I would like to thank a number of people who provided invaluable assistance in bringing the project to completion: my coeditor, Von Hardesty, for his collaboration and work as the translator; Alla Khramova, who provided the preliminary translation of the Finne text; Harry Woodman, whose knowledge of this subject could be published as a book; William T. Judkins, for all his help and for his persistent—and successful—endeavors to find the family of K. N. Finne; Olga Glass Finne, the widow of K. N. Finne, and her family, for their willingness to share historical memories and to allow us access to their late husband and father's papers; Harvey Lippincott and United Technologies Corporation, for allowing me access to the Sikorsky archives and for providing copies of photographs that appear in this work; Peter Grosz, an authority on Austro-Hungarian aviation during World War I, for his generous support of historic photographs and the insert on Paul Meyer; R. E. G. Davies, Curator of Air Transport, NASM, for the excellent maps he prepared for the book; and Ross Serafimovych, a volunteer at NASM, for his consultation with Von Hardesty on preparing the final translation of the book. I wish also to thank Judy Engelberg, another expert Russian-language specialist, for her commentary on the translated work.

The Aeronautics Department at NASM, in particular Anita Mason, provided sustained support for the project. Various curators, staff, interns, and volunteers—Jay Spenser, Efrain Ortiz, Trish Graboske, Mary Pavlovich, Sybil Descheemaeker, Tom Dietz, and Stephen Hardesty—lent a hand. Dale Hrabak and his staff in the photography lab at NASM supplied professional advice and work in preparing the many illustrations for the book. To Felix C. Lowe and the staff of the Smithsonian Institution Press, we owe a debt of gratitude for their patience and encouragement.

On a personal note I wish to thank certain people. Special thanks are owed to my wife, Corinne, who typed a good portion of the first manuscript, and to Norman Good and the rest of my family, all of whom were available when I needed their help. Finally, I am indebted to Konstantin Nikolayevich Finne, who had the presence of mind to put his recollections to paper half a century ago.

CARL J. BOBROW

INTRODUCTION

Igor Sikorsky, The Russian Years is a translation and adaptation of Konstantin Nikolayevich Finne's *Russkiye vozdusnyye bogatyri I. I. Sikorskogo* [Russian air warriors of Igor Sikorsky]. A personal friend and admirer of Sikorsky before the Revolution, Finne wrote this aviation classic in 1930, while living in exile in Yugoslavia. Finne had served as a flight surgeon with the *Eskadra vozdushnykh korablei* (EVK), or Squadron of Flying Ships, during World War I. The Imperial Russian Air Force had organized the EVK as a special squadron to fly Igor Sikorsky's Il'ya Muromets, the world's first four-engine bomber. Finne assumed the role of historian to record for posterity the achievements of Igor Sikorsky and his giant aircraft during the years before the Bolshevik Revolution. For Finne, Igor Sikorsky's design of the Il'ya Muromets represented a major aeronautical achievement. Finne knew at first hand the remarkable wartime feats of the Il'ya Muromets squadron during World War I and Sikorsky's larger contribution to Russian aviation. He believed fervently that the story of this remarkable designer and his aircraft should be told.

This English-language adaptation, *Igor Sikorsky, The Russian Years,* is an abbreviated version of Finne's 1930 work. Finne included in his original narrative a detailed history of Igor Sikorsky's design work in prerevolutionary Russia and a brief concluding segment on Sikorsky's first decade in America. Finne's treatment of the American years was little more than an addendum to his core history of the Il'ya Muromets. Rather than translate this supplementary portion of the Russian-language version, it was decided

Standing next to the IM-Kievskiy at Pskov in 1915 are (left to right) Deputy Commander Staff Captain A. V. Serednitskiy; Commander Staff Captain I. S. Bashko; Mechanic A. M. Lavrov; and Flight Doctor K. N. Finne. *Courtesy of the National Air and Space Museum*

to develop a new epilogue for the American years, one that would provide a unique and comprehensive perspective. To this end Sergei Sikorsky, the son of Igor Sikorsky, has written a special epilogue for *Igor Sikorsky, The Russian Years*. His historical overview serves the same purpose as Finne's supplementary chapter, but it has the added dimension of providing some new insights into Igor Sikorsky's life and the overarching themes that link his Russian and American years.

Conversely, *Igor Sikorsky, The Russian Years* represents a substantial amplification of Finne's original work. Through editorial notes, photographs, maps, bibliography, appendices, drawings by Harry Woodman, and Sergei Sikorsky's epilogue, the present English-language version expands Finne's coverage and documentation. The story of the Il'ya Muromets is complex, involving Igor Sikorsky as the central creative person, the rapid evolution of Sikorsky's original designs, and, as a historical backdrop, a nation caught up in war and revolution. Even Igor Sikorsky's own autobiography, *The Story of the Winged "S,"* published in 1938, provided only a sketchy picture of his career in Russia. In writing this autobiography, Sikorsky made extensive use of Finne's fundamental research and documentation but gave only minimal, if vital, commentary on the Il'ya Muromets aircraft. Through extensive research in Russian and surviving historical materials in the West, the editors of the present volume have been able to illuminate certain obscure aspects of the story and provide more authoritative data on the many variants of the Il'ya Muromets aircraft. *Igor Sikorsky, The Russian Years* embodies an amplification of Finne's original history as well as detailed documentation of Sikorsky's autobiographical work.

Westerners have for the most part defined Igor Sikorsky's aviation career by the substantial achievements of his American years: we know much more about Sikorsky's seaplanes and helicopters, for example, than we do about the Il'ya Muromets or the "S" series of aircraft. Sikorsky's seaplane designs of the 1920s and 1930s have been a familiar and crucial part of the Golden Age of flight. His prototype helicopter, the VS-300, is no less significant. Its appearance during the late 1930s opened the modern phase of the history of vertical flight. While those historical achievements are familiar, Sikorsky's Russian years have remained obscure, a sort of murky prelude to his creative American years. Sikorsky's friendship with Charles A. Lindbergh has remained vivid in our historical consciousness, while Sikorsky's earlier association with Nicholas II and the Russian aeronautical community have passed into historical obscurity.

K. N. Finne wrote his history at a time when Igor Sikorsky had emerged as an important figure in American aviation. Finne's goal, however, was to preserve the prerevolutionary legacy of Sikorsky's technological attainment for the scattered Russian émigré community. For the modern reader seeking a full account of Sikorsky's life and achievements, Finne has supplied an important link to these obscure Russian years—which, it should be noted, anticipated in many ways the boldness and innovation that characterized Sikorsky's work in America. It should also be observed that the Russian phase possessed its own unique accomplishments and style and is a story chronicled from Finne's own historical perspective. In retrospect, Sikorsky's design work in Russia—from his early work on helicopters, through the "S" series of single-engine monoplanes and biplanes, to the building of the Il'ya Muromets bombers—was eclectic. Finne reminds us that these aircraft made a vital contribution to Russia's rich prerevolutionary aeronautical tradition. By implication, Sikorsky's aircraft designs influenced the subsequent evolution of the Soviet aviation community in many profound and subtle ways: the Il'ya Muromets anticipated the Maxim Gorkiy—the Soviet Union's giant eight-engine aircraft of the 1930s.

As a Russian émigré living in Belgrade during the interwar years, Finne realized that the fateful course of war and revolution had cast the Il'ya Muromets, Russia's unique aircraft, into historical limbo. The Bolsheviks, who had triumphed in the revolutionary struggle, displayed little inclination to exhibit, or even to acknowledge, the technological achievements of the late Tsarist period. In Soviet histories, where propaganda interests often gain ascendancy over the reflex for historical objectivity, the old regime under Nicholas II was consistently portrayed as backward and technologically inferior. Official Soviet historiography, then and now, has portrayed Communism as the pathway for Russia to achieve modernity. The year 1917 marked for the new Communist regime not merely a political dividing line but also a technological benchmark; technological leadership fell under the aegis of the Communist party, and its achievements were deemed modern and forward looking in contrast to the Tsarist age, now defined as historically backward.

Igor Sikorsky had embraced life in exile rather than the Bolshevik Revolution; that fateful decision brought in its wake the official indifference of the new Communist regime to his aeronautical work. The silence on Sikorsky's Russian career endured for several decades. For those Russians who knew Sikorsky and took enormous pride in his achievements, there was a keen sense of anger at his being dropped, as it were, down a memory hole, to be forgotten by his own country and to be unknown to the rest of the world. Finne regarded this lacuna of information on Sikorsky's career as a cruel twist of history and endeavored in his own zealous fashion to redress the balance. He wrote in Russian and sought to broaden the awareness of the Russian émigré community to the splendid accomplishments of Igor Sikorsky and the men who flew the Il'ya Muromets.

Born in 1877, K. N. Finne was graduated from the Military Medical Academy in 1903. That same year he entered military service, having been assigned as a doctor in an army hospital. In 1914 Finne entered service with the newly formed *Eskadra vozdushnykh korablei* (EVK). As flight surgeon for the EVK, Finne organized the medical facilities for the four detachments flying the Il'ya Muromets. While at the front, Finne met Olga Glass, the daughter of a commander of a Russian infantry division. She served as a nurse with the Finnish hospital at Pskov, one of the front-line medical facilities that dealt with the enormous problems of providing adequate care for Russia's many wounded and dying troops. They were married in January 1917, just on the eve of the Revolution.

Finne's personal experiences during the revolutionary period were fraught with danger and constant movement. He first saw the breakup of the EVK in 1917, as the western periphery of the former Russian Empire fell into chaos and political upheaval. Once the Bolsheviks had assumed power, Finne felt compelled to join the Whites, or counterrevolutionaries. His motives were identical to those that had sustained him throughout the war years: his profound sense of patriotism and duty. In 1918 he joined General

Staff Captain A. M. Kolyankovskiy prepared a handwritten account of the EVK (Squadron of Flying Ships) while in exile after the Bolshevik Revolution. A close friend of K. N. Finne, Kolyankovsky provided historical data for Finne's larger published work on Igor Sikorsky and the Il'ya Muromets. K. N. Finne took this photograph of Kolyankovskiy in July 1916. *Courtesy of the K. N. Finne family*

Anton Denikin's Army of South Russia, which struggled in vain during the Civil War to overthrow the Bolshevik regime. His brother was arrested by the Bolsheviks, sent to a camp, and later executed. He suffered the tragedy of losing contact with his family forever in the vortex of the Revolution and civil war. Finne finally escaped to Yugoslavia in 1920, where he occupied a number of posts as a doctor.

Moving with his family to Belgrade in 1926, Finne devoted himself increasingly to literary work. He completed his work on Igor Sikorsky in 1930, but Finne's corpus of writings includes many articles on Russian history, short stories, and polemical pieces related to Russian politics in the postrevolutionary period. Finne remained in Europe during World War II, another time of hardship and forced movement of his family. Finding himself among the many displaced persons of Europe, he moved with his wife and three children to New York in 1949. K. N. Finne died in 1957.

Finne left a rich legacy of materials on Russian military aviation of World War I. To reconstruct the history of the EVK, he relied in part on the memories of his fellow exiles who had served with the famed squadron of Murometsy. More than seventy of these giant four-engine aircraft were built by the Russians during the war. Murometsy served the dual role of bombers and reconnaissance aircraft. The Il'ya Muromets was the first large bomber mobilized for the air war in the east; it was deployed for active service long before the Germans launched their heavy bombers against the British.

Finne became a close friend of Sikorsky and M. V. Shidlovskiy, the commander of the EVK, during the turbulent war years. He saw at first hand the combat activity of this remarkable air unit. Finne regarded himself and those who served with the EVK as Russian patriots. He lamented the tragic defeats of Russia in World War I and saw in the Bolshevik triumph a cruel imposition of an alien ideology on the Russian people. In his coverage of Igor Sikorsky and of the EVK, Finne was unsparing in his denunciation of those who, in his opinion, had betrayed Russia. During the war Finne found Russians embracing ideas that were destructive to the political order and undermined the natural bravery of the Russian soldier. In a reading of Finne's history, it becomes quickly apparent that Finne was not a neutral observer or, as in the case of Igor Sikorsky in his autobiography, one willing to ignore many of the underlying political tensions that shaped the history of the EVK and of Russia at large. While Igor Sikorsky was on the whole detached from politics and somewhat philosophical about the fateful turn of events that brought war and revolution to Russia, his former flight surgeon and devoted friend was extremely vocal in his opposition to Communism. Finne was as much a polemicist as a historian.

When Finne approached the Russian Revolution, however, he was always thoughtful, seeking to identify the fundamental weaknesses in the old order that allowed the triumph of the Communists. On the surface, of course, many unpatriotic and revolutionary ideas gained sway in Russian society, in particular in the army. Not all these negative and unpatriotic notions, Finne believed, could be traced simply to the current revolutionary movements of the time. The problem for Finne went much deeper—into the very fabric of Russia's national self-image and approach to the West. Finne lamented the long-standing Russian tendency to ape European ways, no matter how foolish or destructive they might be to the national well-being. Toward that particularly unsavory element in the Russian experience, Finne expresses his intense anger. The tendency among Russians to praise as superior anything foreign in origin and to denounce anything indigenous in inspiration as inferior, as Finne saw it, had led to national suicide in World War I.

In Finne's judgment, Russia's profound sense of inferiority toward the West had extended beyond culture and politics to technology. Sikorsky's unique achievements passed unnoticed or unappreciated even in those years during which he worked in his native land. During the Great War the EVK had fought bravely against the central powers, only to be ignored by the established military authorities and, finally, to be consumed by the revolutionary upheaval and defeatism. Finne looked back on the war years with great bitterness. His retrospective hostility toward those who betrayed Russia, however, is equaled only by his undisguised pride in the great work of Sikorsky and the EVK.

Finne's historical instincts were correct: Sikorsky's aeronautical feats, in particular his contributions during the war years, deserve more global attention and careful historical reconstruction. The present translation is an attempt to rescue Finne's work from obscurity. The original Finne history, however, has exerted a limited but significant influence through the years. It was read by many in the Russian émigré community after 1930, it served as a basis for Igor Sikorsky's own autobiography, and even during the 1980s many Soviet historians have eagerly sought copies of it to fill in gaps in their own understanding of Russian aviation history. Now for the first time, Finne's history appears in the English language.

Igor Sikorsky, of course, occupies a central place in the Finne narrative. This son of a prominent medical doctor in Kiev played a vital and creative role in the development of Russian aviation before 1917. No Russian aircraft designer could match Sikorsky's creative design work or accomplishments as a flier. Sikorsky's family background, moreover, provided a rich environment for personal achievement. Ivan Sikorsky, the father of four children, was a prominent professor in Kiev and an important figure in the new field of psychology. He came from a modest and impoverished background; his father had been an Orthodox priest. Clerical families were typically poor, although many had a modicum of education that separated them from the Russian masses. As a youth, Ivan Sikorsky had displayed an intense interest in learning, had traveled to Kiev, where he became a medical doctor, and later wrote a number of books on psychology. During the years before the Revolution, Ivan Sikorsky emerged as a prominent Russian psychologist, having established professional contacts with Sigmund Freud and other members of the Vienna school. His book *Soul of a Child* was published in several languages, a major work on child psychology.

Igor Sikorsky, the youngest of the Sikorsky children, had two sisters, Helen and Olga, and a brother, Sergei. Igor Sikorsky became an avid reader of Jules Verne and, once he had read the sketchbooks of Leonardo da Vinci, became enthralled with the idea of flight. From Jules Verne he acquired the inspiration for a helicopter. All these formative influences prepared the young Sikorsky for the air age. A visit to France in 1907, after his graduation from the Naval Academy, prompted further interest in aviation and the decision to pursue engineering studies. His interests proved to be more practical than theoretical; for Sikorsky the main challenge was to design and fly airplanes, not to pursue aeronautical theory on an intellectual level only. Sikorsky made several efforts at designing a helicopter, then moved on to his "S" series of aircraft.

The "S" series proved highly successful. Sikorsky's S-6-B won the military aircraft design competition in 1912. The same year, Sikorsky established a number of world records. Those triumphs soon opened the door for further opportunities. In 1912 M. V. Shidlovskiy, then director of the Russo-Baltic Wagon Company, offered Sikorsky the position of chief designer at the firm's new aviation plant in St. Petersburg. Igor Sikorsky was able to persuade his patron that the Russo-Baltic plant should build the first four-engine airplane. Toward aviation Shidlovskiy proved to be as bold as he had been earlier as an industrial entrepreneur; he endorsed the project enthusiastically and gave Sikorsky the required funds to complete the project.

Throughout the winter of 1912–13, Sikorsky labored on the construction of the Russkiy vityaz, which later became known as the Grand. This four-engine airplane, the world's first, became a reality in 1913. The Grand would become, through its highly successful, if brief, flying career, the prototype of the Il'ya Muromets. Sikorsky's creation stood in the face of the prevailing prejudice of the time. Few aeronautical experts believed that a 9,000-pound airplane could fly. Some Western Europeans, always skeptical of Russian engineering skills, referred to Sikorsky's behemoth airplane as "the Petersburg Duck." They warned Sikorsky that multiengine aircraft were inherently unstable. Little was known about the aerodynamics of large aircraft at the time. The great fear was that if one of the engines broke down—a high probability—the aircraft would be thrown into a violent and uncontrollable yaw. Sikorsky, however, did not leap into multiengine designs without careful and systematic testing. The Grand went through several design configurations before Sikorsky installed four engines abreast on the leading edge of the lower wing. The worst fears were not realized. Sikorsky had designed the Grand with long and narrow wings—later to be called high aspect ratio—which gave his huge and underpowered flying ship the necessary margin to fly. Sikorsky would later attribute his success to a blend of intuition and a systematic program of testing and experimentation.

The Grand did fly in 1913, to the amazement of Sikorsky's critics and to the wild enthusiasm of the citizens of St. Petersburg. The Grand not only flew, it cruised above St. Petersburg and its environs for periods of more than six hours, establishing a number of new flight-duration records. At one point Sikorsky took sixteen people and one dog aloft. Even members of the Duma (the Russian parliament) clamored to get a ride on this marvel of the air.

Once they were on board, the Grand offered its passengers unique and comfortable quarters. The pilot flew the aircraft from an enclosed cabin. There were a forward balcony for observation, a passenger cabin with four seats, a comfortable sofa, a table, a washroom, and a closet. Large windows allowed passengers to observe the fine boulevards of St. Petersburg in luxury and comfort. At Krasnoye selo, Emperor Nicholas II himself inspected the unique flying ship. The Grand met an untimely end in 1913, when in a freak accident an engine from a passing airplane broke loose and cracked through one wing. No one was hurt, not even the pilot of the engineless airplane, but the world's first four-engine aircraft had been damaged beyond repair.

The success of the Grand paved the way for building in 1914 the Il'ya Muromets, named after a legendary Russian folk hero and warrior. Sikorsky incorporated into the Il'ya Muromets many design changes, which were derived from the practical tests he had made while flying the Grand. By the summer of 1914, Sikorsky was ready to attempt a long-distance flight of unparralleled scope and boldness, a sixteen-hundred-mile round-trip flight from St. Petersburg to Kiev. Finne gives us a description of this epic flight and suggests that the Il'ya Muromets in 1914 had demonstrated the potential of large aircraft to fly long distances. The military implications of Sikorsky's incredible flight from St. Petersburg to his hometown to Kiev were apparent in 1914, even as Europe went to war.

The actual role of the EVK in World War I was limited in scope, not unlike the air war itself on the Russian front between 1914 and 1917. The enormous length of the Russian front, the scattered arenas of conflict, the occasional and intense fighting, the primitive means of logistics—all made air operations difficult to organize and sustain. Both sides used the airplane, each year with increasing effectiveness, but the principal air operations of the Il'ya Muromets were aerial reconnaissance. There was no occasion or real means to conduct strategic bombing. But there was a perpetual need to know the enemy's movements along the vast sweep of the front that stretched from the Gulf of Finland to the Black Sea. Air-to-air combat and bombing raids became secondary to the primary goal of reconnaissance.

For these reasons, the Il'ya Muromets became a valuable tool for the Russian Army, a fact that Finne describes in detail. The Il'ya Muromets could probe deep into enemy-held territory, stay aloft for more than six hours, and provide a stable platform on which to conduct aerial photography. When required, the Il'ya Muromets could bomb enemy positions, especially railway and communications centers.

The organization of the EVK in 1914 was a bold idea. The aggressive M. V. Shidlovskiy, who had been instrumental in building the Il'ya Muromets, served as the catalyst to organize the squadron. As a patriot, Shidlovskiy strongly urged the Ministry of War to exploit fully the unique aircraft that for a time Russia alone possessed—a long-range, four-engine bomber and reconnaissance aircraft. The reasons given to the Russian government were practical, but behind Shidlovskiy's proposal was the vision of the Il'ya Muromets as a unique and potentially devastating weapon of war.

The Russian Ministry of War, with the concurrence of Nicholas II, quickly approved the idea of the EVK. Although a former naval officer, Shidlovskiy accepted the rank of major general in the Russian Army and command of the squadron. Igor Sikorsky, at the time the sole test pilot for the two Murometsy that had been built, assumed responsibility for the training of pilots and specialists for the EVK. Finne regarded Sikorsky and Shidlovskiy—both prewar business associates—as important figures in making the Il'ya Muromets a great success.

The wartime organization of the EVK was hurried and accompanied by numerous difficulties, all of which Finne described in detail and with a certain degree of bitterness. In 1914 the Imperial Russian Air Force (IRAF) possessed around 250 military aircraft (all light airplanes, most of them of foreign design), two major flight schools (one at Gatchina, outside St. Petersburg, the other at Sevastopol in the Crimea), a small cadre of trained pilots, and a modest supply of spare parts and aero engines. The advent of the EVK, as a special unit, did not spark much enthusiasm within the IRAF.

Few officers in the air force saw much potential in the so-called heavy aircraft. Sikorsky's flight from St. Petersburg to Kiev on the eve of the war represented from their point of view an aerial feat, not a demonstration of military air power. From the point of view of the IRAF, there was no small problem either with Shidlovskiy's appointment as major general and the influence of civilians such as Igor Sikorsky.

To add to these problems, Shidlovskiy made the mistake of committing the two existing Murometsy to combat prematurely in 1914. The Ministry of War had ordered military versions of the Il'ya Muromets into production. At the Russo-Baltic branch plant in St. Petersburg (in 1914 renamed Petrograd) work began on the updated models. Sending the only two Murometsy aircraft available to the front courted disaster. Both airplanes were old and proved to be slow and incapable of maintaining the requisite altitude for combat. In the minds of many air force officers, the Murometsy were ill suited to military operations and prompted outcries that they be removed from front-line service.

Finne shows convincingly that the EVK overcame its failures quickly in 1914 and went on to become an effective squadron right up to the military collapse of 1917. Finne's account is punctuated with numerous asides in which he takes the critics of the EVK to task and describes the numerous challenges faced by the squadron, including Igor Sikorsky himself, who had gone to the front to train pilots to fly the Murometsy.

Finne also provides rare images of the air war in the east. His portrait of the EVK is clear and vivid. At the top, there was General Shidlovskiy serving as commander, only to die a tragic death at the hands of the Bolsheviks. Many Murometsy pilots—Gorshkov, Lavrov, Bashko, and others—performed their tasks with exemplary bravery. Behind the scenes but ever present as a technical adviser and test pilot, was the figure of Igor Sikorsky, who, as Finne demonstrates, made an enormous contribution to the war effort and the success of the EVK.

Being an army officer, Finne gives only slight attention to the more numerous enlisted men who served in the EVK as mechanics and support staff. Their contribution was vital, and only at the end of the story of the EVK, in 1917, does that group receive attention. One of Finne's interesting assertions is the virtual absence of friction between officers and enlisted men. The highly motivated EVK was one of last units of the Russian Army, it would appear, to feel the effects of the revolutionary ferment that brought disintegration of the Russian military and the downfall of the Romanovs.

The story of the EVK mirrors the larger circumstances of the Imperial Russian Air Force. Air units, as a rule, enjoyed high morale. This was true even in the desperate winter of 1916–17. The EVK, especially among its pilots and crews, approached the war with aggressiveness and discipline. Their demonstrated prowess against the enemy in air action, bombing raids, and aerial reconnaissance established a pattern of success, which was lacking in the Russian Army at large. The privations at the front, the logistics problems, and the rivalry with IRAF units were debilitating, but never in a terminal way as long as the EVK maintained its high morale.

Among all the difficulties faced by the EVK, the shortage of aero engines was the severest and most persistent. Before the war, Igor Sikorsky had used 100-horsepower, German-made Argus engines. Once the Il'ya Muromets was put into production, it became evident that a new source of aero propulsion would be required. Sikorsky and his technical staff tried a sequence of engines—Sunbeams, Renaults, and even R-BVZ types produced by the Russo-Baltic Wagon Company—but as the war progressed no satisfactory solution to this critical problem was ever found. All kinds of expedient field modifications and cannibalizations were made to keep the Murometsy in the air. This aspect of the story was not a mere sideshow; in many respects the fate of the EVK was shaped and conditioned by the work of engine mechanics.

Mirrored in the aero engine crisis, of course, was the reality of Russia's lack of preparedness for war. The Russian aviation industrial base, if modern for the time, was small and not geared for mass production. Other categories of war matériel reflected the same grim circumstances. There were acute shortages of guns, ammunition, transport, and equipment. The fact that the EVK maintained their more complex aircraft operational with engines, armament, bombs, and photographic equipment is a testament to the improvisational skill of its ground crews.

When Nicholas II abdicated, in March 1917, the EVK was still at the front and conducting air operations. As mutinies, desertions, and eventual disintegration overwhelmed the Russian Army, the EVK resisted the tide, holding itself together as the storms of revolution swept around the squadron on all sides. Finally, the EVK succumbed; Finne tells, with great bitterness, of the collapse of the squadron. To complete the story, Finne ends his original narrative on a more positive note, covering Igor Sikorsky's impressive new career building seaplanes in America. Other members of the EVK, as the author notes, did not enjoy such good fortune.

The story of the Il'ya Muromets and its four years of military activity in World War I occupies an important place in aviation history. For Igor Sikorsky, those years marked the formative stage of his impressive career in aviation. If Sikorsky left Russia in 1919, his influence lingered there into the Soviet period. Sikorsky had triggered an interest in large aircraft that would persist in the Soviet Union during the interwar years. When the Soviets built the huge eight-engine Maxim Gorkiy in the 1930s, they reflected a tradition of aircraft design that had originated with Igor Sikorsky.

In recent years, Soviet histories have begun to deal belatedly with Igor Sikorsky's accomplishments. P. D. Duz' in his *Istoriya vozdukhoplavaniya i aviatsiya v Rossii (Period do 1914)* [History of aeronautics and aviation in Russia before 1914] (Moscow, 1979), gave substantial coverage to Sikorsky's work in Russia. The famous Soviet aircraft designer, A. S. Yakovlev, in his *Samolety* [Airplanes] (Moscow, 1979), also gave sympathetic and accurate treatment to Sikorsky's contribution to aviation, even providing a photograph of the designer. The most authoritative history of Soviet aviation, V. B. Shavrov's *Istoriya konstruktsiy samoletov v SSSR, do 1938 g.* [History of aircraft design in the U.S.S.R. before 1938], 3d ed. (Moscow, 1985), placed Igor Sikorsky prominently among early Russian and Soviet aircraft designers. This same third edition, with its cover illustration of Sikorsky's Il'ya Muromets, is in sharp contrast to the early years, when Sikorsky himself, if not his aircraft, was given studied neglect.

Today in the Soviet Union there is a growing appreciation of the unique achievements of Igor Sikorsky. Like that of Feodor Dostoevsky, Sikorsky's world reputation compels respect and acknowledgment, even in the face of personal political attitudes that have run counter to the official ideology. His countrymen hold a thinly veiled pride in his impressive career and the fact that a native son has had such a profound effect on aviation technology. At the same time, Westerners acknowledge the need to understand more fully Sikorsky's shadowy Russian years. K. N. Finne provides in his illustrated history a rare view of Igor Sikorsky's first career in Russia in all its dramatic detail.

Von Hardesty, Ph.D.
National Air and Space Museum
Smithsonian Institution
Washington, D.C.
June 1987

PREFACE

Russkiye vozdushnyye bogatyri I. I. Sikorskogo [Russian air warriors of I. I. Sikorsky] is dedicated to the memory of those men who served and perished in performance of their duties as members of the Eskadra vozdushnykh korablei [Squadron of Flying Ships.]

Revolution brings in its wake civil war, terror, and mass emigration. All these tragedies have beset Russia. Beyond the fact that millions of Russians became victims of the bloodthirsty and insatiable God of Destruction, Russia has lost countless cultural treasures, including numerous historical materials that awaited expert evaluation. Those materials related to the 1914–18 war will be difficult—in some cases impossible—to restore; therefore, those who witnessed events at that time and endured the hard times should see to it that surviving materials are gathered, examined, and preserved for the future. It should be done while the participants and witnesses of that time are still alive. In addition, there is still the possibility of correcting the errors and inaccuracies that have arisen. The memoirs of individuals, as a rule, are subjective and reflect the character of their authors, but official documents may be flawed as well. Once these materials have been corrected and amended, they will become valuable for those who will restore the historical truth as it relates to those issues concerning Russian life in both prewar and wartime periods.

This essay is an attempt to compile all the information the present author, the former chief physician of the EVK (the squadron that flew Igor Sikorsky's Il'ya Muromets), was able to observe closely and objectively. It also represents the distinctive and creative thought of the many veterans of this air squadron. Without having a claim on the complete story, this information provides a clear picture of Igor Sikorsky's invention of the Il'ya Muromets and the reaction of Russian society to it.

The subject of this book is the Il'ya Muromets. This large multiengine aeroplane, designed by Igor Sikorsky, reflects the true national Russian spirit. The author extends his acknowledgment to all those individuals who helped him gather and publish these materials.

K. N. Finne
Belgrade
October 1929

Chapter One

THE EARLY YEARS

On May 26, 1913, at about 9:00 P.M., a large crowd gathered on a grass field adjacent to the Korpusnoi Aerodrome in St. Petersburg (renamed in 1914 Petrograd). They waited anxiously to witness an unusual spectacle—the first experimental flight of a large four-engine airplane known as Russkiy vityaz. Milling in the vast crowd eager to see a free show were other observers, more serious spectators, who wanted to see with their own eyes whether a huge, four-engine aeroplane, also known as the Grand, weighing more than four tons could actually take off.[1] Many aeronautical experts of that time considered the proposed flight impossible. If the Grand actually took off, some cynically commented, the aeroplane would crash the moment one of its engines stopped. Russians at the time accepted uncritically the opinion of foreigners on matters of aviation and often quoted them. During those days the phrase "foreigners are of the opinion" was a way of introducing "immutable truth." Many foreign aviation experts had earlier abandoned the idea of building a large flying machine. Therefore, the effort by Russians to fly such an aeroplane in the face of this highly regarded opinion was considered foolhardy, and the project was doomed in advance to failure.

Despite the predictions of both foreign and domestic experts, the Grand not only took off but also, after gaining altitude and circling several times over the field, landed smoothly near its hangar. This aerial spectacular prompted the stormy applause of the gathered spectators.

This successful flight of the Grand belongs in the annals of historic

One of the few photographs of the Grand in flight, taken in 1913. Note passenger in forward balcony. *Courtesy of the National Air and Space Museum*

Igor Sikorsky seated in the cockpit of the Grand, about 1913. *Courtesy of the Archives, United Technologies Corporation*

flights as a triumph of human ingenuity over nature. Russians received the news of this great flight with immense joy and satisfaction. The aerial feat had been achieved by one of our own, moreover, a young student at the St. Petersburg Polytechnical Institute, Igor Ivanovich Sikorsky.[2]

Igor Ivanovich Sikorsky was purely Russian in background. Born in 1889, he grew up in Kiev, where his father, Ivan Sikorsky, was professor of psychology at the Imperial University of St. Vladimir. Professor Sikorsky, the author of numerous scientific articles was well known at the time. The young Sikorsky received his secondary education at one of Kiev's classical secondary schools and later trained with the Naval Cadet Corps. After graduation, he entered the Kiev Polytechnical Institute. He also attended lectures in mathematics, chemistry, and shipbuilding in Paris. As a youth, Igor Sikorsky, by nature a quiet and curious child, demonstrated an aptitude for mechanics. At the Kiev Polytechnical Institute, he became clearly interested in aviation and the construction of a flying apparatus. In fact, he organized and headed a student aviation society. Sikorsky was studying at the St. Petersburg Polytechnical Institute at the time he built the Grand at the aviation branch factory of the Russo-Baltic Wagon Company.[3]

After this initial flight, the young pilot-designer began to fly the Grand over St. Petersburg and its suburbs almost every day. Many people clamored for a ride on one of these flights. Sikorsky made test flights as well to gauge the flying characteristics of his aeroplane. During one of these experimental flights, he shut off the engines in a certain sequence: first, he shut off one engine, then two at a time, then one from the left side and one from the right; finally he shut off both engines on the same side. During all these test flights, the Grand retained its stability, confirming the theory of the young inventor from Kiev that multiengine aeroplanes could fly with one or more engines shut off. Abroad, there was disbelief. Some foreigners had called Sikorsky's aeroplane "the Petersburg Duck."[4]

Flights by the Grand continued during the summer of 1913, and Sikorsky's aeroplane set several records. During this period, the Grand never broke down. It emerged as a unique flying machine—for both Russia and the world. The Grand could not help but attract attention to itself, including the keen interest of military circles.

In the summer of 1913, Emperor Nicholas II expressed his desire to see the Grand. For this Imperial inspection, Igor Sikorsky flew his flying ship to Krasnoye selo, landing on a military airfield near the Emperor's staff headquarters. His Majesty carefully and thoroughly examined the Grand, at one point ascending by a ladder to the front balcony of the aeroplane, where he inspected the cockpit. He also spoke amicably with Sikorsky, expressing to the young inventor his satisfaction with the remarkable flying ship. In memory of this occasion, the Emperor gave Igor Sikorsky a timepiece, which became a treasured gift for Sikorsky, a memento of the Emperor's gratitude and favor.

Emperor Nicholas II confers with Igor Sikorsky in the forward balcony of the Grand at Krasnoye selo in the summer of 1913. *Courtesy of the National Air and Space Museum*

Sikorsky's goal of building a flying machine went back to 1908, when he first attempted to build a helicopter. This helicopter, powered by a 25-horsepower engine, as an experiment, has historical interest as the basis for Sikorsky's subsequent work with helicopters. By 1910, he had built his second helicopter, which had two propellers that rotated in opposite directions. The underpowered craft could only take off without a pilot.[5]

The same year Sikorsky lost interest in helicopters and built his prototype biplane, the S-1, which was powered by a 15-horsepower engine. With his updated S-2, powered with a 25-horsepower engine, he managed to fly as high as 180 meters, setting a new Russian record. His S-3, powered with an Anzani 35-horsepower engine, was built at the end of 1910. Sikorsky's flight in the S-3 lasted for 59 seconds.

Igor Sikorsky with his helicopter no. 2. at Kiev in the spring of 1910. This early version of a helicopter was powered with an Anzani 25-horsepower engine.
Courtesy of the National Air and Space Museum

By 1911, the young inventor had built the S-4 and S-5 aeroplanes. Both types demonstrated good results. In a series of tests Sikorsky achieved an altitude of 500 meters and flights of up to an hour's duration.

At the end of 1911, Igor Sikorsky built his S-6 and in the spring of 1912 his improved S-6-A. At the controls of the S-6-A, Sikorsky won first prize in a competition sponsored by the Russian military.[6] Among the eleven flying machines that participated in the military competition, several were designed and manufactured by famous European aviation firms such as Farman, Nieuport, and Fokker. It should be noted that all Sikorsky's aircraft built before the S-6 were built by the young inventor in a barn on an estate in Kiev that belonged to his father. His subsequent designs, beginning with the S-7 model, were built in St. Petersburg in the aviation branch factory of

Igor Sikorsky at the controls of his BIS-1, powered by a 15-horsepower Anzani engine. This pusher-type biplane, built in 1910, never really flew, but it inaugurated Sikorsky's "S" series of aircraft. *Courtesy of the National Air and Space Museum*

The S-4 was powered by a 35-horsepower Anzani engine, pictured here at an aviation exhibit at Kiev in April 1911. *Courtesy of the Archives, United Technologies Corporation*

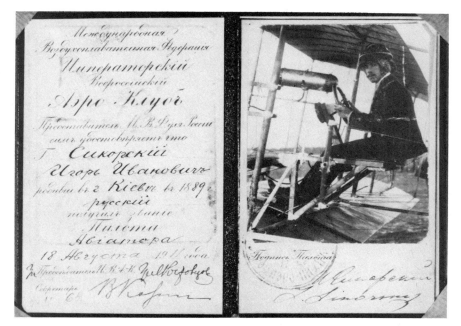

Igor Sikorsky's pilot licence, number 64, issued on August 18, 1911 (old style). The Imperial Russian Aero Club, as an affiliate of the International Federation of Aeronautics (IAF), supervised the licensing of aviators in Russia. The photograph shows Sikorsky at the controls of his S-5, in which he recorded a series of altitude, speed, and distance records. *Courtesy of the National Air and Space Museum*

Igor Sikorsky's S-6 at Kiev in December 1911. This same biplane was modified into the streamlined S-6-A, which won the Moscow aircraft design competition in 1912. *Courtesy of the National Air and Space Museum*

Lieutenant G. V. Yankovskiy, a military pilot who commanded the Il'ya Muromets III (IM-3) in 1916. *Courtesy of the National Air and Space Museum*

The S-7 two-seater monoplane was built in 1912 and was powered by a 70-horsepower Gnome engine. *Courtesy of the Archives, United Technologies Corporation*

the Russo-Baltic Wagon Company (R-BVZ). The R-BVZ had established the aviation branch with the aim of building Russian-designed aeroplanes. This offered Sikorsky a unique opportunity to express his creativity as an aircraft designer.

For the construction of his first flying machines, Sikorsky spent his own money, which was limited. It should be mentioned that his twenty-year-old sister, Olga Ivanovna, gave him financial and emotional support. Olga Ivanova later accompanied her brother to America, where she died on February 14, 1926. Those who knew Olga Ivanova in St. Petersburg remembered her as a genial hostess, one who received guests in the hangar of the aerodrome and served them tea in an improvised tea room.

Igor Sikorsky's coworkers at the Russo-Baltic Wagon Company were the pilots G. V. Yankovskiy and G. V. Alekhnovich, A. A. Serebrennikov, a student from the Polytechnical Institute who worked on aircraft calculations and design, and V. Panasiuk, a motor mechanic. Panasiuk later flew with Sikorsky on the epic flight from St. Petersburg to Kiev.[7]

The first airplane built by Sikorsky at the R-BVZ branch was an S-7 monoplane, which was later purchased by pilot Lerkhe.[8] The same factory at St. Petersburg manufactured the S-7, S-9, and S-10 aeroplanes, respectively, each equipped with Gnome rotary engines. The S-10 was equipped with floats and assigned to Russian naval aviation.

At the beginning of 1913, Igor Sikorsky designed and built the S-11 monoplane. Yankovskiy flew this monoplane to win second prize in a competition in St. Petersburg in the spring of that same year. Alekhnovich won the first prize flying a S-10. By the spring of 1914 Sikorsky had built the S-12 aeroplane, which was designed especially for loops. Flying this aeroplane, Yankovskiy won the first prize in aerobatics during an aviation week held at the Kolomyazhskiy hippodrome.[9] With the same S-12 Yankovskiy set a Russian altitude record of 3,900 meters.

Among Sikorsky's other small aeroplanes manufactured at the R-BVZ branch, his S-16 and S-20 biplanes are worth mentioning. (Only the S-7, S-11, and S-12 were monoplanes; the remainder of his single-engine aeroplanes were biplanes.) The S-16 had a Rhone 80-horsepower engine and a Gnome-mono-Soupappe 100-horsepower engine. Its speed was 140 kilometers an hour and it was lightweight, mobile, and easy to fly. In 1915 the S-16 was modified to become a fighter, by adding a machine gun that fired forward through the propellor. The S-20 was an improved version of the latter. Some of Sikorsky's small aeroplanes were accepted for service in the Russian Army during World War I. Despite their excellent flying characteristics, these aeroplanes were not broadly used, for reasons that will be discussed later. One important reason, of course, was the Russian fascination with all things foreign.

In addition to these aircraft, Igor Sikorsky designed and built an airsled, the first in the world, in 1912, at the R-BVZ Branch in St. Petersburg.

Many of Igor Sikorsky's designs were used by the Russians in World War I. The S-10 biplane, equipped with floats, was flown near the Baltic sea during 1913–15. *Courtesy of the National Air and Space Museum*

Igor Sikorsky reached the conclusion as early as 1911 that the future belonged not to small, single-engine aeroplanes, but to large aircraft with two or more engines. This belief stemmed from an unusual incident: a mosquito accidentally got into a carburetor jet and stopped the engine, nearly costing Sikorsky his life. Fortunately, Sikorsky avoided the danger by landing his aeroplane between some railroad cars and a wall. In Sikorsky's opinion, large multiengine aeroplanes possessed certain advantages over single-engine types, in particular their high load-carrying capacity and range. Large flying machines, moreover, would be operated not by one pilot, but by a crew, in the same manner as a ship at sea. Having not one, but several engines, the large aircraft were safer: if one engine stops, the rest continue working. In addition, pilots flying multiengine aeroplanes can choose more suitable places for landing in emergency situations.

Igor Sikorsky expressed his ideas about a large flying ship to Mikhail Vladimirovich Shidlovskiy, the chairman of the Russo-Baltic Wagon Company. Shidlovskiy's branch facility in St. Petersburg until that time had been

Igor Sikorsky's S-12a single-seat monoplane powered by an 80-horsepower Le Rhone engine. This photograph was taken at a forward airfield at the front about 1915. The two pilots at the left are dressed in the typical flight suits of the Imperial Russian Air Force. The presence of the binoculars and map suggest the reconnaissance role played by most single-engine aircraft at the beginning of World War I. *Courtesy of Sergei Sikorsky*

An airsled, designed and built by Igor Sikorsky at the Russo-Baltic Wagon Company (R-BVZ). Igor Sikorsky is seated at the wheel, and to his left is M. V. Shidlovskiy, director of the R-BVZ. *Courtesy of National Air Space Museum*

In 1913 Igor Sikorsky built his first flying ship, the Bolshoi Baltiiskiy [Great Baltic], later given the official name Russkiy vityaz [Russian Knight], which soon acquired the popular name "the Grand." This rare photograph shows the Grand being modified in the spring of 1913 with a second pair of Argus engines in tandem. *Courtesy of the Archives, United Technologies Corporation*

building only small, single-engine aircraft. Shidlovskiy familiarized himself with the details of Sikorsky's project, carefully examining the drawings and calculations for the large aeroplane. After listening attentively to the young inventor, Shidlovskiy accepted the proposed project with enthusiasm and gave directions to begin work immediately on the construction of this unique aircraft. On August 30, 1912, actual construction began on what became known as the Grand. The Grand was the first four-engine aeroplane to fly, the forerunner of all present-day giant aircraft.

Chairman Shidlovskiy played a leading role in construction of the Grand and later the development of Russian "heavy" aviation. He possessed considerable entrepreneural talent and wide-ranging achievements as an industrial leader in Russia. Shidlovskiy was descended from an old family of landowning nobility in Voronezh province. As a young naval officer, Shidlovskiy had traveled around the world as crewman on board the clipper ship, the "Plastun." Later, shortly after his graduation from the Alexandrovskiy Military and Law Academy, he resigned from the Russian navy and transferred to the Ministry of Finance. As a high-ranking government official, Shidlovskiy became an influential figure who served on the State Council until his appointment as commander of the *Eskadra vozdushnykh korablei* (EVK) or Squadron of Flying Ships. The EVK became a special squadron organized to fly Sikorsky's Il'ya Muromets bombers during World War I.

As chairman of the Russo-Baltic Wagon Company in Riga, Shidlovskiy quickly increased the productivity and profitability of the firm. The R-BVZ manufactured railroad cars, not only for domestic needs but for foreign export as well. In addition to his contribution to the creation of Sikorsky's Grand and later the Il'ya Muromets aircraft, Shidlovskiy supervised the manufacture of the first and only Russian-made automobiles, known as Russo-Baltic. These automobiles were manufactured especially for primitive Russian roads and had to pass a series of difficult road tests. Their quality was demonstrated in the Nagel Rally conducted in Russia, western Europe, and northern Africa. The use of Russo-Baltic automobiles during the war, even on primitive roads by military drivers, further established their reputation for ruggedness. Some of these Russo-Baltic automobiles were driven during the war without repairs for thousands and thousands of versts.[10] Another of Shidlovskiy's wartime contributions was the production in 1915 of the first and only Russian aero engine, the R-BVZ, built at the Russo-Baltic factory.

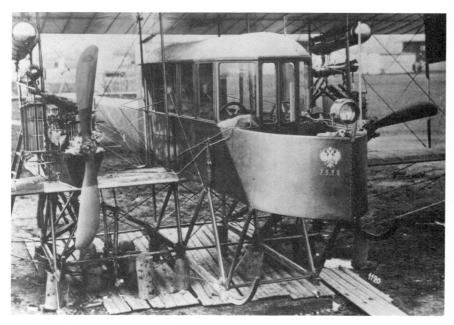

The Grand (original name, Bolshoi Baltiiskiy) rests on blocks for repairs at St. Petersburg in 1913. This particular photograph shows the early tandem version of Sikorsky's first flying ship. *Courtesy of the Archives, United Technologies Corporation*

1882—1896.

АКЦІОНЕРНОЕ ОБЩЕСТВО

РУССКО-БАЛТІЙСКАГО ВАГОННАГО

ЗАВОДА.

Основной капиталъ 9.600.000 руб.

ПРАВЛЕНІЕ: Спб., улица Гоголя, № 13.

Телеф. 2-74, 568-24 и 508-18.

Адресъ для телеграммъ: СПБ., Вагонобалтъ.

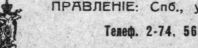

АВІАЦІОННЫЙ ЗАВОДЪ.

Спб., Строгановская наб., 1. — Телеф. 199-14.

Адресъ для телеграммъ: Спб., Аэробалтъ.

Акціонерное Общество Русско-Балтійскаго Вагоннаго Завода первое въ Россіи крупное предпріятіе, строящее аэропланы. Авіаціонный заводъ Общества изготовляетъ аэропланы своей системы (И. И. Сикорскаго) и всѣхъ другихъ типовъ.

Бипланъ «Русскій Витязь» системы И. И. Сикорскаго. Величайшій въ мірѣ аппаратъ. Мощность моторовъ 400 лошад. силъ; расчитанъ на подъемъ 12 человѣкъ.

Смѣты высылаются немедленно по полученіи твердаго запроса.

I-й призъ на военномъ конкурсѣ 1912 года
— и другія высшія награды и отличія. —

Advertisement for the Russo-Baltic Wagon Company (R-BVZ), about 1913. Pictured at the center is the Russkiy vityaz [the Grand], which is described as an aircraft with 400 horsepower, capable of taking twelve people aloft. *Courtesy of the National Air and Space Museum*

Igor Sikorsky's Russkiy vityaz [the Grand] pictured in 1913 in its final configuration with four Argus 100-horsepower engines mounted on the leading edge of the lower wing. *Courtesy of the National Air and Space Museum*

M. V. Shidlovskiy was arrested in 1919, together with his son, while attempting to cross the Finnish frontier to escape the Bolsheviks and was brutally murdered.

The building of the Grand in the spring of 1913 owed much to the generous patronage of Shidlovskiy. This flying machine, even during its initial flight, justified his decision to support Igor Sikorsky's idea of constructing the world's first four-engine aeroplane. The Grand performed as expected. It is worth adding that Shidlovskiy was so confident of the safety of the Grand that together with his family he went for a flight with Igor Sikorsky. Later he demonstrated the same confidence in the Grand's successor, the Il'ya Muromets.

The Grand was made of wood and weighed just over 4,000 kilograms. This large flying ship was designed with a spacious enclosed cabin with large windows for both the crew and passengers. From the cabin or cockpit the pilot had an exit to the balcony, located in the forward section of the aeroplane. There were also side exits leading to the lower wings, providing access to the engines for repairs in flight. Four 100-horsepower German-made Argus engines provided power. These automobile-type engines were located on the lower wings, two engines on each side of the fuselage. The Grand could carry aloft a load of 737 kilograms and cruise at a speed of ninety-six kilometers an hour. Sikorsky's initial test flights of the Grand proved that his concept of large multiengine aircraft was sound. These same flights also exposed defects in the original design that required attention, in particular the inability of the Grand to attain high altitude.

Igor Sikorsky stands next to the damaged Grand in September 1913 at St. Petersburg. The Grand was damaged in a freak accident when an engine (center, on the ground) broke loose from a passing airplane. *Courtesy of the Archives, United Technologies Corporation*

Encouraged by the Grand's success, Sikorsky began construction of his second flying ship, a larger one, which he named Il'ya Muromets.[11] The Il'ya Muromets also had four 100-horsepower Argus engines. The dimensions of this new version were as follows: it weighed nearly 5,000 kilograms, it had a wing span of 31 meters, and the length of the midwing extended 17 meters with a total surface area of 150 square meters. Subsequent variants of the Il'ya Muromets, as with the original Grand, were constructed of wood.[12]

Construction of the Il'ya Muromets began in the fall of 1913 and was completed in January 1914. In general, its configuration was similar to the original design of the Grand, but on the second version Sikorsky removed the forward balcony. He equipped the cabin with six large windows on each side. The new Il'ya Muromets was furnished with comfort in mind. There were wicker chairs in the cabin. Heating for the enclosed compartments was

Rare photograph of the R-BVZ factory at Petrograd with a section of the fuselage of the original Il'ya Muromets. Date unknown. *Courtesy of the National Air and Space Museum*

provided by exhaust gases (from the inboard engines channeled through pipes that acted as radiators). Electric lighting was generated by a special wind driven generator. In addition to the pilot's cabin or cockpit, there were a room for passengers, a bedroom, and even a toilet.

Sikorky's test flights on the Il'ya Muromets were conducted under unfavorable winter conditions. During the late winter thaws the ground turns wet and soggy. It was decided to fit the Il'ya Muromets with skis. This was the only way the flying ship could take off. These tests demonstrated that the new version was superior to the Grand. Under normal conditions the Il'ya Muromets required a distance of 400 paces to take off. In spite of its great weight and identical Argus engines, the Il'ya Muromets could carry aloft a larger useful load than the Grand to an altitude of 1,000 meters.

In February 1914 Sikorsky took the Il'ya Muromets aloft with sixteen passengers. On this memorable flight, there was another passenger on

The original Il'ya Muromets, summer of 1914. Details of the forward cabin and balcony, engines, radiators, fuel tanks, and undercarriage are clearly evident. *Courtesy of the Archives, United Technologies Corporation*

The interior of the Il'ya Muromets. For Igor Sikorsky and his crew, the round-trip flight from St. Petersburg to Kiev in July 1914 offered unique comforts, in contrast to the usual primitive flying conditions during the era of early flight. Note the interior electric light. *Courtesy of the Archives, United Technologies Corporation*

The Il'ya Muromets lands at Korpusnoi Aerodrome, near St. Petersburg, in February 1914. Note passengers on top of the fuselage. *Courtesy of the National Air and Space Museum*

board—a four-legged traveler, the beloved mascot at the aerodrome, a dog named Shkalika. This unusual flight with its numerous passengers was an unprecedented aerial feat. The useful load for this trip over St. Petersburg was 1,300 kilograms. Following the pattern of the Grand, the Il'ya Muromets made many flights over the imperial capital and its environs. Quite often, the Il'ya Muromets flew over the city at low altitude—around 400 meters. So confident was Sikorsky of the safety factor provided by several engines that he was not afraid to fly at such a low altitude. Pilots who flew small, one-engine aeroplanes during these early days typically avoided flights over any city, especially at low altitudes, because failure of an engine and the accompanying forced landing could be fatal.

During these flights by the Il'ya Muromets it was possible for passengers seated comfortably in the enclosed cabin to observe the stately squares and boulevards of St. Petersburg. Every flight by the Il'ya Muromets brought traffic to a standstill as crowds gathered to look up at the behemoth aeroplane with its noisy engines.

Aerial view of St. Petersburg, about 1914, showing the Admiralty, the Neva River, and the Peter and Paul Fortress. *Courtesy of the K. N. Finne family*

Igor Sikorsky (center) stands with a group of friends in front of the Il'ya Muromets in March 1914. It was in this flying ship that Sikorsky made his epic flight from St. Petersburg to Kiev in the summer of 1914. *Courtesy of the K. N. Finne family*

By the spring of 1914, Sikorsky had built a second Il'ya Muromets flying ship. It was equipped with more powerful Argus engines, the two inside engines rated with 140-horsepower and the two outside engines with 125-horsepower. The total engine power of the second model attained 530-horsepower, exceeding the power of the first Il'ya Muromets model by 130-horsepower. Accordingly, the greater engine power meant a greater load-carrying capacity and speed and the capacity to attain an altitude of 2,100 meters. On a preliminary test flight this second Il'ya Muromets carried aloft 820 kilograms of gasoline and six passengers.

Notes

1. [Editors' note.] There has been a considerable amount of confusion surrounding the name of Igor Sikorsky's first four-engine flying ship. Some historians have assumed mistakenly that there were two variants built in 1913. The confusion lies with the multiple names used for the same prototype. The Bolshoi Baltiskiy [Great Baltic], was first built in 1913 as a twin-engine tractor version; later, a four-engine tractor-pusher version was known widely but unofficially as "the Grand." In June 1913 Sikorsky modified the Great Baltic by moving the rear engines forward and adding a pair of rudders. This version had all four engines on the leading edge of the lower wing. Sikorsky gave this modified version of the original flying ship the official name of Russkiy vityaz [Russian knight]. The name "Grand," however, persisted as the most commonly used designation for Igor Sikorsky's first four-engine flying ship.

2. [Editors' note.] Igor Sikorsky had studied in France, where he became interested in a aviation. Before World War I, France was the center of European aviation.

3. [Editors' note.] The main factory of the Russo-Baltiiskiy Vagonnyy Zavod (R-BVZ) [Russo-Baltic Wagon Company] was in Riga. Here the R-BVZ company built railroad cars, rolling stock, and automobiles. The aviation branch was located in St. Petersburg (Petrograd).

4. [Editors' note.] St. Petersburg was the capital of the Russian Empire and, as the home of the Imperial All-Russian Aero Club (IRAC), the center of Russian aeronautical life. The capital boasted several modern aerodromes, including the Komendanskiy aerodrome, where the IRAC was headquartered. There were several military aerodromes and training facilities in St. Petersburg for aviation and ballooning.

5. [Editors' note.] Igor Sikorsky flew his prototype helicopter, the VS-300, in 1939, signaling an important new phase in his American career. Before 1939 Sikorsky had designed and manufactured seaplanes in the United States.

6. [Editors' note.] The Imperial Russian Army, in order to promote military aviation, sponsored special competitions for new designs. Sikorsky's S-6-A (and later the S-6-B) represented an important benchmark for the small Russian aeronautical community. The S-6-A had been successful in competition with foreign designs, and this achievement exhibited the growing sophistication of indigenous Russian designs.

7. [Editors' note.] In addition to A. A. Serebrennikov, Igor Sikorsky invited several other engineers to join him at the

R-BVZ branch plant in St. Petersburg: K. K. Ergant, M. F. Klimikseyev, A. S. Kudoshev, and G. P. Adler. In two years this design team produced more than twenty experimental airplanes.

8. [Editors' note.] This passing reference may be to M. G. Lerkhe, a noted prewar Russian aviator. Lerkhe was licensed by the Imperial Russian Aero Club in 1911 (license number 26), and participated unsuccessfully in the St. Petersburg-to-Moscow Air Race in July 1911.

9. [Editors' note.] The Kolomyazhskiy hippodrome was located on the northern outskirts of St. Petersburg. In this same area, the Imperial Russian Aero Club opened its own facility, the Komendanskiy aerodrome.

10. [Editors' note.] A prerevolutionary Russian unit of measurement, the verst was equal to 1.067 kilometers or 0.663 miles.

11. [Editors' note.] The name Il'ya Muromets is that of a legendary warrior of byliny tales. Il'ya Muromets, as a warrior [*bogatyr*], embodied the ideals of heroism and courage, a defender of the Russian lands against its enemies.

12. [Editors' note.] The Russkiy vityaz was damaged in a freak accident in September 1913. A. M. Gaber-Vlinskiy, a well-known Russian aviator, was flying over the parked Russkiy vityaz in his Moller Type 2. Suddenly the engine in Gaber-Vlinskiy's airplane broke free and fell to the ground, tearing through the left wing of the Russkiy vityaz. Gaber-Vlinskiy managed to land safely, but Igor Sikorsky's flying ship had been seriously damaged. In the aftermath of this accident Sikorsky decided to build a new giant aircraft, not to repair the Russkiy vityaz. During the winter of 1913–1914 he built his first Il'ya Muromets type, which had a monoplane third wing with a span of 17 meters attached to the fuselage behind the main wings. After several tests, this feature of the design was eliminated. The data given by K. N. Finne incorporate this early variation.

Chapter Two

AN EPIC FLIGHT

The flights of the Murometsy convinced Igor Sikorsky that long-distance flights, even unprecedented ones, were now possible. He decided the time had come to make a long-distance journey to demonstrate the capabilities of his new flying ship. For this aerial trek, he chose as his ultimate destination the city of Kiev, a distance of nearly 1,200 kilometers by direct flight southward from St. Petersburg. Sikorsky's flight plan called for one refueling stop, at Orsha, then a flight along the winding Dnieper to Kiev.

Sikorsky selected a crew of three to accompany him: Lieutenant G. I. Lavrov to serve as a pilot and flight navigator, Staff Captain Kh. F. Prussis also to serve as a pilot, and V. D. Panasiuk to assist as a mechanic. On board there were nearly 1,100 kilograms of gasoline, spare engine parts, two spare propellers, an extra tire, wires, bolts, and water containers.

Sikorsky left at 1:00 A.M. on June 30, 1914. In the still air and natural light of St. Petersburg's "White Nights," the Il'ya Muromets took off from the Korpusnoi Aerodrome.[1] The weather was clear, with no air turbulence. Heading southward, the Il'ya Muromets attained the altitude of 1,500 meters. At this elevation, the engines were throttled back to cruising speed. The three pilots alternated at the controls every half hour, thereby affording each person an opportunity to admire the beautiful scenery unfolding below.

About five hours into the flight, a breakfast of sandwiches and hot coffee was served. At 8:00 A.M., the Il'ya Muromets flew over the city of Vitebsk, and the crew observed a large number of people and carriages

A group of officers at the Gatchina Military Flying School in 1915. Staff Captain K. F. Prussis, who flew with Sikorsky on the flight from St. Petersburg to Kiev, is seated at the front, second from left. *Courtesy of the K. N. Finne family*

gathered in one of the squares. Telegrams had been written on board, which were put into a small tube tied with a long ribbon and dropped over Vitebsk with money enclosed to cover the costs of sending the messages. The same method would be used on the return trip, and in both instances the messages were delivered on time.

As the city of Orsha approached, the Il'ya Muromets descended to a lower altitude for landing. While on approach to Orsha, the Il'ya Muromets flew into air currents and whirlwinds. At this hour, about 9:00 A.M., the cool still air of the morning had given way to humid turbulent air. The large flying ship was thrown from side to side, but the turbulence did not prevent Sikorsky from making a safe landing after a nonstop flight of eight and one half hours.

The landing of the Il'ya Muromets at Orsha, to be sure, attracted a large crowd of people, who stared curiously at the huge and unfamiliar flying machine. Sikorsky's crew had to explain many things to the crowd, even as they worked to refuel the Il'ya Muromets with 1,100 kilograms of gasoline. Refueling required a considerable amount of time because the gasoline had to be pumped manually, without any special devices, through small openings in the tanks.

It was only with difficulty that Igor Sikorsky managed to escape the crowd to inspect and to measure the improvised field from which the Il'ya Muromets would take off. The strip was narrow, 50 paces wide and 400 paces long. The contour of the field sloped downward toward the steep bank overlooking the Dnieper River. Sikorsky decided that despite a tailwind the direction for takeoff would be down the slope toward the river.

It took about two hours to refuel the aeroplane and roll it into a position for takeoff. At this point the sun was high in the sky and it was very humid. Sikorsky propelled the large flying ship down the sloping field. During the takeoff run, the Il'ya Muromets became airborne at the moment its chassis passed over the precipice. Sikorsky then banked the aircraft, which skimmed over the rooftops of Orsha and began to climb slowly, heading southward.

After reaching an altitude of 150 meters, the Il'ya Muromets encountered severe turbulence, sometimes air pockets up to 50 meters in depth, which made its further climbing difficult and complicated the pilots' work at the controls. The flight plan called for the Il'ya Muromets to pass over a vast and diverse terrain, which included the forests and lakes of northern Russia. Sikorsky anticipated that there would be zones of strong air turbulence, and, as long as the aeroplane carried a maximum load of gasoline, there would be dangers. However, he decided to continue the flight.

Fifteen minutes after takeoff, Sikorsky, who at that time was at the wheel, faced the frightened gestures of his mechanic, Panasiuk, who pointed to the inboard left engine. It was on fire! Because of the engine noise, it was difficult for the crew to communicate. It happened that a fuel line to the engine had broken and the engine had stopped. As gasoline poured out on the wing and burst into flame, the fire engulfed a large area. Lieutenant Lavrov and Panasiuk crawled out onto the ramp across the lower wing with fire extinguishers and, in the turbulent air stream, put out the fire.[2]

After flying a certain distance with only three engines, Sikorsky then decided to land. He and his crew chose a suitable location and landed safely. An examination of the aeroplane showed that there was little damage. The gasoline line was quickly repaired. It was too late, however, to resume the flight with any hope of reaching Kiev before dark. Accordingly, Sikorsky decided to postpone the flight until the following morning, and the crew spent the night in the cabin of the aeroplane. It rained throughout the night. By morning the rain had stopped, but the weather was overcast and cloudy. The Il'ya Muromets took off at around 4:00 A.M. and flew over the fog-shrouded town of Shklov at an altitude of 500 meters.

Soon afterward, the Il'ya Muromets flew into a large bank of clouds. As the air turbulence increased, the task of keeping the aeroplane under control became more difficult. To maintain a sense of direction, a compass was used. Suddenly it started to rain heavily, and a heavy stream of water battered the wind shield. It became so dark that the wing tips of the Il'ya Muromets were barely visible. After the turbulance diminished, the Il'ya Muromets abruptly nosed downward to the left and started to fall rapidly. Sikorsky's efforts to move the steering wheel did not help! In a few seconds the aeroplane had fallen 200 meters; it then straightened out and continued flying through the enveloping dense clouds.

During this sudden fall, it was noticed that the compass dial made two or three full turns. Evidently, the Il'ya Muromets had flown through electric-charged storm clouds that influenced the magnetic pointer. Once the compass had stabilized and the crew had recovered from nervous shock caused by the rapid descent through the clouds, it was noticed that Il'ya Muromets was heading east instead of south. The decision was made to descend beneath the clouds in order to determine the position of the aeroplane. At an altitude of 400 meters the grounds became visible again, but because of the rain it was impossible to determine the exact location of the Il'ya Muromets. Therefore, the heading was changed to a westerly direction in the hope of reaching the Dnieper River, which alone could reestablish the proper flight path. The Il'ya Muromets cruised at the same altitude, just below the clouds, pitching severely, but gradually stabilizing itself. After about 10 kilometers, the Dnieper came into view, allowing the crew to orient themselves properly again. At this point, their estimated position was south of the river town of Rogachev, about 270 kilometers north of Kiev.

In order to avoid the persistent rain and air turbulence, Sikorsky decided to climb up through clouds. Gaining altitude was relatively easy now, for the Il'ya Muromets had consumed some 328 kilograms of gasoline. At an altitude of 1,000 meters, the rain ceased, and at an altitude of 1,500 meters, the Il'ya Muromets began to fly smoothly. Sikorsky now assumed a cruising altitude of 200 meters above the vast ocean of clouds. This cloud layer below took on dazzlingly white and fantastic configurations! The crew observed this dramatic vista as the Il'ya Muromets cast its moving shadow on the endless cloud layer that stretched to the horizon.

After cruising at this altitude for the next two hours, Lieutenant Lavrov announced that he estimated the Il'ya Muromets to be 10 kilometers from Kiev. Sikorsky then put the aeroplane into a descent toward Kiev. Once again the large aeroplane passed through the clouds and the turbulent air currents.

At an altitude of 600 meters, the Il'ya Muromets suddenly broke through the clouds. Below, the Dnieper came into view. Straight ahead the Tsennoy Bridge was visible, and on the right, the crew could see the golden domes of the Kiev-Pechersk Monastery. After passing over the city, the Il'ya

Igor Sikorsky (center) with assistants during World War I. Vladimir Panasiuk, Sikorsky's mechanic, is standing in back at the right. *Courtesy of the National Air and Space Museum*

Muromets landed on the airfield of the Kiev Aeronautical Society (Kurenev Aerodrome). The Il'ya Muromets had completed the first leg of its long-distance flight, a flight in which the young and brave crew had had to cope with many difficulties and dangers.

Naturally, the city of Kiev gave Sikorsky and his crew a warm and enuthusiastic reception. The flight of the Il'ya Muromets stirred considerable interest among the citizens. The Kiev City Duma (City Council) elected Igor Sikorsky an honorary citizen and the Kiev Polytechnical Institute awarded him an honorary degree in engineering. During the stay in Kiev, Staff Captain Prussis had to abandon the idea of returning with Sikorsky to St. Petersburg because his leave from the army would soon expire.

After remaining in Kiev for a short period, Sikorsky flew the Il'ya Muromets from Kiev on July 12, at about 4:00 A.M. for the return flight to St. Petersburg. By 8:00 A.M., the Il'ya Muromets flew over Mogilev. The weather was so clear that when the aeroplane was flying between Mogilev and Orsha, the crew could see both cities. Cruising altitude was 1,500 meters. At 11:00 A.M., the Il'ya Muromets landed safely in Novo-Sokolniki for refueling. This time the task of refueling took only half an hour, since gasoline was pumped under compressed air pressure.

The weather during the return flight was very humid. At an altitude of 600 meters, the aircraft encountered turbulent air. It was very difficult for the Il'ya Muromets, loaded with gasoline, to gain altitude and maintain control. Also, beyond the city of Novo-Sokolniki there was continuous fire in the woods and peat bogs. It was decided to press on with the flight in order to fly from Kiev to St. Petersburg in the shortest possible time.

At this point on the return flight, the Il'ya Muromets flew into the severest air turbulence. One dangerous moment came when the flying ship was at an altitude of 200 meters. Suddenly, it plunged downward 100 meters, forcing the crew to throw overboard several containers of extra fuel and water to avoid crashing. Such air pockets made the flight very difficult, especially between 200 and 500 meters from the ground.

After an hour Sikorsky and his crew finally reached the zone of the forest fires. It was very hot, and they could smell smoke. The flight proceeded at an altitude of 700 meters because air pockets made it difficult to gain additional altitude. Another anxious moment came somewhere between Novo-Sololniki and St. Petersburg, when the Il'ya Muromets suddenly banked to the left wing and fell. Chairs and other furniture not tied down slid abruptly to the left side. Sikorsky, who was resting in the passenger cabin, could hardly make it back to the cockpit.

Despite all his efforts to turn the steering wheel to correct the leftward tilt, the Il'ya Muromets continued its rapid descent. Below, there was a large lake with banks covered by woods. When the falling aeroplane finally straightened out, the altimeter showed 250 meters. Probably the cool water of the lake in combination with the woods, heated by fire, caused the formation of a large air pocket 500 meters deep, into which the Il'ya Muromets had plunged. At a low altitude over the lake, the air was relatively tranquil, enabling the aeroplane to pull out of the spin.

After escaping this danger, Sikorsky took the Il'ya Muromets upward to a tranquil air zone of 1,000 meters, which allowed the crew to relax after their difficult passage through the air pocket. At 5:00 P.M., they flew over Pavlovsk and Tsarkoye selo. A few minutes later, after passing over the

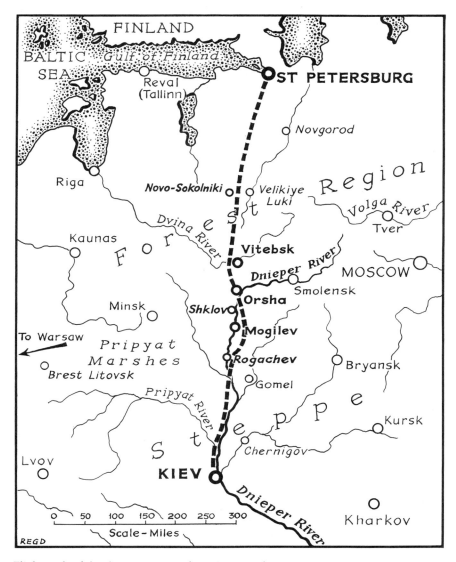

Flight path of the Il'ya Muromets from St. Petersburg to Kiev, 1914.

Moscow road and the Obvodniy canal, Sikorsky made a circle over St. Petersburg and landed at the Korpusnoi Aerodome.

The flight from Kiev to St. Petersburg had taken thirteen hours. This flight set a world long-distance record, which could not remain unnoticed either in Russia or abroad.

His Majesty Nicholas II again showed his high regard for Igor Sikorsky by visiting the Il'ya Muromets in person and speaking warmly with the crew. Shortly afterward, Sikorsky received the Order of St. Vladimir, Fourth Degree, which at that time was a very high decoration. By nature a modest man, Sikorsky never liked ostentation, but he was proud of this award. In addition, Sikorsky was given 100,000 rubles for further development of his large flying ship.[3] To pursue his design work, Sikorsky was now exempt from the draft.

In July 1914, at a large Imperial military review at Krasnoye selo on the occasion of the visit to Russia by President Poincaré of France, Nicholas II gave the Il'ya Muromets the name "Kievskiy." The Il'ya Muromets—a flying ship equal to its name—was situated on the right side of the aviation units. The large flying machine attracted the keen attention of the French president, who was reviewing the troops with the emperor. The pilots who participated in this ceremony remembered that Poincaré, while seated in a carriage next to the empress, not only kept looking at the Il'ya Muromets while passing by, but continued to look back in order to get a better view of this unique Russian "Knight of the Air."

Although the Il'ya Muromets attracted considerable public attention and stirred the still water of Russia's Philistine swamp, the broad strata of Russian society remained indifferent. Surprisingly, little interest in or sympathy for Igor Sikorsky's work was shown, despite its originality and Russian national character. Only a few people realized that Sikorsky's flying ship was the first large multiengine aircraft in the world, a design that had launched a new phase in aircraft design.

With the help of Sikorsky's design the future development of air transport would assist Russia in overcoming its vast geography, endless plains, and primitive means of transport. At the time, no one took any serious steps to organize financial support for the construction of a special factory to manufacture Sikorsky's flying ship and the engines necessary for it. This general attitude demonstrates a substantial difference between Russians, who slavishly ape everything foreign, and non-Russians.

Recall how the Germans treated Count von Zeppelin, the creator of the large dirigible. The first zeppelin, built in 1900, crashed as a result of defects in design. The general public, however, collected funds for the construction of not one, but several new dirigibles, at considerable expense. It is remarkable that at the beginning Kaiser Wilhelm and those in powerful government circles in Germany treated Count von Zeppelin as a dreamer and a crazy man. Help came from the majority of the German people, who made it possible for this dreamer to improve his invention and build entire squadrons of these dirigibles before World War I. Zeppelins, however, did not exactly meet the high expectations of the public. They were easily hit by artillery fire and were therefore unsuitable, not only for reconnaissance missions in the enemy rear, but also for daytime flights. Owing to the widespread support of a patriotic people, these airships reached the highest degree of improvement in the technical sense of the word. Zeppelins during the war had considerable effect as an aerial weapon, making numerous night missions over London, Paris, and other vital centers of population.

There is an aphorism that states, "Flies could move a man provided they acted unanimously." It is regrettable that Russians worship all things foreign and pay little attention to the good things that their own countrymen do. It is a pity that we did not acquire from the Germans their most important qualities: a deep love of their country, mutual support, efficiency, and a conscientious attitude toward work.

It is even more painful to admit that this passive attitude of Russian society toward Sikorsky's aeroplanes occurred at the same time that some Russian intellectuals were working actively to create conditions that led to the destruction of the Russian nation.

These same people did not consider it necessary to support the development of the Il'ya Muromets because of the fact that the project was supported by the hated Imperial government. The majority of Russians thought that it was not their business to support Igor Sikorsky's invention. So what? Who cares if some aeroplanes are being built? It would have taken a great effort to prompt them to think, to distract them from the leisure pursuits, the card games, and other "serious" occupations that filled their lives.

If Sikorsky had chosen Moscow, not Kiev, as the location for his flight, he could have taken a bow before the Moscow patrons of the arts and sciences. Probably this would have accomplished something and amazed Europe. But the engine noise of the Il'ya Muromets never reached Moscow. The construction of Sikorsky's Il'ya Muromets continued in the small St. Petersburg workshop of the Russo-Baltic Wagon Company.

The timing of Sikorsky's flight should be taken into consideration. It was just after the assassination of Archduke Francis Ferdinand, the heir to the Austro-Hungarian throne, in the city of Sarajevo. Storm clouds quickly gathered, not only over the Balkan peninsula but also over Europe. Finally the clouds burst, bringing on an unprecedented war that turned the entire world upside down.

It was at this time that broad public support, thoughtful planning, and organization for the construction of the Il'ya Muromets was most necessary. Unfortunately, these steps were never taken.

Notes

1. [Editors' note.] St. Petersburg, Russia's "window on Europe," was built on the marshlands at the mouth of the Neva River, adjacent to the Gulf of Finland. The sun at this latitude during the brief summer stays above the horizon except for a few hours at night. This phenomenon gives rise to St. Petersburg's "White Nights."

2. [Note by K. N. Finne.] The members of the Imperial Russian Firefighters Society elected the crew of the Il'ya Muromets to membership in their society.

3. [Editors' note.] According to Igor Sikorsky, certain members of the State Duma (the national parliament) worked to provide 100,000 rubles for the support of his work with giant aircraft, but this state aid never materialized.

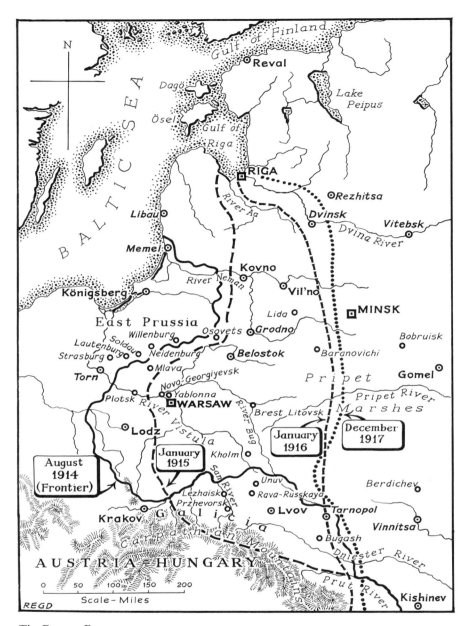

The Eastern Front, 1914–1917.

Chapter Three

THE GREAT WAR

It could be argued that the reversals suffered by the Russian army during the opening days of World War I might have been avoided if there had been more enthusiasm for building the Il'ya Muromets. Perhaps the reverses under the command of General Samsonov could have been averted.[1] In the aftermath of these defeats the German army gained an undeserved reputation for invincibility, a perception which, in turn, made a deep impression on Russian troops. Our abrupt retreat from East Prussia led to bloody battles near Lodz, Warsaw, Ivanograd, and other places where some of our best army corps perished.

When World War I was declared, in July 1914, only two Murometsy were ready for military operations. On orders from the Ministry of War, Murometsy were ordered into production at the R-BVZ aviation factory in Petrograd.[2] German Argus engines, ordered for these Murometsy, did not arrive, so they were replaced with Salmson engines made in France. The Salmson engines unfortunately proved less useful for the Il'ya Muromets than the Argus types.[3] In fact, the French-made engines contributed in a significant way to the negative attitude of military pilots toward the Il'ya Muromets. At the beginning, these pilots had enthusiastically greeted the Il'ya Muromets as a truly Russian flying machine, but as time passed they joined the chorus of opponents of the large, multiengine aeroplanes.

The decision was made to arm and equip existing Murometsy for military use as soon as the war broke out.[4] As a first step, it seemed wise to determine what requirements could realistically be met by this type of aero-

The Il'ya Muromets (type B) equipped with Salmson engines at Petrograd shortly after the beginning of World War I. *Courtesy of the K. N. Finne family*

The blessing of the Il'ya Muromets II at Korpusnoi Aerodrome, Petrograd, taken on the eve of its flight to the front in late September 1914. The commander of the flying ship was A. V. Pankrat'yev. Note the priest, the band, and the film crew in the foreground. The Il'ya Muromets II was equipped with Salmson engines and was one of the first Murometsy committed to the war effort. *Courtesy of the K. N. Finne family*

plane in a wartime situation, to analyze its strengths and weaknesses, and to consider how well prepared its commanders were for military service. These necessary tasks, however, were not conducted properly or with high seriousness—not surprising, for aviation at the time was still in its infancy and important questions about its role remained to be answered. Many prewar ideas quickly proved untenable. For example, the best altitude for air operations had been considered to be 1,000 or even 800 meters. Once the hostilities broke out, this altitude proved to be too dangerous.

In December 1914 we set the combat altitude at 1,700 meters, but by the beginning of 1915 we revised it upward again, to about 3,000 meters. No one had given much serious thought to the nature of air combat. Typically, when enemy aeroplanes encountered ours at the front, they dispersed and returned to base. Only pilots such as Staff Captain Peter Nesterov actively sought out the enemy. As is well known, this courageous military pilot perished while ramming an enemy fighter. The role of antiaircraft artillery at that time, moreover, was limited and in practice ineffectual.

As a result of all this confusion in military aviation, we covered the Murometsy with steel armor and equipped it with a 37-mm Hotchkiss cannon for "shooting at zeppelins." To fire, or, more precisely, to hit a target with this gun while in flight proved difficult.

There was another effort made to adapt weapons to meet wartime requirements. At the beginning of 1915 we installed a three-inch gun on board the Il'ya Muromets. This gun, weighing about 100 kilograms, was an effective and original weapon. We mounted it on a very light platform without compressors, to eliminate the recoil. This unusual cannon, invented by a young Russian artillery officer, fired two projectiles simultaneously in diametrically opposite directions. It was loaded with a single cartridge.[5]

Because of this general ignorance within Russian military aviation circles at the time, the Putilov factory sent armor made of beautiful well-hardened two-millimeter steel for testing on Sikorsky's flying ships as modern-day knights' armor. Clad in this armor, crew members on the Murometsy could hardly move. One can understand how these airborne cannons and the personal armor from the Putilov factory dramatically increased the weight of each flying ship, thereby reducing the useful load available for combat operations.

Other attempts were made to adapt the Il'ya Muromets as a flying machine for universal military use—by equipping it with floats, for example, to serve as a seaplane. One Il'ya Muromets, fitted with these floats, was transferred to the island of Ezel and put under the command of a naval pilot, Lieutenant G. I. Lavrov. It made several flights, but these experiments assumed little military significance. The Murometsy had demonstrated excellent results in peaceful applications, but the difference between peacetime uses and military operations turned out to be quite dramatic. All these novel

An Il'ya Muromets fitted with Argus engines and a 37-millimeter Hotchkiss cannon. Russian War Minister V. A. Sukhomlinov is fourth from the left. General M. V. Shidlovskiy (fifth from left) and Sikorsky (seventh from left) are also pictured. *Courtesy of the National Air and Space Museum*

Rear view of an Il'ya Muromets equipped with floats, about 1914. *Courtesy of the Archives, United Technologies Corporation*

An Il'ya Muromets (type B) equipped with floats at the Libau Naval base on the Baltic Sea. The two inboard engines are 200-horsepower Salmsons. The two outboard engines are 115-horsepower Arguses. This photograph was taken in June 1914, a month before the outbreak of World War I. *Courtesy of the Archives, United Technologies Corporation*

experiments, of course, took a considerable amount of time and effort, but each in turn had to be rejected as impractical.[6]

One of the most important wartime tasks was the training of pilots to fly the Murometsy. In reality there was a world of difference between operating a small one-engine aeroplane and flying a giant 5,000-kilogram, four-engine Il'ya Muromets. It was the officer-instructors at the Gatchina Military Flying School who became future Il'ya Muromets pilots. Igor Sikorsky, already occupied with the design and manufacture of the aeroplane, assumed the responsibility for this training, or, to be more specific, retraining.

These military pilots, who had already accumulated experience flying small aeroplanes, considered themselves to be an elite in the world of Russian aviation and authoritative spokesman on all matters related to aviation. Nevertheless they were asked to undergo new training in the war emergency, to be transferred from positions as instructors at Gatchina to the status of cadet-trainees under the overall supervision of a civilian. All these circumstances, as might be imagined, bruised their egos.

It should also be mentioned that these pilots were spoiled by the public attention that had been showered on them. They had been treated like movie stars. Accustomed to performing aerial stunts, they now had to

Officers of the EVK at St. Petersburg just before going on active duty: (1) V. A. Ivanov; (2) B. N. Firsov; (3) G. G. Gorshkov; (4) Colonel Ulyanov; (5) A. V. Kostenchik; (6) G. V. Alekhnovich; (7) M. P. Spasov; (8) V. M. Brodovich; (9) I. S. Bashko; (10) M. V. Smirnov; (11) Mechanic Kisel; (12) Lieutenent Shestov; (13) Artillery Officer Nekrasov. *Courtesy of the National Air and Space Museum*

switch to the boring routine of training, to perform takeoffs and landings, and to learn about the operation of the Il'ya Muromets.

Understandably, they displayed little zeal for their training. As events turned out, these future Murometsy commanders explained their inevitable failures and mishaps by placing the entire blame on the Il'ya Muromets aircraft. The Il'ya Muromets, to be sure, had defects, but no more than other aeroplanes. These pilots doted on foreign aircraft and expressed disdain for indigenous flying machines. As usually happens, certain defects of the Il'ya Muromets, hitherto unnoticed, began to attract more attention than the large flying ship's obvious advantages, the very characteristics that had prompted popular enthusiasm before the war. Inevitably failures and breakdowns did occur during this training. Predictably, these pilots attributed each problem to inadequacies of design in the construction of the Il'ya Muromets.

It should be noted that no serious mishaps took place when Igor Sikorsky flew the Grand or variants of the Il'ya Muromets. It was only in October 1915 that an Il'ya Muromets with Sikorsky at the controls had an accident worthy of mention. During a landing with this flying ship Sikorsky "touched" a Farman aeroplane that was flying beneath. The chassis on the Il'ya Muromets was broken. The pilots and passengers on both aeroplanes landed safely, however, and no one suffered any injuries. Even serious accidents with Murometsy aircraft, in most instances, ended safely for the crew.

Once an Il'ya Muromets hit a fence during its training flight at the Korpusnoi Aerodrome, crushed it, then completely cut down seventeen birch trees in an adjoining field. None of the eight officers on board suffered any serious injury, although the aeroplane was broken into pieces. The basic cause of this mishap was the lack of experience of the pilot. This event, of course, became an occasion for the opponents of Il'ya Muromets to renew their arguments for single-engine aeroplanes. Soon this kind of recrimination against the Murometsy became commonplace. . . . Many younger pilots became agitated with the delays in organizing the Murometsy squadrons and with all the problems that arose with the Salmson engines.

These pilots and future Il'ya Muromets commanders were anxious to enter military action and expressed their displeasure and lack of faith in large aircraft. Their continued preference for small aeroplanes led to their absence from training sessions at the 1st Aviation Company aerodrome, where the Murometsy hangars were located. Eventually these pilots completely withdrew, switching to single-engine aeroplanes. It would not be fair, however, to blame these officers for their actions. The worst behavior was exhibited by those pilots who, while remaining in command, strongly criticized the Murometsy.

Dostoyevsky once said, "Give a Russian student a map of the heavens and he will submit it to you the next day with corrections." Obviously, these young future Murometsy commanders displayed this national trait.

The Il'ya Muromets squadrons, first organized in August 1914, required special attention and thorough planning for their development. At that time, however, our aviation squadrons lacked an established and coherent organization. The Murometsy were different in character from the army's single-engine aeroplanes. As an original aircraft design, the Il'ya Muromets differed significantly from all light aviation types in the army. For the operation of Sikorsky's flying ships, you could not borrow parts from abroad—as we loved to do—because there were no such aeroplanes outside Russia. Because of the war emergency everyone was overburdened and, as a consequence, the organization and training of the Il'ya Muromets squadrons took on a certain improvised character. There was great uncertainty about what the future would hold for the Murometsy.[7]

In addition to fighting zeppelins, the Murometsy were considered to be useful in offensive operations against enemy fortresses. Yet there was little clarity about the exact combat role for the Il'ya Muromets. An incident occurred in 1915 that illustrated this confusion. The chief of staff of one of our armies proposed to Captain G. G. Gorshkov, commander of the Il'ya Muromets "Kievskiy,"[8] that he should fly to a German aerodrome in the town of Sanniki, land, scatter the enemy with machine-gun fire, then burn enemy aircraft and hangars. Captain Gorshkov responded to this proposal with wit and humor, stating that he would fly the combat mission for the St. George's Cross and that someone should deposit the medal at the German aerodrome in advance for him to pick up.

After consideration of these circumstances, it becomes clear why there was confusion. Some errors were made in the construction of a special depot and central repair shop for the Murometsy. Without these facilities, the new aviation detachment could hardly be expected to be organized properly and to operate efficiently. The organization of technical, administrative, and sanitary aspects of these squadrons reflected well the context of "wartime conditions."

According to military staff estimates, the organization for each squadron called for the appointment of a commander, a deputy commander or assistant, an artillery officer, a junior officer serving as an adjutant, a mechanic, and forty recruits drawn from the lower ranks. For each air unit there were four cars assigned, two of which were to be manufactured at the Russo-Baltic factory, and two models modified as ambulances for transporting the wounded. Each squadron was also assigned two trucks. As it turned out, some squadrons had five cars. It became apparent that those who were in charge of personnel aimed to provide every officer with at least one automobile. It is necessary to add that squadron commanders, even those who were expert pilots and courageous officers, did not always have the qualities or the experience to command small air units.

It was under such conditions that the Murometsy were prepared for war. It would be difficult to expect that this preparatory phase would bring good results. It was impossible in this initial period for the Murometsy to fulfill the many expectations and radiant hopes placed on them or to become an independent, national, and determined instrument of war.

The authorities worked hurriedly to send the Il'ya Muromets to the front. In the middle of September 1914 the Il'ya Muromets I (IM-1), the same type flown by Sikorsky from St. Petersburg to Kiev, was dispatched prematurely to the front.[9] The result of this hasty preparation of both the aircraft and the crew became evident immediately. The flight from Petrograd to Belostok, in four stages, covering a total of 912 kilometers, took 23 days to complete. When the IM-1 departed from Korpusnoi Aerodrome, the wind was not strong. Later the wind velocity increased dramatically, at times to gale force, compelling the IM-1 to fly at a speed of 27 kilometers an hour. Six hours into the flight the flying ship ran out of fuel, having covered only 193 kilometers. Finally, it made a forced landing on Count Tiran's estate in the Petrograd province, breaking its undercarriage.

The IM-1 took 13 hours and 52 minutes to complete a flight from Petrograd to Belostok, the approximate amount of time it had taken Igor Sikorsky to fly from Kiev to St. Petersburg in 1914. Once the IM-1 reached Belostok, the headquarters staff of the Northwestern Front ordered the

The Il'ya Muromets at St. Petersburg in the fall of 1914. Captain G. G. Gorshkov is visible in the cockpit. This photograph provides excellent detail of the front of the fuselage and the Argus engines. *Courtesy of the K. N. Finne family*

flying ship to conduct a series of aerial reconnaissance missions. The dispatches from the commander of the IM-1 clearly indicate that the flying ship did not accomplish its assigned mission.

[This section contains an abbreviated version of the original report.] In two reports to the Field Inspector General of Aviation, dated October 21, 1914, and January 10, 1915; the commander of the Il'ya Muromets outlined his many objections to the Muromets type of aeroplane. His complaints centered on the difficulties encountered in flying the IM-1 from Petrograd to Belostock, which took nearly 24 hours. Serious problems arose later, when the IM-1 was assigned to aerial reconnaissance operations. The flying ship, he stated, could not maintain the required operational altitude. There were difficulties as well with the reliability of the power plants. The aero engines for the Murometsy were regularly serviced and, with each of the many breakdowns, given a thorough inspection, but to no avail. The commander reported that even Igor Sikorsky himself arrived in November 1914 to inspect the flying ships and recommended a series of remedies to solve the altitude problem. Despite these detailed instructions, according to this report, the IM-1 in various aerial reconnaissance flights for the headquarters staff of the Northwestern Front failed to achieve the necessary optimum altitude. [End of abbreviated section].[10]

These reports by the commander of the IM-1 did not sound like regular military reports. On the contrary, they took on the form of a legal document, as if submitted for an inquest into the unsuitability of Il'ya Muromets–type aircraft. The reports suggested that the Il'ya Muromets was an "abnormal" type of flying machine and made an appeal to the R-BVZ company and Igor Sikorsky. The author of the reports, however, could hardly be considered an objective judge. As the commander he was supposed to be responsible for the good condition of his aeroplane.

Time, the best and most objective judge, showed that many of these complaints made by the commander of the Il'ya Muromets I to demonstrate the inferior design of his flying machine as compared to "regular" aeroplanes were the expression of his own bias for French-designed flying machines. At that time the Russian Army used Farman, Nieuport, Deperdussin, Morane Saulnier, and Voisin aeroplanes.[11]

These so-called inadequacies in engine design did not prevent Il'ya Muromets flying ships from performing quite adequately in subsequent combat missions. By April 1917 Murometsy had conducted more than 100 combat missions deep into the enemy rear. The IM-1 engines were removed and installed on board the Il'ya Muromets III IM-3,[12] which made duration flights (up to 6 hours) over enemy territory, sometimes as far as 213 kilometers from the front line.

After the IM-3 had been damaged, its engines were installed on board the Il'ya Muromets Kievskiy (IM-Kievskiy), which served until the end of the war, from May 1916 to April 1917.[13] Both Murometsy helped the headquarters of the First and Third armies in significant ways. They expressed their appreciation with unusual displays of flattery, comparing the Murometsy with single-engine aircraft. The same Argus engines which were used by Igor Sikorsky during his round-trip flight from St. Petersburg to Kiev were installed on the IM-Kievskiy and were used until April 22, 1916. At that time the engines were refitted on the Il'ya Muromets XIII (IM-13).[14] Finally, these same engines were put into storage in May 1917, having had a lifetime of two years, with nearly 700 hours of flying time.

The fact that IM-1 could not attain an altitude above 1,350 meters, as described in the commanding pilot's report, should not be attributed to the design shortcomings of the flying ship. In fact, Igor Sikorsky took this same rather worn-out aeroplane aloft on March 17, 1915, above the town of Yablonna and into a strong wind, and easily reached an altitude of 2,100 meters with a weight of 1,065 kilograms on board. Sikorsky's flight in the IM-1 caused a storm of controversy in military aviation circles, where many tended to doubt the data from the barogram because of their profound bias against the Murometsy.

It could be argued that if the commander of the IM-1 had been more

The Il'ya Muromets VI (IM-6), equipped with two Salmson engines, was used as a trainer. This particular variant was destroyed in a training flight at Yablonna in February 1915. *Courtesy of the K. N. Finne family*

sympathetic to Russian-built aeroplanes than to so-called "regular" types—that is, French-designed flying machines—those shortcomings of the IM-1 that he pointed out in his telegram certainly could have been eliminated. Concerning the accusation that the carburetors froze at −5 degrees C., it should be noted that a little later, when Murometsy made flights of long duration, their carburetors did not freeze, even at −30 degrees C.

Consequently, the first unsuccessful tests of the IM-1 should be explained by the preference of the commander for light aviation, not by design defects. Certain inadequacies in design were apparent earlier, at the time of Sikorsky's flight from St. Petersburg to Kiev. The bias of the commander was evident throughout his report, with his constant reference to small single-engine aeroplanes. At one point he asked for two such aircraft to be assigned to the squadron.

While the commander's reports were accusatory in nature, the resolutions of the Field Inspector General of Aviation in fact sounded a death knell for Sikorsky's Russian air knight, the Il'ya Muromets. As a result of these negative reports, the headquarters staff of the Northwestern Front refused to accept delivery of the Il'ya Muromets II (IM-2) that had been allocated for its use.[15] Stavka issued a directive that "aeroplanes not suitable for military use should not be dispatched to the army and that no new aeroplanes be ordered from the Russo-Baltic factory, and that existing orders be considered void."

While correspondence and bureaucratic entanglements persisted, the Murometsy, whether good or bad, were being prepared for shipment to the army at the front. Following the example of the IM-1, the IM-2 made an attempt to get to the front by air. At Rezhitsi, as the IM-2 was flying toward the front, our troops opened fire, forcing the IM-2 to make an emergency landing. One consequence of this incident was serious damage to the landing gear of the flying ship. The crew of the IM-2 decided to complete their journey by railway. Once the crippled IM-2 finally arrived at Brest-Litovsk, it was much like its legendary namesake, forced to sit there until its later transfer to Yablonna, near the fortress of Novo-Georgiyevsk, in January 1915.

It is necessary to state that the IM-2, as opposed to the IM-1, had French-made Salmson engines. The inboard motors had 170 horsepower, the outboard motors 130 horsepower, giving the IM-2 around 600 horsepower. As pointed out earlier, these Salmson engines were not effective.

Among the five Murometsy squadrons, there is not much to state because they were not really operational. Some of these squadrons did not have commanders, others did not have any flying ships in their inventory, or if they had them, they lacked engines. In other words, these squadrons were far from being "military prepared."[16] Nevertheless, all these squadrons were dispatched to the town of Yablonna on December 25, 1914. Here they awaited further orders. The future was not promising. In reports, as cited above, both the Stavka and headquarters of the Northwestern Front considered the Murometsy unsuitable for military operations, and in many aviation circles they were regarded as "incapable of lifting off the ground."[17] There is an old Russian proverb which says, "good reputation remains still while the bad kind travels fast." This proverb describes well the situation of the Murometsy at the beginning of the war.

Notes

1. [Editors' note.] General Alexander V. Samsonov (1859–1914) commanded the Russian Second Army in the disastrous battle of Tannenberg in August 1914.

2. [Editors' note.] In an expression of war-induced nationalism, St. Petersburg was renamed Petrograd in 1914. The purpose was to give the Imperial capital a more Russian-sounding name.

3. [Editors' note.] The Salmson engines did not perform well on the Murometsy for a number of reasons. The four large radiators produced a significant aerodynamic drag. These same radiators often failed because of engine vibration. The Salmsons also failed to deliver their rated horsepower, but this may have

been the result of an inappropriate type of propeller, the quality of the fuel and oil, or both. Despite the augmented horsepower, the Salmson engines failed to give the Murometsy the anticipated increases in speed and ceiling.

4. [Editors' note.] At this point there were two models of the Il'ya Muromets in existence.

5. [Editors' note.] The gun mentioned here is probably a recoilless type, developed by two Russian inventors, a Lieutenant Colonel Gelvig and a Captain Oranovskiy. Two experiments were conducted with the gun on the Il'ya Muromets.

6. [Editors' note.] In May 1914, on the eve of World War I, the original Il'ya Muromets (Type B [Beh], no. 107) was sent to the Libau Naval Facility for tests and evaluations as a hydroplane for the Russian navy. Floats were adapted to the flying ship, along with a new engine configuration—two inboard Salmson 200-horsepower engines and two outboard Argus 115-horsepower engines. When World War I broke out, the Il'ya Muromets was assigned to Ezel Island, but its subsequent fate remains unclear.

7. [Editors' note.] When World War I broke out, the Russian Army possessed around 250 military aircraft. The Russian navy possessed a number of seaplanes that operated out of modern facilities at two bases, one on the Baltic, the other on the Black Sea. The Russian navy's base at Sevastopol was modern and active during the war.

8. [Editors' note.] Nicholas II added the word "Kievskiy" to the name Il'ya Muromets, on the occasion of the flying ship's round-trip flight from St. Petersburg to Kiev in 1914. The "Il'ya Muromets Kievskiy" also became the name for three subsequent Murometsy. The original, the IM-Kievskiy (Type V [Veh]) was built in 1914 and flown by Captain G. G. Gorshkov. The second IM-Kievskiy was probably a Type G-1 and built in 1916. The third flying ship with this name was the IM-Kievskiy (Type G-2) was equipped with four Beardmore 160-

horsepower engines. I. S. Bashko flew all three versions. See appendix 6.

9. [Editors' note.] The IM-1, Type B (Beh). See appendix 6.

10. [Editors' note.] See appendix 3 for a complete translation of this report. The report was probably written by Yevgeniy V. Rudnev, a well-known military pilot in the prewar years.

11. [Editors' note.] K. N. Finne found the positive attitude of the commander of the IM-1 toward foreign aviation technology typical, a "cosmopolitanism" that Finne detected in the Main Military Technical office, which in the prewar years oversaw Russian military aviation. In a footnote to his narrative Finne lamented the fact that Russian-designed airplanes, in particular the S-16, which possessed a synchronization gear apparatus for firing through the propeller, were largely ignored during the war.

12. [Editors' note.] The Il'ya Muromets III, Type V (Veh). See appendix 6.

13. [Editors' note.] The Il'ya Muromets Kievskiy (second version, probably Type G-1). See appendix 6.

14. [Editors' note.] Il'ya Muromets XIII, Type G-1. Il'ya Muromets Kievskiy, Type V (Veh). See appendix 6.

15. [Editors' note.] Il'ya Muromets II, Type B (Beh). See appendix 6.

16. [Note by K. N. Finne.] Among the flying ships, there was the Il'ya Muromets VI, Type B, an improved version with Salmson engines. The commander of the IM-6 was war military pilot and Staff Captain B. N. Firsov. The IM-6 crashed on a training flight at Yablonna on February 26, 1915.

17. [Editors' note.] Later, in March 1915, Finne notes: "I had a conversation with an army engineer, a Colonel P. K., who was surprised that the Il'ya Muromets was still being flown. According to this engineer the Murometsy were considered in industrial circles to be the product of a corrupt scheme by which the Russo-Baltic Wagon Company had manipulated the government to obtain valuable contracts.

Chapter Four

THE ESTABLISHMENT OF THE EVK

The military pilots at the front had greeted the Il'ya Muromets with keen disappointment at the beginning of World War I. This attitude, as stated earlier, was in sharp contrast to the prewar enthusiasm for the great flights of Igor Sikorsky and his Murometsy flying ships. The negative response of the military pilots had many causes: the failure of the Salmson engines, the delays in mobilizing the Murometsy into a separate squadron, the poor organizational work of the army, and the failure of the Il'ya Muromets I.

The larger story of the Murometsy is more important than the way the military pilots acquired their negative attitudes. While this attitude threatened to doom the entire Russian cause, it should be pointed out that there were people who strongly defended Sikorsky's flying ships at the time. M. V. Shidlovskiy, the chairman of the Russo-Baltic Wagon Company, was one important defender of Sikorsky. On the basis of Sikorsky's flight from St. Petersburg to Kiev, Shidlovskiy argued in a report that the Il'ya Muromets was a powerful war machine and warned that any refusal to use these flying ships would be criminal.

The Stavka agreed with Shidlovskiy's position and suggested that he should take personal command of a new squadron of Murometsy, to be called the Squadron of Flying Ships, or *Escadra vozdushnykh korablei* (EVK).[1] The Stavka appointed Shidlovskiy as commander of the EVK in December 1914. As a high-ranking civil servant and former councilor of state, Shidlovskiy was promoted to the rank of major general in the Russian Army. For the position as his assistant, Shidlovskiy chose a professor at the

Yablonna, located near the Novo-Georgiyevsk fortress in the Warsaw area, became the forward air base for the EVK in 1915. *Courtesy of the National Air and Space Museum*

Nicholas Military and Engineering Academy, Colonel V. F. Naidenov, who had earlied served in military aviation and was well-known in aeronautical circles.[2]

It was not difficult to imagine the reaction in military circles, especially in the air units, to the appointment of a civilian as major general. At that time there were no generals except the Field Inspector General of Aviation attached to military aviation units. Some people asked cynically about this appointment, whether the Russo-Baltic Wagon Company had played a corrupt role in obtaining the appointment.

At that time, officers brought up in the traditional army organization could not easily reconcile themselves to the fact that their new commander was a "civilian" general. Shidlovskiy's earlier military service in the navy was unknown to many people. When Shidlovskiy arrived at Yablonna, the air base for the EVK, he had immediately to face the thinly concealed hostility of his subordinate officers. The officers of the EVK, moreover, had with great reluctance to surrender their post quarters in the house of Countess Pototsky's estate manager to their new commander.

General Shidlovskiy had to begin his military career under these difficult circumstances. His flying ships were not in operational readiness. These conditions did not bode well for General Shidlovskiy's future. There was, moreover, the opposition of the Field Inspector General of Aviation, who had earlier opposed the appointment of Shidlovskiy. The Stavka, if supportive, was distant and overburdened with other military problems.

Despite all these obstacles, General Shidlovskiy managed to organize flights by the EVK from Yablonna shortly after his arrival in January 1915. Igor Sikorsky in the IM-3 made a test flight on January 24. Two days later, the IM-Kievskiy made its flight, commanded by Captain G. G. Gorshkov, with twelve passengers on board. The IM-Kievskiy attained an altitude of more than 2,500 meters in 49 minutes. During this flight, when the IM-Kievskiy was flying near Warsaw, it was approached closely by a Morane Saulnier, one of the Russian airplanes used for special assignments. The Morane was stationed in Warsaw and was humorously called Bristolskiy after a famous hotel and restaurant in the suburbs of Krakov. The pilot of Morane said later that he had taken the Il'ya Muromets for an enemy aeroplane and had been prepared to fire his revolver [sic!] because it was a common belief in his squadron that the Murometsy could not reach such an altitude. This incident illustrated how little Russian military pilots knew about Sikorsky's flying ships and the fact that the EVK aerodrome which was located only eighteen kilometers from Warsaw. At the same time, this story reveals to us how single-engine aeroplanes, operating as fighters at the time, were armed for air combat.

During this same period the IM-3 type was adapted for military use. The cabin of these military versions did not have the comfortable accommodations of its passenger type, but they weighed less by 410 kilograms.[3] The same Argus engines that were used on the flight from St. Petersburg to Kiev were installed on the IM-Kievskiy. With a load of about 1,200–1,300 kilograms, the flying ship reached the much higher altitude of 3,700 meters. This same type had been built at the R-BVZ factory in seven weeks, commencing with completion of drawings. During its construction, Captain G. G. Gorshkov, the future commander of Murometsy, made certain recommendations, which stemmed from his experience in military aviation, and many were later taken into consideration.

Although talk about the inability of the Murometsy to fly gradually subsided, there was still a lot of work to do to form a squadron capable of effective military air operations. (For work done to put the EVK in order, Major General Shidlovskiy was awarded Order of St. Vladimir, Second Degree). General Shidlovskiy, a newcomer to aviation, had not only to correct errors made while the EVK was being formed, but he had also to struggle against the pervasive mistrust by military pilots of large aeroplanes. Shidlovskiy's situation was aggravated by the fact that the majority of his officers sympathized with light aviation. The Field Inspector General of Aviation and his staff, already alienated from heavy aviation because of the test flights of the IM-1, did not conceal their negative attitude toward General Shidlovskiy.

This attitude toward the EVK can be illustrated by an incident that occurred during the inspection of the squadron on February 3, 1915. When the Field Inspector General of Aviation, seated in the new Russo-Baltic automobile that had been sent for Igor Sikorsky's use, loudly, in front of the

Grand Duke Alexander Mikhailovich (left), appointed by Nicholas II to head Russian military aviation in World War I, visits Yablonna in 1915. To the left of the grand duke is General M. V. Shidlovskiy, commander of the EVK. The grand duke is pictured here inspecting the Il'ya Muromets I (IM-1). *Courtesy of the National Air and Space Museum*

squadron officers, said sarcastically to Major General Shidlovskiy, pointing at the automobile, "What is this? A gift from the Russo-Baltic Wagon Company for the EVK commander?"

This mistrust of General Shidlovskiy became in time more acute and serious. It brought about isolation for heavy aviation. Its effect was negative. Such attitudes hindered the normal development of the Il'ya Muromets squadron and retarded the broad application of this technology in military operations.

Such behavior demonstrates a typical Russian or, to be more precise, Slavic characteristic, the tendency to consider those who disagree with you to be your worst enemies, even in minor things, rather than recognize that the real enemies are outside the country.

It is well known that Russia has constantly suffered from irreconcilable differences and conflicts among independent princes, boyars, and finally, in modern times, political parties. History has taught us few lessons. The words, spoken in ancient days by the revered Yurodivy, or "God's fools," concerned the Russian people: "We Russians do not need any bread to eat since we eat each other to satisfy our hunger."[4] This observation has remained true until now. We find it relatively easy to forgive the errors of those who are close to us; we cannot forgive them, however, if they notice our own mistakes. *Chi offende, non perdona* ["The one who offends is never forgiven"], says an Italian proverb. Has not this attitude easily put our beloved country under the oppression of our enemies, whose yoke has been many times bitterer than that of the Mongols?[5]

Therefore it is not surprising, under these conditions of disagreement or, more accurately, open hostility between advocates of light and heavy aviation, that our air knights, the Murometsy, could not develop as comprehensively as the Russian national situation might have allowed. Ultimately it would be the foreigners who would take full advantage of the creative work of Igor Sikorsky.

After preliminary experimental and training flights, the IM-Kievskiy began its first combat flight at eight o'clock in the morning, February 27, 1915. It carried enough gasoline for three and a half hours of flight with a bomb load of 246 kilograms. The crew included the pilot, Captain G. G. Gorshkov; his deputy commander, Lieutenant I. S. Bashko; the artillery

The Il'ya Muromets I (IM-1) at Yablonna in March 1915. Seated in the tail section, left to right, are Captain G. G. Gorshkov, Ensign Andreiyev, and Lieutenant I. S. Bashko. *Courtesy of the Archives, United Technologies Corporation*

The Il'ya Muromets I (IM-1) with members of the EVK at Yablonna in 1915.
Courtesy of the National Air and Space Museum

officer, Staff Captain A. A. Naumov; and one engine mechanic. The combat mission lasted 1 hour and 51 minutes. The IM-Kievskiy flew at an altitude of 2,800 meters, having achieved this cruising altitude in 40 minutes. Because of clouds, the flying ship returned to the aerodrome after reaching only the city of Plotsk.

The military baptism of the IM-Kievskiy actually took place the following day, on February 28, 1915. During this second flight with the same crew, it flew over enemy territory, bombing their trenches. During this flight, which lasted 2 hours and 30 minutes, it was discovered that there were no bridges over the Vistula near Plotsk.

It is probable that the flight of the IM-Kievskiy prompted the Germans to take notice of the aerodrome of the Murometsy. German aircraft began to appear over Yablonna regularly, twice a day. They dropped bombs on the aerodrome on February 28, just three hours after the IM-Kievskiy returned from its first combat mission. In most instances, these bombs dropped from enemy aircraft did no damage to the Murometsy, but in the city of Yablonna some people were wounded and killed.

During one enemy raid, on March 19, 1915, Igor Sikorsky was almost injured. A bomb fell close to him and a mechanic who had been assigned

from the R-BVZ factory. The mechanic was seriously wounded by fragments from an exploding bomb. Besides the bombs, the Germans also threw
flechettes (sharp-pointed arrows) with the inscription *Invention française,
fabrication allemande* [French invention, made in Germany]. These flechettes, which possessed considerable penetrating power, did not do much
harm, but, to tell the truth, they made an unpleasant impression on those
victimized on the ground.

The first military flight of the IM-Kievskiy abruptly altered the attitude
at the Stavka. This flight signaled further military applications for the
Murometsy. It would be appropriate to mention the commander of the IM-
Kievskiy, Captain Gorshkov. Georgiy Georgiyevich Gorshkov (later Colonel), was born into the family of an officer of the Urals Cossacks. He was
graduated from the Orenburg Cadet Academy, the Neplynyevsky Cadet
corps, and the Nicholas Engineering College. For a short time he served in a
field-engineer battalion in the Russian army. Interested in aeronautics,
Gorshkov later entered the Officers' School of Aeronautics (near St. Petersburg), where he was graduated and joined the staff as an instructor.

He participated in many prewar flights in balloons, called among common people "bubbles," including a long-distance flight begun in St. Petersburg with a landing in the Saratov region. In spite of the defects in these
aerostats and dangers during landings, Gorshkov used to recall these flights
with affection. He found that among his flights on free-flying balloons,
dirigibles, and aeroplanes, he enjoyed flying balloons most because they
were completely silent. Therefore, all the sounds reaching the balloon from
the ground, such as dogs barking, roosters crowing, and the sound of wind
in the trees, made an especially pleasant impression on him.

These 64-kilogram bombs,
dropped by a German zeppelin
on the Osovets fortress in 1915,
did not explode. The artillery
officer of the Il'ya Muromets V
(IM-5), Staff Captain
Zhuravchenko, is shown
disarming the bombs.
*Courtesy of the National Air
and Space Museum*

At the Officers School of Aeronautics, Captain Gorshkov served for a while as a dirigible commander. He did not like this duty. Once aeroplanes appeared, he took up flying. Subsequently he was sent to France to learn aviation. There he flew aeroplanes of almost all designs. Gorshkov first flew on an Il'ya Muromets in 1914, when he was deputy commandant of the Gatchina Military Flying School. Later he assumed command of the IM-Kievskiy.

Before Shidlovskiy's arrival at Yablonna, Gorshkov commanded the five Murometsy flying ships stationed there. After having made several military flights as commander of the IM-Kievskiy, he received the Order of St. Vladimir, Fourth Degree with Swords. In addition, he was promoted to the rank of lieutenant colonel, was appointed commander of the Murometsy group at Lvov (the IM-3 and IM-Kievskiy), and was later commander of an EVK detachment near Riga.

Unfortunately the antagonism between light and heavy aviation, with which Gorshkov's entire life had been connected, prevented him from giving all his energy to EVK activities. By nature straightforward and abrupt, Gorshkov found it difficult "to sit between two chairs." Therefore in February 1916, because of the aforementioned antagonism, he left the EVK, at a time when his energy and talent had a wide field for their application. No doubt General Shidlovskiy and Captain Gorshkov, shared a mutual respect. Their strength and energy had contributed to the development of the Il'ya Muromets.

When Shidlovskiy resigned his post after the Revolution, Gorshkov assumed command of the EVK, but he could not do much. After the Russian Army had collapsed and the Germans had invaded, Gorshkov, in an effort to preserve whatever remained of Russian aviation, joined the Ukrainian army, where he was appointed deputy commander of Ukrainian aviation under Pavlenko.

When the Bolsheviks took power, G. G. Gorshkov joined the Volunteer's Army, where he was received, not as one of the outstanding and experienced representatives of Russian aviation, but rather as a competitor. He was threatened with a trial and was forced to leave Ekaterinodar for Odessa, where he was captured by the Bolsheviks and later executed.

On March 9, 1915, the IM-Kievskiy took advantage of favorable weather and made a three-and-one-half-hour flight over East Prussia. At the time the flying ship was assigned to the First Army Headquarters under the command of Cavalry General Litvinov. After circling twice over the city of Willenburg, one of the places where General Samsonov's army had perished earlier, the IM-Kievskiy dropped 17 large bombs—16 to 32 kilograms each—on the railroad station, hangars, and horse-drawn wagons. It also conducted a thorough reconnaissance mission over the area with the purpose of gathering information on German troop movements around Mlava. Finally, it took photographs of the certain enemy positions and returned safely to the aerodrome.

The Il'ya Muromets Kievskiy in flight over Yablonna air base near Warsaw in 1915.
Courtesy of the K. N. Finne family

On the following day, the IM-Kievskiy repeated the sortie. This time, it dropped forty-five bombs on Willenburg, ten of which were 16-kilogram bombs. As a result, a railroad station and its rolling stock were destroyed. According to information received later at the Russian First Army Headquarters the raid had caused considerable panic. In addition to the destruction of the railway station, trains, and warehouses, two enemy officers and seventeen enlisted men had been killed. The railway station superintendent was wounded as well. In one German newspaper received in Petrograd, it was reported that the Russians possessed special aeroplanes that had caused great damage and were not vulnerable to artillery.

As a result of these successful missions, the general attitude toward the Murometsy changed abruptly. The Northwestern Front headquarters, for example, which had refused earlier—on March 27, 1915—to accept the IM-2, made the following request of the Stavka: "I hereby request that you inform us whether it would be feasible to assign an Il'ya Muromets of the Kievskiy type for the Northwestern Front."

The Stavka then withdrew the EVK from the command of the field inspector general of aviation and placed it under direct supervision of the Stavka. This action was prompted as well by the successful flights of the IM-1 in March 1915 by Sikorsky in which he attained an altitude of 2,100 meters; the same flying ship under its former commander had reached an altitude of only 1,350 meters. Especially flattering were the remarks made by the First Army Headquarters and the superintendent of the Novo-Georgiyevsk fortress, General Bobyr. The chief of staff for the fortress was Lieutenant General Yel'chaninov, a former professor at the military academy.

The Headquarters Staff of the Russian First Army sent the following telegram to the field inspector general of aviation:

> The IM-Kievskiy made six flights, ordered by the staff of the First Army. These flights consisted not only of reconnaissance work, but also of the mission to destroy railroad stations. The resulting reconnaissance information was highly valued, owing to the convenience of observing and taking photographs of each targeted enemy area. According to our information received from secret agents, the bombing of the railroad stations was met with great success. It was the experience gained from the first flight that demonstrated that aeroplanes of this type could be efficient both in reconnaissance and in bombing operations. The flights were normally conducted at an altitude of 3,200 meters and took four and one half hours to complete. We surmise that aeroplanes of this type, regarding their flight characteristics, deserve encouragement and their future actions depend entirely on how well they are staffed with experienced pilots.

The commandant of the Novo-Georgiyevsk fortress gave the following testimony about the Il'ya Muromets:

> The flights of the Il'ya Muromets aeroplanes demonstrated the great advantages of this type of aeroplane over other types. Reconnaissance from on board the Il'ya Muromets can be conducted thoroughly and with ease, owing to the convenience of observation and the possibility of taking photographs. These factors allow for excellent intelligence gathering. Reconnaissance may be also conducted with serenity and assurance. Since the flight ceiling—the last flight was made at an altitude of more than 3,200 meters with little difficulty and easily maintained—makes the Il'ya Muromets almost unvulnerable to enemy anti-aircraft fire. Reconnaissance, finally, also may be carried out at long range, deep in the enemy rear. The Il'ya Muromets can conduct flights of long duration owing to its sizable load-carrying capacity–that is, the capacity of the flying ship to carry large quantities of gasoline and oil. The Il'ya Muromets is capable as well of maintaining high speeds and covering long distances.
>
> The Il'ya Muromets may be considered to be a dangerous offensive weapon with its awe-inspiring armament and impressive bomb load. In addition, the Il'ya Muromets is a formidable weapon with its maneuverability and accurate bombing.[6] Flights at Yablonna and later combat reconnaissance sorties established excellent results.
>
> It is also necessary to add that the pilot's cabin was comfortable. There was a comparatively high degree of reliability with most engines, which were

easy to repair and maintain while in flight. It was relatively easy to repair light damage to the aircraft in flight. Another advantage was the extreme difficulty for the enemy to determine the actual distance between themselves and the Il'ya Muromets. This confusion was caused by the unusually large size of the Muro-metsy, which created a deceptive impression of distance and size.

These military flights showed quite well the results that can be expected from the Il'ya Muromets type, namely the Il'ya Muromets III. This aeroplane, even during its experimental flights over Yablonna, demonstrated significant advantages over such aeroplanes as the Il'ya Muromets Kievskiy that had already been tested in military actions.

German pilots captured near Prasnysh told us that they knew about the existence of our large flying machines and that Germany lacked aeroplanes of this type. It is also noted that from the first day one of these Murometsy had been assigned duty at the aerodrome and until March 6, no German aeroplanes have appeared.

It is necessary to state that the Il'ya Muromets I, earlier considered unsuitable for military flights, was kept in Brest-Litovsk and Lvov for a while. Nevertheless, it attained an altitude of 2,200 meters in a flight to Yablonna in less than one hour after takeoff with a 115-kilogram load aboard. This same flying ship also demonstrated in flight some remarkable characteristics in making turns, acceleration, rate of climb, descent, and landing.

In general, I assume the Il'ya Muromets–type aeroplanes will be outstanding for military actions when their crews finally prove worthy of them. This is now being achieved. Even if we do not consider these aircraft to be quite perfect, all the same, a giant step forward toward conquering the air has been made. The honor for this success, to our great pride, belongs and will always belong to Russia.

Out of all flights made by IM-Kievskiy at that time, the one made on March 31, 1915, is worth mentioning, since it provided the Headquarters of the First Army with extraordinary intelligence information. In the middle of March, the Austro-German Supreme Headquarters Command began to concentrate troops in Galicia. At that time, the Russian First Army staff received information that a considerable German force had been moved to their sector of the front.

Alarmed over these developments, the First Army Headquarters ordered the IM-Kievskiy to investigate the enemy rear areas thoroughly in order to determine enemy troop movement and deployment. Captain A. A. von Goerst, an intelligence officer from the Russian First Army, was added to the regular crew of the flying ship, which included Captain G. G. Gorshkov, the commander; Lieutenant I. S. Bashko, deputy commander; and Staff Captain A. A. Naumov, the artillery officer.

The IM-Kievskiy carried 524 kilograms of gasoline, 98 kilograms of oil, a total of four machine guns—two Maxims and two Madsen guns—and two cameras, a Potte and an Ul'yanin. The mission lasted for four hours. It was conducted at an altitude varying from 3,200 to 3,600 meters and covered a distance of about 533 kilometers. The target area for the reconnais-

The Il'ya Muromets Kievskiy returns to Yablonna after a mission over East Prussia on March 31, 1915. *Courtesy of the Archives, United Technologies Corporation*

sance flight roughly covered the frontier line with Germany, including such geographical points as Willenburg, Neidenburg, Sol'dau, Lautenburg, Strasburg, Torn, and certain terminal points of railway lines that transported German troops.

At Torn, the flight proceeded over the upstream side of the Vistula River to Plotsk, then to the north, then toward Mlava, and then to the east. The Il'ya Muromets then turned south and flew back to the front line from its eastern end to the west toward Plotsk. As a result, the front-line zone of the enemy was thoroughly reconnoitered. The most important points and all the large cities were photographed; a total of fifty photographs was taken.

It became clear that the enemy had not relocated any troops in this area. The conclusion was obvious. False information had been sent to the Russian First Army Headquarters. On the contrary, this reconnaissance flight, contradicting what had been observed during previous flights, demonstrated that enemy forces from this area had been relocated elsewhere. A copy of this report was dispatched to the Stavka of the Russian Army.

The Argus engines were removed from IM-3 type B (Beh) and installed on board IM-3 type V (Veh), the latter being of the same type as the IM-Kievskiy. This field modification made possible the joint participation of these flying ships in military action. By the time the modification had been made new aeroplane commanders had reached the squadron.

On April 20, 1915, the IM-Kievskiy completed a mission to destroy the Sol'dau railroad station. The crew consisted of the following: the commander, Lieutenant Bashko; deputy commander Lieutenant M. V. Smirnov; the artillery officer, Staff Captain Naumov, and Ensign Andreyev. The IM-Kievskiy circled six times over the Sol'dau station, in which fifteen trains were parked, then bombed the trains. The crew noticed and took a photograph of a locomotive explosion, just as the locomotive started moving.[7] During this mission, both Staff Captain Naumov and Ensign Andreyev got out on a wing and repaired an engine oil line which had broken in flight.

About half an hour later, after the IM-Kievskiy's flight, the IM-3, under the command of Staff Captain Brodovich, bombed the same railway station. This second mission caused an even greater panic. The crew of the IM-3 noticed another locomotive moving away from the station at full steam, probably in reaction to the panic caused when the IM-Kievskiy had destroyed a locomotive in the first raid. Both flying ships dropped forty bombs, of which thirty weighed more than 16 kilograms each.

Among other flights by the Murometsy, it is worth mentioning the flight on April 19, 1915, to Mlava by the IM-Kievskiy. For this mission, the crew consisted of the commander, Lieutenant Bashko; the deputy commander, Lieutenant M. V. Smirnov; and the artillery officer, Lieutenant Yu. G. Boiye. The IM-Kievskiy destroyed the railway station at Mlava. Commander Bashko and his crew dropped eleven 16-kilogram bombs and six 20-pound bombs. The IM-3, the crew consisting of the commander, Staff Captain Brodovich; the deputy commander, Lieutenant M. P. Spasov; and the artillery officer, Lieutenant Gagua, had flown over Plotsk, where the bridge over the Vistula, spanning both banks, undamaged the day before the flight, had been ripped open.[8]

In addition, the IM-Kievskiy dropped bombs on the German aerodrome at Sanniki. These bombs destroyed a tent hangar and an aeroplane. Over Bzura, the IM-3 encountered intense antiaircraft fire. For the Germans, the most serious raid by the Murometsy took place on April 24, 1915, when both these Murometsy flew over East Prussia. During this raid the IM-Kievskiy dropped eleven 16-kilogram bombs and one 82-kilogram bomb on the city of Neidenburg. The IM-3, one hour later, completed the destruction begun by the IM-Kievskiy. As a result, a railroad station was destroyed, and fires ignited by the bombing raged all night.

Lieutenant Colonel Gasler, of the Stavka, who had arrived on the eve of the flight and participated in it, was quite pleased with both the mission and its spectacular results. It must be assumed that the destruction inflicted on Neidenburg by both Murometsy was considerable, because on the follow-

Aerial reconnaissance photograph from a bombing mission of the Il'ya Muromets on the Mlava railway station. Note the bomb falling on a train that is visible below. The lower half of the photograph shows the time and altimeter setting at the time the photograph was taken. *Courtesy of Sergei Sikorsky*

ing morning, six German aeroplanes attacked our base at Yablonna. These Germans aeroplanes dropped twenty-six bombs and broke the glass in the house of Countess Pototskiy's estate manager. One old aeroplane, the Il'ya Muromets V, (IM-5), which was no longer used for military operations was slightly damaged.[9] There were no casualties.

The Russian First Army Headquarters staff were quite satisfied with these flights by the Murometsy, especially with the destruction at Sol'dau. The Germans, alarmed by the raids, reinforced their defenses in Willenburg, Mlava, Sol'dau, and other points in East Prussia. They also installed numerous antiaircraft artillery batteries in these cities.[10]

All these flights by the Murometsy took place in East Prussia, in the same area where General Samsonov's army had perished in August 1914. Somehow the Germans associated this victory with the name of Tannenberg, which has been well remembered since 1410 as the place where the Slavs totally vanquished the Teutonic knights.

In his memoirs, *Aus meinem Leben* (1920), Hindenburg wrote the following in reference to these days:

> Tannenberg! This word awakens difficult recollections for the mighty German order of Knighthood, the rallying cry of triumphant Slavs, a memory still fresh in history despite the passing of more than five hundred years.

The Germans probably wished to associate the name of Tannenberg with their new victory and as a symbol of revenge over the Slavs. They referred to the latter with their usual epithet *Schweinehund,* or with such phrases as the "manure for German culture" [*Dunger-Volk*].

As a consequence, the Il'ya Muromets flying ship, as an original and purely Russian weapon, paid a debt owed to the arrogant Teutons by visiting and bombing them in East Prussia. Here in the battle of Tannenberg in 1914 the Germans, with a larger and technically superior army, surrounded

This twin-engine variant of the Il'ya Muromets was equipped with British-made Sunbeam engines and was used as a trainer. *Courtesy of the K. N. Finne family*

and defeated the Russian Army. By fighting at Tannenberg, it should be noted, the Russians took on German power and saved France from the steel of German fists. [Tannenberg is the very place where in the Napoleonic war of 1806–07 Russian troops under Count Benigsen fought numerous skirmishes. Before that time Napoleon had been invincible. By virtue of these Russian victories under Benigsen Prussia had been saved.]

While both the IM-Kievskiy and the IM-3 completed the above described missions, other Murometsy at Yablonna were being prepared for combat action. English Sunbeam engines, which were expected to work much better than the ineffectual Salmson engines, arrived for installation. Unfortunately, the Sunbeam engines, despite our high hopes, demonstrated only slightly better results than Salmson engines. The Sunbeams, moreover, were far behind Argus engines. Murometsy equipped with "Sunbeam" engines were quite incapable of climbing to a higher altitude than 2,900 meters. Since better engines for Murometsy were not available, both training and combat flights had to be made with these Sunbeam engines. For example the Il'ya Muromets I (IM-1) (Commander Lieutenant G. I. Lavrov), the Il'ya Muromets II (IM-2) (Commander Staff Captain A. V. Pankrat'yev), and the Il'ya Muromets V (IM-5) (Commander Lieutenant G. V. Alekhnovich) made several combat flights to Lovich, Skernevitsi, Yedinorozhets, Tsekhanov, and other places during June and July 1915.[11] During a flight by these three Murometsy on July 17, a large concentration of enemy troops was spotted on the Narev front.

By the beginning of May 1915, the number of personnel in the EVK had been expanded and the number of flying ships in the squadron had in-

Inspection of the Il'ya Muromets II (IM-2) at Yablonna by Grand Duke Kirill Vladimirovich on May 29, 1915. The grand duke is seated in the machine-gun position in the fuselage. *Courtesy of the National Air and Space Museum*

creased from seven to ten, the newly established limit. The shortage of well-prepared commanders for the Murometsy had become obvious. In order to fill these positions, the Office of the Field Inspector General of Aviation had sent some officers from the ballooning corps, officers who had remained unengaged owing to the disbanding of dirigible detachments. These dirigibles had proven to be absolutely unsuitable for military action.

These officers were unfamiliar not only with the Il'ya Muromets aeroplanes and their operation, but also with that of small aeroplanes. They were soon dismissed from the EVK.

Among the few military pilots who had been graduated from the aviation school and had reported to the EVK was Lieutenant N. G. Severskiy-Prokofiyev, a well-known opera artist, who had never served in the army before. Having developed a great interest in aviation before the war, he enlisted as soon as the war began. He was given the rank of lieutenant, then entered the Gatchina Military Flying School, from which he was posted to the EVK. By that time he had grown sons who were officers serving in naval aviation.[12]

Lieutenant Severskiy-Prokofiyev did not remain long in the EVK. While on duty, he caught a cold, developed pneumonia and was evacuated to the rear. Soon afterward he departed the EVK for a unit flying single-engine aircraft.

On May 24, 1915, the IM-Kievskiy flew to Lvov. This flight took 4 hours and 15 minutes. Some time later, on May 27, the IM-3 joined the IM-Kievskiy at Lvov. The relocation of the two best flying ships to Galicia was necessitated by the concentration of German troops in the area. At that time, the Russian Army, which did not then have sufficient artillery, ammunition, or even rifles, had begun a retreat from the Carpathian Mountains. These Murometsy helped our troops by flying reconnaissance missions over the advancing troops and by bombing enemy railway stations, warehouses, command posts, and other targets. This period of active combat work is considered to have been the most efficient in the history of the EVK. It can be said that this was its most impressive phase as far as aggressive military actions and combat results are concerned.

Unfortunately, soon after the Murometsy arrived in Lvov, the IM-3 commander, Staff Captain Brodovich, submitted a request to be dismissed and transferred to light aviation. It was, to be sure, done under the influence of the light aviation headquarters, which, as mentioned earlier, did not look with favor on the Murometsy and the EVK, which had been removed from their command.

The resignation of this commander who was considered a serious pilot and an excellent officer, was another blow to the operations of the Murometsy which had just begun to be effective. In addition to the unpleasant impression that his resignation made on the morale of the squadron officers, the loss of one of the best commanders came at a time when other EVK commanders were expected to be involved in intense and responsible work.

German Pilot Observes the Il'ya Muromets Galicia 1915

This dramatic photograph of an Il'ya Muromets was taken by Lieutenant Paul Mayer of the German Air Force on a long-range reconnaissance flight in 1915. His airplane flew toward the Il'ya Muromets from above and at a distance. The approximate altitude of Mayer's aircraft was 3,000 meters. This was the normal approach toward the giant Russian bomber, since it possessed considerable defensive firepower.

German airmen referred to the Murometsy as "Sikorskies." Lieutenant Mayer flew with the Fliegerkompagnie 9, stationed at Rohatyn, which was located southwest of Tarnopol in Galicia. The huge Il'ya Muromets bombers, with their capacity for long-range flights deep into enemy rear areas, had no rivals on the Russian front, and for this reason they drew the intense interest of German fighter squadrons who were keenly desirous of downing one of the behemoth flying ships. During the entire course of the war on the eastern front only three Murometsy were downed by enemy action.

Lieutenant Mayer's photograph was taken on the morning of August 9, 1916, during a two-hour reconnaissance flight that covered 210 kilometers, a flight that began at 6:20 A.M. and concluded at 8:20 A.M. Mayer indicates that "the Sikorski was spotted and photographed near the town of Darachow."

The incident could not help but cause an interruption in military operations. On the one hand, the majority of the EVK officers, who had no settled views on the Il'ya Muromets aeroplanes, could not help but look back fondly at single-engine aeroplanes. On the other hand, there was an acute shortage of well-trained pilots ready to assume command of Il'ya Muromets bombers.

Notes

1. [Editors' Note.] The term "Stavka" refers to the Supreme High Command or Supreme Headquarters of the Russian military in World War I. The Field Inspector of Aviation oversaw Russian military aviation. This position was held by the Grand Duke Alexander Mikhailovich, who during the prewar years had been an advocate of airpower and the impetus behind building an "air fleet" for Russia. The EVK, as it evolved, became a self-sufficient air unit with its own supply and technical staff. When fully operational, the EVK possessed its own mobile workshops, motor pool, and railway cars.

2. [Note by K. N. Finne.] Colonel V. F. Naidenov held the position of deputy commander of the EVK under General Shidlovskiy. He was seriously injured in an automobile accident in June 1915 and was evacuated to the rear hospital. Naidenov never returned to the EVK. He died in Petrograd in a famine under Soviet rule. [Editors' note. Finne is probably referring to the period of the Russian Civil War, 1918–21.]

3. [Note by K. N. Finne.] This version was a Type V or "narrow wing." The forward cabin or cockpit had windows that allowed the pilot to look forward and downward for maximum visibility.

4. [Editors' note.] The *Yurodivy,* or "God's fools," were pilgrims or wanderers, highly revered by Russians for their spirituality, who preserved through oral tradition many folk stories, songs, and poems. They occupied a special, if unofficial, place in the life of the Russian Orthodox Church.

5. [Editors' note.] The Mongols, a nomadic tribe, invaded and overran the Russian lands in the thirteenth century. The subsequent Mongolian rule or Tartar yoke lasted for two centuries.

6. [Note by K. N. Finne.] The accuracy of the target bombing by the Il'ya Muromets stemmed from a special aiming device or military target instrument designed by Igor Sikorsky and later improved by Staff Captain V. A. Ivanov, who worked independent of one another. The same instrument was improved through the labors of Lieutenant Gagua, an artillery officer. Lieutenant Gagua was later killed in an air crash at Gatchina in 1916. Sergeant Major Fogt, a mechanic and another contributor to this project, was killed earlier, on November 15, 1915, in the crash of the IM-3.

7. [Note by K. N. Finne.] Nikolskiy, in his book *Tactics of Aerial Bombardment,* records the following German report: "On April 20, 1915, the Sikorsky aeroplane appeared over Sol'dau. While it was circling over the railway station it dropped thirteen bombs. Two bombs hit the train. One locomotive was destroyed. There were many railway workers and some soldiers killed or wounded." [Editors' note: This may refer to M. N. Nikol'skoi (1888–1969), who once served as a mechanic with the

EVK, joined the Red army in 1918, and wrote several books on aviation tactics in the Soviet period.]

8. [Note by K. N. Finne.] On April 18, 1915, the IM-Kievskiy dropped bombs on the bridge, destroying two barges as well as some buildings in the embankment near Plotsk.

9. [Editors' note.] The Il'ya Muromets V, Type B (Beh). See appendix 6.

10. [Note by K. N. Finne.] In a German report, quoted in Nikolskiy's *Tactics of Aerial Bombardment,* it is stated: "In Mlava, thirteen bombs were dropped [by the Il'ya Muromets] with six soldiers killed and sixteen wounded, and several horses killed. There is an obvious lack of antiaircraft guns for defense of our troops."

11. [Editors' note.] Il'ya Muromets I, Type V (Veh); Il'ya Muromets II, Type V (Veh); and Il'ya Muromets V, Type V (Veh). See appendix 6.

12. [Editors' note.] His son, Alexander Seversky, served with distinction as a Russian naval pilot in World War I. Seversky, following the pattern of Igor Sikorsky, emigrated to the United States and pursued a career as an aviation industrialist.

Chapter Five

THE EVK IN ACTION

During the spring of 1915 the Austrians and Germans launched an offensive against the Russian Third Army under the command of General Lesh. Two Murometsy, the IM-Kievskiy and the IM-3, arrived in the combat zone and conducted aerial reconnaissance missions deep into enemy territory. These aircraft were very helpful to the Third Army, by vigilantly monitoring the movements and positions of the enemy. According to one newspaper correspondent, the capture of 15,000 enemy troops near Lublin in 1915 was made possible through the reconnaissance work of an Il'ya Muromets. Light aircraft at the time lacked sufficient range to penetrate deeply behind the front lines of the enemy. Only the Murometsy were able to conduct long-distance reconnaissance missions. They patrolled the shores of the river San and beyond, gathering information on enemy communication lines, the movement of trains, the transfer of reserves to the front, the appearance of new aerodromes, and the concentration of supplies and matériel.

As a consequence of this aerial reconnaissance activity, the staff of the Third Army acquired a clear and detailed picture of enemy activity, not only along the front lines, but also in the rear areas. The intelligence staff deeply appreciated this valuable reconnaissance work. Murometsy bombarded enemy positions in the rear areas as well, dropping huge bombs on railroad stations, trains laden with war supplies, warehouses, and transport vehicles.

During one of those flights, on June 27, 1915, the IM-Kievskiy flew over the Przhevorsk railroad station, located just south of Yaroslav. This four-

Bombs from IM-Kievskiy set off an explosion of an Austrian train at Przevorsk in Galicia on June 27, 1915. The photograph was taken from an altitude of 3,000 meters. *Courtesy of the Archives, United Technologies Corporation*

hour mission included reconnaissance work in the district of the San River and the dropping of four bombs on the trenches at Lezhaisk. Over Przhevorsk the IM-Kievskiy circled three times, then dropped seven bombs on an ammunition train. The crew of the Il'ya Muromets observed exploding bombs, tongues of flame, and bellowing smoke among the five ammunition trains parked at the station. After several minutes of bombing, the station at Przhevorsk was filled with smoke and shells bursting in the air. According to the testimony of prisoners of war, later confirmed in German newspapers, approximately 30,000 artillery shells had been destroyed.

For the enemy, there was loss of life at the Lezhaisk station. In addition, the raid produced great physical destruction at the railway station and interrupted communications in the district. Panic had also arisen as a consequence of the raid by the Il'ya Muromets. For this mission Lieutenant I. S. Bashko, the commander of the IM-Kievskiy, and Staff Captain A. A. Naumov, the artillery officer, were awarded the Order of St. George, Fourth Degree. Deputy commander Lieutenant M. V. Smirnov received the St. George sword, and the mechanic Shkudov received the St. George Cross. These were the first men in the EVK to achieve the knighthood of St. George.[1]

Bombs hit Yaroslav railway
station. This photograph,
taken from the attacking Il'ya
Muromets bomber, with the
accompanying photo-
interpretation overlay,
illustrates both the bombing
accuracy of the Murometsy
and the highly sophisticated
aerial reconnaissance
techniques employed by the
Russians in 1915. *Courtesy of
Sergei Sikorsky*

Bombs being loaded onto an Il'ya Muromets. Note the blurred image of the upper machine-gun position near the fuel tanks. *Courtesy of Harry Woodman*

It is evident that the enemy resented these bold missions by the EVK. When flying at an altitude of 3,000 meters, the Murometsy were done little harm by the enemy's antiaircraft batteries. At the same time, German fighters chose to keep away from our well-armed Russian knights of the air. These circumstances prompted crewmen on Murometsy to approach their combat missions with high confidence, an attitude that is an indelible feature of the Russian character.

This feeling of invincibility almost led to tragedy for the crew of the IM-Kievskiy. Having been able to fly deep into enemy territory without challenge or apparent danger, the crew decided to remove some of the aircraft's machine guns to allow for a greater useful load of bombs for a mission on July 19, 1915. Three or four machine guns were removed, leaving the flying ship armed only with one rapid-firing Madsen gun and one carbine. During the mission three Brandenburg-type aircraft attacked the IM-

Kievskiy over the town of Shebrzheshin, which was about forty-eight kilometers from the Russian lines and to the south of the Krasnostav-Kholm line.

One enemy fighter, taking advantage of its superior speed, passed undetected beneath, turned sharply, and flew head on toward the IM-Kievskiy, firing its machine gun at close range. From the IM-Kievskiy it was possible to see clearly the faces of both the pilot and the observer in the approaching enemy aeroplane. The IM-Kievskiy returned fire, forcing the enemy pilot to dip his wing sharply and dive away in the manner of a falling leaf. The other two enemy fighters, flying parallel to the IM-Kievskiy at a respectful distance, continued to fire, but with no effect.

During this air battle the IM-Kievskiy was hit by sixty rounds of enemy fire, which pierced the oil tanks, radiators, and gas tanks and shattered the glass panes of the cockpit. Two engines on one side were knocked out. Lieutenant Bashko, the pilot in command, suffered head and leg wounds.

Interior of an Il'ya Muromets equipped for combat, looking backward toward the tail. Note the bomb rack at the left. Straps for securing the bombs are also on the floor. A carbine is evident on the right.
Courtesy of Harry Woodman

Yet he was able to direct his flying ship back to our lines, then glide to a safe landing on the soggy airstrip of the 24th Aviation Squadron (commanded by military pilot Captain Mul'ko). The two remaining operable engines of the IM-Kievskiy had stopped just above the aerodrome.

This was the first unpowered landing by an Il'ya Muromets aircraft. Until this time it was believed that an unpowered landing was not possible or, at a minimum, extremely dangerous. While landing, the wheels of the IM-Kievskiy became stuck in the muddy soil, abruptly snapping the left side of the chassis. This mishap broke four struts and the propeller of the second engine, plus other supporting struts and ribs. It took a day to repair the damage to the IM-Kievskiy.

Because of the great interest in this air battle—the first for an Il'ya Muromets aircraft—Captain Gorshkov, the ranking officer of the EVK, submitted the following report:

> For the Commander of the EVK, submitted on July 19, 1915. Report No. 125. City of Vlodava.
>
> I hereby report on the flight on the above-cited date for the Il'ya Muromets Kievskiy.
>
> > Crew members: Pilot in command, Lieutenant Bashko; deputy commander, Lieutenant Smirnov; artillery officer, Staff Captain Naumov; mechanic, Lieutenant Lavrov
> >
> > Load: Gasoline, 491 kilogram; oil, 98 kilogram; ten 16-kilogram bombs, five 11-kilogram bombs; twelve incendiary bombs; a light machine gun; a carbine; and 260 rounds of ammunition.
> >
> > Weight: 1163 kilogram;
> >
> > Flight Path: Vlodava–River Bug–eastward of the village of Grabovets–Unuv'–Belzhets–Shebrzheshin–Krasnostav–Kholm.
> >
> > Duration of Flight: 4 hours, from 4:00 to 8:00 A.M.
>
> Our reconnaissance indicated that there were three enemy artillery batteries near the village of Gostynnoye, and to the north and west of Unuv' there was an enemy aerodrome, equipped with several tent hangars and an antiaircraft battery. At the Lyubych station there were three enemy trains consisting of 50 cars. To the north of Unuv' there were nearly 400 horse wagons. In the area farther north our information suggested that there were no trains. In Shebrzheshin there was a small train consisting of 60 horse wagons.
>
> During the raid we dropped five bombs on the aerodrome near Unuv'. In addition, we dropped four bombs on a train near the Belzhets station and five bombs on the Lyubych station. Our twelve incendiary bombs were dropped on fields to the south of Shebrzheshin.
>
> Three German pursuit airplanes attacked us during the mission at our cruising altitude of 3,200–3,500 meters. The first enemy aircraft was spotted through the lower hatch approaching about fifty meters from below. At the

time of the attack, the IM-Kievskiy, with Lieutenant Smirnov at the controls, was flying over Shebrzheshin, which was about forty-two kilometers from the trenches. At once, Captain Bashko replaced Smirnov as pilot. Meanwhile the German fighter, with its greater speed, quickly took up a position fifty meters above and to the right of the IM-Kievskiy and opened fire with its machine guns. Within the flying ship, the crew assumed their battle stations. Lieutenant Smirnov remained next to Commander Bashko, Staff Captain Naumov opened fire with his light machine gun, and Lieutenant Lavrov fired at the enemy with a carbine.

On the first pass, the enemy machine-gun fire pierced the overhead fuel tanks, the fuel filter of the right engines, the radiator, the fuel lines leading to the left engines, and the windows on the front and right side of the cockpit. Once the fuel line to the left engines had been pierced, the valves supplying fuel to the left side were shut off. Now the IM-Kievskiy continued to cruise with just two engines on the right side operating. The German aircraft again resumed its attack, now from the left side, but this time the enemy faced the concentrated defensive fire [of the rapid-fire gun and carbine] of the Il'ya Muromets. The German then banked sharply to the right, dove, and careened downward toward Zamost'ye.

In the aftermath of the attack Lieutenant Smirnov took the controls of the flying ship, and Lieutenant Lavrov attended to Captain Bashko, who had been wounded in the head and leg. In a brief time, Bashko once again took over the controls, while Smirnov Lavrov took turns covering the ruptured fuel filter with their hands in order to stop the leakage of fuel. During the first enemy attack, the machine gun had fired twenty-five rounds in the one cassette and fifteen rounds in the second cassette before the weapon jammed. It was later discovered that the recoil spring had broken.

Another German aircraft appeared, made one pass on the left side, and opened fire with its machine gun. Smirnov returned fire with the carbine. Lavrov unfortunately was in the cockpit next to the filter and was unable to respond. Naumov tried in vain to repair the light machine gun. Smirnov then passed the carbine to Naumov, while replacing Lavrov at the ruptured filter. Lavrov's wrists had been severely frozen while trying to block the fuel leak. Fortunately the second enemy fighter did not make another pass.

When the IM-Kievskiy reached the trench line, a third German fighter attacked at long distance, approaching from above and to the left. The enemy rained down a burst of fire from his machine guns. At the same time, enemy artillery fire opened up from below. The IM-Kievskiy was flying at an altitude of 1,400–1,500 meters when this attack occurred.

While approaching the city of Kholm at an altitude of 700 meters, the engines on the right side abruptly stopped, having run out of fuel. The crew then made a crash landing on a boggy pasture field near the village of Gorodishche, which was located about four or five kilometers from Kholm. The site of the emergency landing was near the aerodrome of the twenty-fourth aviation detachment. The IM-Kievskiy was mired in mud up to the chassis of the suspension. There was damage to the left side of the chassis, to four struts, to the propeller of the second engine, to the engine suspension, and to other small ribs and spars.

During the inspection of the aircraft after landing, the crew discovered serious damage from enemy machine-gun fire—the propeller of the third engine was pierced in two places; the iron frame or mount holding the number three engine was damaged; the hood of engine number two was also pierced; the magnetos of engine number two were hit; the frame of engine number two had been struck; and there were dents and bullet marks across the entire surface of the aeroplane.

Despite his wounds, Captain Bashko had landed the IM-Kievskiy. His wounds were attended to in the small village of Gorodishche. Later he was taken to the hospital of the All-Russian Society of Noblemen in Vlodava. Bashko had been hit by machine gun fire in the calf of one leg, above the knee, and in the buttocks. There had also been superficial wounds to the head when a bullet had exploded on his right side.

/Signed/
SENIOR OFFICER OF THE EVK
CAPTAIN GORSHKOV

The same air battle of the IM-Kievskiy was mentioned in the following telegrams from the Stavka (no. 373) to Lieutenant Bashko.

The Supreme High Command (Stavka) has directed us to express our sincere gratitude to you and your comrades for your heroic action.

/Signed/
YANUSHKEVICH
No. 10,977

By the order of the Stavka, Lieutenant Bashko and Lieutenant Lavrov were promoted and given the Cross of St. George, Second Degree. Staff Captain Naumov and Lieutenant Smirnov both received decorations. The telegram written by Captain Gorshkov, describing the air battle, was sent to Nicholas II.

At that time, the home aerodrome of the IM-Kievskiy and the IM-3 was located in Vlodava, where the Murometsy had arrived after having been stationed earlier in Lublin. Soon after the above-described episode of air combat, the IM-Kievskiy was reunited with the EVK, which was located at Lida in the Vilnius region.

The IM-3 alone continued its arduous combat duty at the front until the fall of 1915, flying in support of the Russian Third Army. It conducted many missions deep into the enemy rear, sometimes as far as 200 kilometers or more. Many of these missions called for the crew of the IM-3 to remain aloft for more than six hours. The IM-3 had the responsibility of checking the deployment of enemy troops. Under the command of Staff Captain Ozerskiy, this flying ship executed its tasks aggressively, at times dropping

Wartime Russian sketch of an Il'ya Muromets in aerial combat with a German fighter. *Courtesy of the National Air and Space Museum*

bombs while flying through heavy enemy antiaircraft fire. Twice a day for one week, the IM-3 hit the railroad station of Belzhets near Rava-Russkaya, the terminus of the railway line on the Austrian sector of the front. These attacks prevented the enemy from running trains during the daylight hours.

After the Russian Army had retreated from Brest-Litovsk, the IM-3 flew to Slutsk, where it continued bombing enemy positions at Kartuz-Berezu, Skobelevskiy Lager' and Baranovichi. The combat contribution of the IM-3 was so highly valued by the staff of the Third Army that the chief of staff, Major General Romanovskiy, expressed at one point this sentiment: "Give me just three Murometsy and take all the light aeroplanes and I will be satisfied." The Council of St. George, on the recommendation of the staff of the Third Army, awarded the officers of the IM-3 the St. George sword.

It is important to remember that the higher echelons of the various armies were not alone in appreciating the contributions of the Murometsy. The front-line troops, who often had little positive to say about light aeroplanes, displayed high regard for the Murometsy. These soldiers had too often seen numerous enemy aeroplanes directing artillery fire and flying unchallenged over the Russian positions. They wondered why the Russian fighters could not meet the challenge of enemy aviation. Russian troops in the trenches regarded the inactivity of our pilots flying light aircraft as evidence of the fact that certain pilots did not want to risk their lives.

By contrast, the Murometsy, flying directly into the enemy rear areas and against intense antiaircraft fire, made an impression on our troops. Sometimes it was possible from our front-line observation positions to see the huge bombs dropped by the Murometsy exploding and to see the accompanying fires. For these reasons, our troops welcomed the appearance of the Murometsy in their sector. Officers, enlisted men, even entire units of soldiers and the teaching staff of regiments often appeared at the aerodromes of the Murometsy to inspect with awe the huge Russian flying machine.

As the author of this memoir, I once heard the enthusiastic account of one artillery brigade, probably the seventy-eighth, who reported that their battery was saved by an Il'ya Muromets. The incident took place somewhere near the Narev front. Here the Germans had launched an assault on the Novo-Georgiyevsk fortress with an intense artillery bombardment on our position and our immediate rear. The artillery fire was so powerful that retreat by our troops was impossible. The IM-5 flew over the German lines at the time of the attack and dropped bombs on the German artillery batteries. This action distracted the enemy artillery fire sufficiently to enable the Russian battery to rest and to rearm itself.

A great misfortune occurred on November 15, 1915, when for reasons unexplained the IM-3 crashed south of Baranovichi near Priluki. According to Captain Gorshkov, who participated on an investigation committee looking into the air catastrophe, the cause of the crash may have been the decision of Staff Captain Ozerskiy—the courageous commander of the IM-3—to remove the supplementary controls from his flying ship to increase the cruising speed, which was normally 120 to 130 kilometers an hour. This alteration in fact reduced the stability of the large aeroplane.

Before entering the EVK, Staff Captain Ozerskiy had been an instructor at the Gatchina Military Flying School. Ozerskiy was unusual because he did not share the hostility of many of his fellow officers toward heavy aviation. In fact, Ozerskiy chose service with the EVK over an assignment with an air unit that flew single-engine aeroplanes. He was convinced that the Murometsy would make a valuable contribution to the war effort. Before catering the squadron, Ozerskiy had belonged to the First Grenadier Guards of Emperor Alexander II.

For Ozerskiy's fateful flight, the IM-3 had fuel for five hours and a bomb load of 425 kilograms. On board the IM-3 there was a crew of three in addition to the commander, Ozerskiy: deputy commander, Lieutenant M. P. Spasov; Lieutenant Colonel Zvegintsev, a member of the State Duma;[2] and the mechanic warrant officer Fogt.

During this mission the IM-3 came under enemy fire while bombing Baranovichi. The IM-3 dropped eight bombs on Baranovichi, hitting the

Deputy commander of the Il'ya Muromets III (IM-3), Lieutenant M. P. Spasov, and M. M. Rykachev of the meteorological unit of the EVK. *Courtesy of the Archives, United Technologies Corporation*

railway station. German antiaircraft fire evidently exploded near the flying ship, damaging cables leading to the ailerons. Ozerskiy observed the damage to the left aileron and turned back, using only the rudder for directional control.

While descending from an altitude of 2,800 meters, the IM-3 suddenly banked to the left and downward. Ozerskiy could not correct the steep dive or bring his flying ship under control. Now earthbound, the IM-3 fell into a deep dive, the nose pointing downward, and crashed. All the crew died except Lieutenant Spasov, who somehow miraculously survived, although he suffered many fractures and injuries.

Also worth mentioning is the fact that the bombs still on board were slightly cracked during the crash, but none exploded. Our Russian-made bombs, according to airborne observations, were of high quality, with a dependable triggering mechanism that worked unfailingly when they were dropped from the air.

As a consequence of this air catastrophe one of the best combat flying ships in the EVK was destroyed. The crash of the IM-3 was a heavy loss for everyone. But this great loss did not weaken the spirit of those willing to work tirelessly to develop our unique and national air weapon, the Il'ya Muromets, and to struggle against the enemy to a victorious end.

Notes

1. [Editors' note.] The Military Order of St. George was awarded to officers for bravery. The Cross of St. George was given to enlisted men for bravery. The Sword of St. George, a separate award, consisted of a small dirk that the recipient wore on his uniform, the hilt containing a miniature of the order.

2. [Note by K. N. Finne.] Before entering the EVK in July 1915, Staff Captain Ozerskiy was an instructor at the Gatchina Military Flying School. Despite the hostility of most officers at Gatchina to heavy aircraft, Ozerskiy joined the Murometsy squadron rather than serve as a commanding officer with an air unit flying light aircraft. He believed that the Murometsy would make a useful contribution to the war effort. Before Ozerskiy entered the air force, he served in the First Grenadier of the Life Guards of Emperor Alexander II.

Chapter Six

THE EXPANSION
OF THE EVK

The Squadron of Flying Ships abandoned its base at Yablonna in July 1915. At the beginning of the month, the Germans had already launched an attack on the fortress of Novo-Georgiyevsk. The enemy offensive forced the EVK to make several relocations, first to Belostok, then to Lida in the region of Vilensk. At Lida there was a beautiful aerodrome available, the former base of the dirigible Astra. There were also workshops and barracks for use by the squadron. In peacetime Lida had been the base for aviation and ballooning units.

The new situation provided an opportunity not only to assemble and to repair the Murometsy, but also to organize a program of systematic training for the officers of the squadron. This aviation training consisted of practical and theoretical lessons on various types of machine gun, a course on firing these guns, and continuing instruction on flying Murometsy aircraft for future pilot commanders.

The IM-2 appeared on August 2, 1915, the day of aviation (Prophet Elijah's day). This flying ship was equipped with engines manufactured at the Russo-Baltic Automobile plant in Riga.[1] The R-BVZ aero engine, designed by the engineer Kireyev, was in fact of an automobile type. It was a six-cylinder, two-stroke, water-cooled engine with the radiators mounted on the sides. Positive results followed with the installation of these Russian-made power plants on the IM-2. They proved to be superior to the Salmson and Sunbeam engines in both quality and performance. These Russian engines were not only comparable to the German Argus engines, but in several

The huge hanger at Lida that once housed Russian dirigibles is shown with Murometsy and S-16 fighters. The photograph was taken in July 1915. *Courtesy of the National Air and Space Museum*

A group of EVK officers at Lida in July 1915: (left to right) Mechanic N. V. Sirotin, Lieutenant G. I. Lavrov, Staff Captain A. V. Pankrat'yev, Lieutenant G. V. Alekhnovich, Staff Captain Chechulin, Lieutenant A. V. Konstenchik, Lieutenant Krzhichkovskiy, Lieutenant Lukinskiy, Mechanic Kisel, Staff Captain A. V. Serednitskiy, Igor Sikorsky, Lieutenant Loiko. *Courtesy of the Archives, United Technologies Corporation*

An Il'ya Muromets II (IM-2) under construction in Petrograd in the summer of 1915. Note the R-BVZ engines and airframe serial number 167. *Courtesy of the National Air and Space Museum*

respects were superior to them. The flying ship, with a load of 820 kilograms, reached an altitude of 3,450 meters on its first flight.

The IM-2 underwent tests carrying the huge 400-kilogram bomb. No Murometsy had ever carried such a heavy bomb load. This giant bomb, nearly two meters in height, could have become a devastating primary weapon for the squadron. When it fell to the earth, it tore open a crater three meters wide. A test bomb was loaded with sand, but one can imagine the crater that the bomb would make if loaded with more than 300 kilograms of TNT.

After the evacuation and fall of the Kovno, Novo-Georgiyevsk, and Brest-Litovsk fortresses and the abandonment of Vil'no in August 1915, the Murometsy had to leave Lida. In the face of the advance of German troops on the Northern Front below Riga, the EVK moved to Pskov. The 710-kilometer flight from Lida to Pskov took place on August 27, 1915. At that time the squadron comprised six Murometsy: the IM-1, IM-2, IM-4, IM-5,

The Il'ya Muromets II (IM-2) with R-BVZ engines. At the center is a 400-kilogram bomb. Igor Sikorsky is fourth from the left and General M. V. Shidlovskiy is third from the right. *Courtesy of the Archives, United Technologies Corporation*

IM-6, and IM-Kievskiy.[2] The flight had to be made in difficult weather, forcing the squadron to fly through fog and rain to its relocated aerodrome. The habit of most commanding officers was to fly without the use of a compass. Only Lieutenant G. I. Lavrov, flying the IM-1, avoided the weather by taking his flying ship above the clouds, then descending through the inclement weather to land at Pskov.

Lavrov had flown with Igor Sikorsky in the 1914 St. Petersburg-to-Kiev flight and had acquired experience flying the Il'ya Muromets over the sea with the aid of a compass. Staff Captain Bashko flew the IM-Kievskiy. Bashko displayed some scepticism about his compass and, moreover, feared that his flying ship might fall into the hands of the Germans, who at the time were advancing on Vil'no. So he decided to fly to Pskov under the clouds—at times at an altitude of only 100 meters. By this route, Bashko took five hours and fifteen minutes to reach Pskov. The IM-5, commanded by Lieutenant G. V. Alekhnovich, landed on an estate some twenty kilometers from Pskov. The IM-2, commanded by Staff Captain A. V. Pankrat'yev, lost its way and landed finally at Novo-Sventsyani.

Each of these Murometsy later reached Pskov. Only the IM-4, commanded by Lieutenant M. V. Smirnov, had to remain in Rezhitsa—a fateful place for Murometsy, to judge from the previous flights of the IM-1 and IM-

Nina Bouroff

Nina Bouroff first met Igor Sikorsky before World War I, while he was building the Grand and working at the Russo-Baltic Wagon Company's aviation branch in St. Petersburg. The young wife of P. N. Bouroff, a general in the Russian Army, Nina Bouroff was acquainted with the Russian political and military elite during the last years of the Romanov dynasty. Her recollections of those days include one formal ball at an officers' club, where she danced with Igor Sikorsky. The young designer from Kiev had emerged in 1913–14 as a prominent figure in aviation, with his impressive flights in the Grand and later in the Il'ya Muromets on the round-trip flight from St. Petersburg to Kiev.

Nina Bouroff soon discovered that World War I would bring a unique and unexpected occasion for her to fly in Sikorsky's Il'ya Muromets. When the war broke out, she had volunteered to serve with the Russian Red Cross. Eventually service with the Red Cross brought her to Kovno, near the front lines, in 1915. Shortly after Nina Bouroff's arrival at the front, the Germans launched their 1915 offensive. The advancing enemy approached Kovno on three sides, leaving only the road on the north side as a tenuous link with outside for the besieged Russians.

With the city about to be occupied by the Germans, it was decided that Nina Bouroff and a small group of Red Cross workers and wounded soldiers would be evacuated by air. On June 22, 1915, as Nina Bouroff recalled, she arrived on the north side of the city early in the morning to board the Il'ya Muromets. The flying ship had landed on the road that served as an improvised runway. The takeoff went well, and the Il'ya Muromets began an arduous four-hour flight to Gatchina aerodrome, outside St. Petersburg.

For Nina Bouroff, the flight was a memorable one, filled with dangers and anxiety. The weather was overcast, dark and stormy. The passengers were seated uncomfortably on two long wooden benches which had been placed in the interior along the walls of the fuselage. "The airplane," she recalled, "appeared much like a boat." Her most vivid memories were of the turbulence that accompanied them throughout the flight and the roar of the engines. The pilot worked energetically to keep the aircraft stable and on course. The long flight ended without a mishap. Nina Bouroff then returned to her home and family in the Imperial capital.

The period of the Russian Revolution, especially after the Bolshevik takeover in November 1917, brought new and for-

Photograph of Nina Bouroff, about 1916. *Courtesy of Nina Bouroff*

midable challenges to Nina Bouroff. She became separated
from her husband, who, in the chaos of the Revolution, had
joined the counterrevolutionaries, or Whites, to struggle
against the Bolsheviks. As the wife of a former Tsarist general, Nina Bouroff became suspect in the eyes of the revolutionaries and was arrested. Later she escaped, and she, too,
served with the Whites. After the Russian Civil War, Nina
Bouroff emigrated to Paris, where, with her two children, she
was reunited with her husband. Eventually Nina Bouroff
moved to the United States, but only after spending the years
of World War II in Nazi-occupied France.

---

2 during the autumn of 1914, when they were on their way to join the
Russian Army at the front.

While en route to their new aerodrome, the Murometsy cruised at low
altitude over the county of Ostrog in Pskov province. Many peasants who
had never seen such a large aeroplane or heard the loud noise of their
engines took flight into the forest.

During September, part of the Murometsy flew to the town of Zegevol'd, near Riga. On September 16 they bombed Mitava, which at the
time was occupied by the Germans.

Three Murometsy, the IM-2, the IM-5, and IM-9, bombed the railroad
station at Freidrichstadt on October 18, dropping forty-eight 16-kilogram
bombs on the enemy. During this raid the IM-9, commanded by Captain
R. L. Nizhevskiy, dropped one bomb that weighed 245 kilograms, which
alone wrecked two buildings completely. Nizhevskiy had joined the squadron just before the mission. Before his posting with the EVK Nizhevskiy had
served on the staff of the School of Aeronautics (ballooning) and had been
the commanding officer of a dirigible. He became one of the best pilots
flying the Il'ya Muromets. He also served capably as an instructor in the
squadron's school and as chairman of the technical commission for the
acceptance of dirigibles and small aircraft for military service.

Nizhevskiy was one of the first to demonstrate that an Il'ya Muromets,
like a light aeroplane, could be landed with the engines shut off. As mentioned earlier, Lieutenant Bashko had performed the same feat on July 19,
1915, landing about five kilometers from Kholm after a combat mission in
which the engines had been damaged. Captain Nizhevakiy landed his Il'ya
Muromets at night, with a full moon, on a snow-covered airfield that was
considered a very dangerous, if not impossible, place to land.

Elements of the Squadron of Flying Ships remained in Lida following
the safe flight of the Murometsy to Pskov: the staff of the EVK, some
personnel, and the maintenance and equipment crews. It was only with
great difficulty that we transferred the disabled and nonflying Murometsy

A Russian 75-mm antiaircraft battery placed on a railway car at Lida in April 1915. *Courtesy of the K. N. Finne family*

out of Lida along with the 75-mm antiaircraft battery. In this setting of retreat, Lida became a congested railway center. The railway station was filled with troops being shifted to the northern front and trains congested with artillery pieces, strategic goods and property being evacuated from Brest-Litovsk, Warsaw, and Osovts, and civilian refugees. Lida was an almost impossible bottleneck.

Fortunately, enemy aeroplanes and zeppelins did not appear over Lida, perhaps as a result of the bad weather. An enemy air raid during our retreat could have been devastating, with the railway station crowded with ammunition cars filled with explosives and bombs. Such an attack could have brought paralysis of movement at an important railway center and disruption of communications. The transport of the squadron's equipment was greatly facilitated by the women workers who had built the railway branch from the aerodrome to the Lida station. At the time there were few men available to perform such a task. The railway tracks on this improvised branch were solidly laid, and they served well in handling the railway cars that evacuated our aeroplanes, bombs, and war matériel.

Finally, the EVK, with its shops, warehouses, and hangars, was relocated near Pskov, about five kilometers outside the town, on the grounds of an agricultural school. The new airstrip selected for the aerodrome had

The agriculture school located at Kresty near Pskov, where the Il'ya Muromets squadron was quartered in 1915–16. *Courtesy of the K. N. Finne family*

Trinity Orthodox Cathedral at Pskov. The cathedral was located inside the old kremlin, or city fortress. *Courtesy of the K. N. Finne family*

been a marsh, which was much like the marshy terrain of the area that existed on both sides of the highway. The personnel of the agricultural school helped us by digging drainage ditches, which dried up the marshy field.

These ditches caused no small number of problems for the aerodrome. The necessity of recovering them at certain points caused many delays. As indicated earlier, the majority of combat-ready Murometsy had flown over to Riga from this aerodrome, and by the middle of September they were active in military operations.

The commanding officers of these Murometsy were already in a contest of courage among themselves. On October 16, 1915, the IM-Kievskiy conducted a five-hour flight in the enemy rear, near the city of Shavli, the headquarters of the commander of the German front and his staff. The IM-Kievskiy had flown from Petrograd to Pskov on October 10 and subsequently from Pskov to Zegevol'd on October 13. At Shavli, the Russian flying ship appeared suddenly, dropping bombs and frightening the slumbering German staff, who soon changed their location.

One of the raids of the IM-Kievskiy almost ended in tragedy. During a mission on October 19, 1915, over the town of Bausskiy, about 53 kilometers from the front lines, all four engines stopped. Water that had collected in the fuel lines had frozen. Staff Captain Bashko, who was at the controls of the IM-Kievskiy, turned back, putting the aeroplane into a glide toward the Russian trenches. Two crew members, Staff Captain Naumov, the artillery officer, and Warrant Officer A. V. Serednitskiy, the deputy commander, attempted to warm the fuel lines with their hands.

With considerable difficulty two engines were restarted, but they performed sluggishly. In order to lighten the aircraft, the crew had to jettison not only the bomb load, but machine guns and ammunition as well. The IM-Kievskiy flew on two engines at a hundred meters over the enemy trenches. The Germans spotted the lumbering Russian flying ship and opened fire with rifles and machine guns. Some sixty-four bullets struck the IM-Kievskiy, but most of them in the rear section, allowing the crew to escape injury. Having cleared the front lines, the IM-Kievskiy landed safely in Russian-held territory near the town of Olai.

This had been a harrowing episode for the crew. Owing to the presence of mind of the commander and the crew, everything turned out fine.[3] When the IM-Kievskiy landed, Russian soldiers (Siberian sharpshooters) rushed forward, thinking Bashko and his crew to be Germans. Despite the fact that one of the crew embraced one of the soldiers out of joy, the Siberian troops stubbornly believed that the airmen were German spies and threatened to shoot them.

Although by the fall of 1915 the Murometsy, unlike light aeroplanes, had displayed superior combat effectiveness, criticisms persisted. The Murometsy had made bombing raids deep into enemy territory, had con-

Olga Glass, the future wife of K. N. Finne, is pictured at the extreme right, seated in the sleigh. Dr. A. N. Khornborg, head of the Finnish Hospital, is seated next to Olga Glass. The picture was taken in December 1916, at Kresty near Pskov, when Olga Glass worked as a nurse in the Finnish Hospital. *Courtesy of the K. N. Finne family*

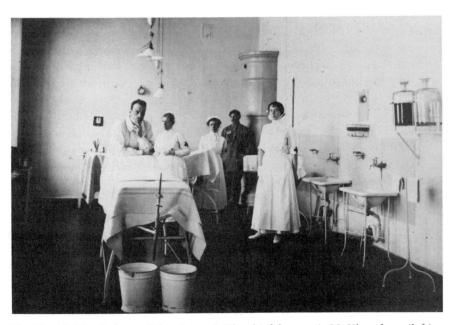

The Finnish Hospital near Pskov in 1916. The chief doctor, A. N. Khornborg (left), is pictured in the operating room with nurses and an orderly. *Courtesy of the K. N. Finne family*

The Il'ya Muromets Kievskiy at Kresty in 1916. Left to right: A. V. Serednitskiy; I. S. Bashko; A. M. Lavrov (mechanic); and A. M. Kolyankovskiy (seated). *Courtesy of the K. N. Finne family*

ducted aerial reconnaissance, and had engaged enemy aeroplanes in air-to-air combat. Yet harmful criticism continued unabated. If they were not able to bring accusations against the Murometsy as "imperfect" aeroplanes, they attacked the commander of the EVK, General Shidlovskiy. Sadly, the circulation of these accusations—more properly labeled gossip—could be traced to certain members of our squadron—men who had joined the squadron as replacement commanders for the Murometsy or their deputies. Some of these "commanding officers," who had never flown one mission in an Il'ya Muromets flying ship, outdid many of the stubbornest and harshest critics of the Murometsy of the past. Yet these men continued as officers in the very squadron they sought to slander. They found support among the staff of the Northern Front headquarters, which was located in Pskov. Among these

Inspection of an Il'ya Muromets by the French military mission led by General D'Amade at Pskov in October 1915. *Courtesy of the National Air and Space Museum*

Officers of a Japanese military mission inspect the Il'ya Muromets V (IM-5) at Pskov in May 1916. Left to right: Senior officer of the EVK, Lieutenant Colonel K. K. Vitkovskiy; Japanese officer Captain G. Takeda; Commander of the IM-5 Lieutenant G. V. Alekhnovich; two Japanese officers, and one Russian officer. *Courtesy of the National Air and Space Museum*

high-ranking officers was General Bonch-Bruyevich, the commander of the northern front, who later occupied an important post in the Soviet armed forces.[4]

This situation interrupted the normal development of the Murometsy as air weapons for Russia. Yet more and more interest was awakened in the Il'ya Muromets despite this sad state of affairs. Visits to the squadron aerodrome by important officials and even foreign missions increased dramatically during these difficult days. On October 13, 1915, a French military mission visited the EVK. This party included the French generals De Laguiche and D'Amade. They examined every detail of the Il'ya Muromets, and one French officer actually flew in one of the Murometsy. This French pilot remarked repeatedly that the cabin of the Il'ya Muromets did not lack, in his words, "beaucoup du confort."

In addition to the French, a Japanese military mission inspected the squadron aerodrome in May 7, 1916. All these visits by foreigners, some involving high-ranking military officers, were received with typical Russian warmth and hospitality. The Russian hosts regaled these visitors at meetings, showing them photograph albums and allowing them to inspect the aircraft.

When the Japanese visited, they smiled pleasantly, bowed, and did not let one detail pass unnoticed. A visiting British officer not only scrutinized the IM-Kievskiy and the IM-3, the two best Murometsy at Vlodava aerodrome in July 1915, attentively, he took measurements in a businesslike manner and snapped many photographs with his Kodak camera.

One incident cannot be remembered without bitterness and shame. The visiting Japanese officers, out of gratitude for the reception by the commander of IM-5, sent a bottle of state vodka "with the white head" to Lieutenant G. V. Alekhnovich. They had followed the advice of the Russian officer who had accompanied them. It is true that at the time such a bottle of vodka was rare indeed. Lieutenant Alekhnovich, however, a teetotaler, took offense. But Alekhnovich did not return it, not wishing to create "diplomatic" problems.[5] The vodka was then consumed for the health of the Allies. So this is how we Russians maintained our prestige in the eyes of foreigners in those days.

Despite the small number of Murometsy in the EVK in 1915, they had an effect on the conduct of the war. It should be remembered that from the very onset of combat activity, the Murometsy flew about a hundred missions and dropped nearly 20,000 kilograms of bombs. In 1915 two aircraft, the IM-Kievskiy and the IM-3, flew about seventy combat missions. The usefulness of these aerial reconnaissance flights deep into the enemy rear has already been discussed. At that time, light aircraft in the Russian air force could not penetrate far into rear areas of the enemy, for there was the high risk of engine failure and a forced landing in enemy-occupied territory. This very thing happened to the French pilot, Gresau, who flew with our air force against the Germans. In May 1915 he was forced down behind German

Lieutenant G. V. Alekhnovich and a member of the Japanese military mission at the EVK aerodrome near Pskov in May 1916. *Courtesy of the National Air and Space Museum*

lines and taken prisoner. For our single-engine aeroplanes, there was also the high probability of attack by enemy fighters when they were flying over enemy lines.

The successful work of the Murometsy in 1915 led to an augmentation of EVK personnel. Our numbers increased by about twenty. Unfortunately, not all the twenty flying ships available to the squadron deserved combat rating. Among them were Murometsy that had not accomplished a single combat flight. Two of these had accomplished one combat mission each in two years and two had made two combat missions each during the same period. Four of the Murometsy flew fewer than ten missions each—typically from four to eight missions—during two years.

It is true that the majority of these Murometsy had been equipped with Sunbeam motors, which were considered inferior to the Argus or R-BVZ types. But the main reason for this poor performance was not the engines. Even those Murometsy with Sunbeam engines that were being flown by aggressive pilots anxious to engage the enemy achieved great feats, which may now be considered the greatest embellishment in the pages of the history of Russian aviation.

All the greater is the heroic record of these officers. Some gave their lives in air combat, some were wounded, and others were crippled. All these brave airmen served with great integrity, proving that they were born "to soar rather to creep." The Murometsy performed about four hundred combat missions during the three years Russia participated in the Great War.

Consequently, the reasons for the limited activity of the Murometsy is not to be found in any defects in structure or design of these aircraft or in the inferior performance of the engines, but largely in the insufficient number of commanding officers with the necessary qualities to be military pilots.

The commander in chief of the Northern Front, General A. N. Kuropatkin, visited the EVK at Pskov on March 8, 1916.[6] He inspected the aerodrome and talked with officers of the squadron. General Kuropatkin remarked on his visit that General Shidlovskiy had taken "all the best pilots in order to integrate them into his own squadron." If one can judge General Kuropatkin's views on German Zeppelins, it is apparent that he knew little about aviation, even lacking a clear understanding of the difference between zeppelins and aeroplanes. It has to be surmised that General Kuropatkin's comment that the best pilots had been transferred, a view often heard later, had been prompted by someone of rank in his staff who was not well disposed toward the squadron.

The idea of a good pilot and the best pilot is very little comprehended. The commanding officer of the IM-Kievskiy, for example, Military Pilot Bashko, was not a graduate of the Gatchina Military Flying School, yet he was among the best pilots flying the Murometsy. Some officers of the squadron who occupied the post of commanding officer as well as that of deputy commander had not held the rank of military pilot, although they held the rank of officer while serving in the squadron. Officers of this category were Captain R. L. Nizhevskiy, Lieutenant G. V. Alekhnovich, Warrant Officer A. V. Serednitskiy, Lieutenant Krotkov, and so on. Some of those who were formerly considered excellent pilots—the commanding officers—after having joined the squadron never flew twice on an Il'ya Muromets in combat. Sometimes the reason was that these pilots, as it was said, had "lost heart."

One officer who had been considered a good pilot had joined the squadron and had flown light aeroplanes. While on his way to his new air base, he was downed by friendly troops, who mistook his aircraft for an enemy flying machine. Along with other officers he was wounded. After recovering from his wounds this pilot joined our squadron, but he had lost heart. He avoided not only combat missions but any kind of flying whatever.

There were some commanding officers who never lost heart, because they never possessed heart. They became active foes of the Murometsy, although they remained members of the EVK. These men took every occasion to criticize the squadron.

Fortunately, such cases were rare. Yet it can be stated without exaggeration that the majority of officer-pilots did not even try to stop gossiping about the Murometsy and the squadron; at times their talk reached the point of inanity, and on occasion they engaged in criticism of their superiors—a serious weakness, as everyone knows.

One incident will serve to illustrate this phenomenon. One young pilot who showed considerable promise and had demonstrated skill as a pilot of the Il'ya Muromets was assigned to assist a commanding officer on an important combat mission. The young pilot mimicked his senior officers by complaining about the Murometsy at every opportunity. Not having been disciplined for his behavior, the young officer soon became lax in fulfillment of his duties. The matter ended when he missed the deadline for a mission. His commanding officer decided not to wait and departed on the flight without the young officer.

This *enfant gâté* [spoiled child] had to travel by train, creeping along the tracks rather than flying on his mission as assigned. This incident came about only because the senior members of the squadron found it fashionable to be critical of the Murometsy and the squadron, always keeping their loyalties to light aviation.

When the squadron organized its own school of aviation, concrete steps were made to overcome the shortage of competent command pilots. This complicated matters as well. In order to train, many pilots were absent from their regular duties aboard front-line Murometsy. Yet this interruption was necessary. During the war there were also irresponsible and cynical officers who entered aviation from the regular army to wear two uniforms and to do nothing. Candidates of this kind for pilot training did get into the school and certainly spread rumors concerning "the dreadful state of training."

For those who genuinely desired to work, the squadron offered many opportunities. After leaving our squadron training school many pilots went on to become the best. Among these graduates was Warrant Officer A. V. Serednitskiy, commander of the IM-18.[7] (Serednitskiy went on to serve with the new Polish air force after the Revolution. During the postrevolutionary years he continued to fly, making one flight from Warsaw to Paris. He died in an air accident in 1926.)

These were the circumstances surrounding the development of the Murometsy. The war had come suddenly to Russia, which in the years of peace had depended heavily on foreign-made aircraft. The manufacture of the Murometsy had been launched hurriedly without broad planning or a solid foundation. In addition, the German occupation of Courland and conquest of parts of Liflandia Guberniya menaced Riga, where the Russo-Baltic Wagon Company was located. German front-line positions were only twenty-one kilometers from Riga. The order was then given to evacuate into the Russian hinterland. As a consequence, the Russo-Baltic Wagon Company did not manufacture its first aero engine until the fall of 1915. The Russo-Baltic factories in Petrograd produced about seventy Il'ya Muro-

Officers of the EVK at Kresty, near Pskov, in April 1916. Left to right: Captain V. Lobov; Lieutenant Romanov; Staff Captain Zagurskiy; Lieutenant G. V. Alekhnovich; Staff Captain Koz'min (seated); Captain In'kov; Lieutenant Plotnikov; and Lieutenant Desilos. *Courtesy of the K. N. Finne family*

mets flying ships (without engines) between 1914 and 1918. Not all of these aircraft ever reached the front, and many of them, in particular after the Revolution, were not really airworthy. The revolutionary situation brought disintegration and an end of support for the Murometsy.

Meanwhile foreign aeronautical technology continued to advance. During 1916, as the Murometsy developed slowly for the reasons described, both the enemy and the Allies were able to build faster light aircraft, almost twice as fast as the Il'ya Muromets. There is nothing surprising about this situation if it is remembered that Russian industry during the prewar years was not highly developed in comparison to that of other industrial countries. Russian battleships became obsolete even before they were launched from the shipyards.

One fact not quite clear to many is the failure of the Allies to assist

Russia in building aero engines. Yet Russian-made aero engines proved to be superior to those made by the French and the British. This fact was reflected in the combat operations that I have already described. It is obvious that the Allies found it more convenient merely to dump quantities of inferior war matériel onto Russia, the rubbish for which they had no need.

In Russia it is customary to regard as valuable everything with a label: "Made in England," "Made in Germany," and so on. It goes without saying that if any sort of rubbish had a trademark, it was considered valuable. If dumped on Russia, moreover, it was accepted as a sign of a magnanimous act on the part of the Allies. (In 1919, for example, the author of this memoir observed a disaster that involved six Russian pilots who were flying a British-made aircraft given to the White "Armed Forces of South Russia," under General Denikin.[8] These pilots were all burned to death while test-flying these foreign-manufactured aeroplanes.) Time has shown "conclusively" that the Allies did not desire a strong and independent Russia. Instead they wanted cannon fodder to weaken Germany. For this reason the development of our national industry was not part of their plan.[9]

At the time that the Il'ya Muromets was slowly maturing as an air weapon, Germany started to make use of Sikorsky's concept. They began to build their own large, multiengine bombers. The need for heavy aviation, as already mentioned, was echoed in the comments of German and Austrian prisoners of war.

The huge German Gotha bomber appeared in 1917 and had a devastating effect in raids on Paris, Dunkirk, and other important targets.[10] In turn, this made the Allies reconsider once more the importance of heavy aviation. This point, at least, was expressed by General Golovin, a professor at the Nicholas Military Academy, in his article "The Past and Future of Aviation." The Murometsy had paved the way for large bombers.

Notes

1. [Editors' note.] Earlier in his career Kireyev had worked as an engineer at an engine plant in Germany. The R-BVZ plant, located at Riga, was evacuated during the German offensive of 1915. As a consequence, only five engines were finished and available to the EVK. Production was resumed later.

2. [Editors' note.] The Il'ya Muromets I, Type V (Veh); Il'ya Muromets II, Type V (Veh); Il'ya Muromets IV, Type V (Veh); Il'ya Muromets V, Type V

(Veh); and Il'ya Muromets Kievskiy. See appendix 6.

3. [Editors' note.] The fourth member of the crew was Staff Captain K. K. Vitkovskiy.

4. [Editors' note.] Finne refers here to General M. D. Bonch-Bruyevich (1870–1956). From August 1915 to February 1916, Bonch-Bruyevich was chief of staff for the Northern Front. During the Revolution he was one of the first Tsarist generals to go over to the Bolshe-

viks. He served with the Red Guards in the defense of Petrograd in 1918 and later with the Red Army against the Whites during the civil war. His subsequent career included several technical commands in the Red Army and work as a military historian.

5. [Note by K. N. Finne.] Lieutenant (later Staff Captain) Alekhnovich joined the Bolsheviks during the Revolution. At one point in the Civil War, he saved an Il'ya Muromets from an advancing White Army in Tambov Province. He died shortly afterward in an air crash. Alekhnovich made the bold proposal that the Il'ya Muromets should be flown to the North Pole.

6. [Note by K. N. Finne.] General A. N. Kuropatkin (1848–1925) was a general of the infantry whose long career in the Russian Army went back to the Russo-Turkish War of 1877–78. He served in Manchuria during the Russo-Japanese War of 1904–5. During World War I, he commanded the Russian Fifth Army, and from February to July 1916 he was commander of the Northern Front. He was sent to the Caucasus in 1916, where, as governor-general, he endeavored to put down a revolutionary uprising. He was arrested by revolutionaries in 1917. Later he emigrated to France, where he died in 1925.

7. [Editors' note.] The Il'ya Muromets XVIII, Type G. This was probably a G-2 variant. See appendix 6.

8. [Editors' note.] General Anton Denikin led a large White Army in an abortive attempt to overthrow the Bolsheviks in 1919. He commanded the Army of South Russia.

9. [Editors' note.] The wartime emergency led to a severe shortage of aero engines for the EVK. The German-made Argus engines ceased to be available after 1914. The French-made Salmson proved unsuitable as a substitute for the Argus. The British supplied the Sunbeam engines, which had been used earlier by the Royal Naval Air Service. The British had used the Sunbeams with expert mechanics and an ample supply of spare parts, none of which were available on the Russian front, with its harsh conditions and chronic shortages. In addition, the Russians had great difficulty getting the engines to the front from the remote allied depots in the far north and south of Russia. Many engines arrived damaged. Russian airmen considered the Sunbeams inferior and perceived that they had been passed along to the eastern front as surplus or "trash." The Sunbeams, in fact, were not as inferior as the Russian critics maintained, but they did perform poorly.

10. [Editors' note.] The Germans built a series of giant aircraft, or *Riesenflugzeuge,* that, included the Gotha bombers. German bombing missions to London raised the specter of destructive potential air power, especially that of the bomber.

Chapter Seven

A CRUEL FATE

In 1916 the work of the Murometsy at the front became more difficult. The Germans had strengthened their antiaircraft forces and, after the failure of their zeppelins, quickly turned their attention to building up the number of fast fighters. Despite these circumstances, the Murometsy had appeared along the entire eastern front in 1916: on the northern front, near Riga; on the western front, near Minsk; and on the southwestern front, near Galicia. On all these fronts the Murometsy gave valuable service to our armies.

During the fall of 1915, the German offensive near Riga had been stopped and the lines had become stabilized. At the beginning of 1916, when preparations for a large-scale Russian offensive in east Galicia began, a detachment of Murometsy was assigned to the sector. The IM-Kievskiy arrived at the village of Kolodziyevka, about forty kilometers from Tarnopol. The first combat squadron of the EVK under the command of Staff Captain Pankrat'yev, the commander of the IM-2, was located at Tarnopol. Both these flying ships soon began combat operations and provided concrete assistance to the Seventh Army, supplying precise intelligence about the numbers and positions of enemy batteries and about movements of troops and also conducting flights into the enemy-held rear areas. Several cities were bombed—Bugach, Yazlovets, Monasterzhisko, Podgaytsy, Brzhezany, Rogatin—and other locations and railway stations in this region.

In the town of Monasterzhisko, bombs from the Murometsy destroyed many buildings, the very targets that our artillery could not reach. When

The EVK on the move. The squadron was compelled to relocate several times in the face of German offensives. The Il'ya Muromets II (IM-2) has been disassembled and placed on a railway car for shipment. The officer with the bandaged head is Staff Captain S. N. Nikolskiy, and at the extreme left is Staff Captain A. V. Pankrat'yev. *Courtesy of Harry Woodman*

our troops entered this town it appeared as if there had been an earthquake. The inhabitants of Monasterzhisko spoke of how the arrival of the Murometsy prompted everyone to run and seek cover. The days of these raids were described as the most fearful of the war.

Clashes between the Murometsy and enemy fighters were not rare. Enemy pilots received orders to down the huge multiengine Russian bombers. Two enemy fighters attacked the IM-2 on April 1, 1916. The crew of the IM-2 repelled this attack, downing one enemy fighter. [In later years, a group of former Austrian officers talked to me about this air battle. They described the bombing of Bugach and the number of people that had been killed. The downed enemy fighter was apparently a Brandenburg, flown by the German pilot Captain Mackensen. When the German fighter crashed into the forest, Mackensen was severely wounded and later died. The other airman on the Brandenburg, a Lieutenant Bogomil Marek, escaped with only minor injuries.]

The IM-2 encountered minor damage during this air battle. Several struts and the radiator of one engine were hit. The crew, however, suffered severely: the mechanic, Warrant Officer Ushakov, was killed, and Military Pilot Lieutenant Fedorov, the deputy commander for the mission, was seriously wounded in the arm.

During the month of May, these two Murometsy, now joined by the IM-13, commanded by Staff Captain V. A. Soloviyev, participated in the Russian offensive in Galicia, which ended in great triumph. These Murometsy gathered considerable information on the enemy through aerial reconnaissance missions deep into enemy territory. They conducted very effective bombing raids, moreover, dropping small and large bombs with great precision on railway stations, warehouses, and other facilities in the enemy rear. These raids drove panic into the hearts of enemy troops, who frequently fell into a disorganized retreat.

After Russian troops occupied the towns of Yazlovets and Bugach, we saw more clearly the devastating effects of the Murometsy raids. It was possible to see the physical destruction of buildings, the choked railway tracks cluttered with train cars, the abandoned hospital, and the impossible roads. To seek safety from the Russian knights of the air, the Murometsy, the Austrians had abandoned their positions in haste and panic.

The panic was all the more intense because the Murometsy had attacked the Austrians twice a day. The detailed account of the combat work of Murometsy in the Galician detachment of the EVK, and especially the work of the IM-2, can be examined in the special order of the Russian Seventh Army, dated October 19, 1916, in which Staff Captain A. V. Pankrat'yev, the commander of the IM-2, was awarded the Order of St. George, Fourth Degree.[1] Here is a portion of the order:

The Order of St. George, Fourth Degree, is awarded to

Staff Captain and Military Pilot Aleksei V. Pankrat'yev, Commander of the 1st Combat Detachment, EVK, and Commander of the Il'ya Muromets II.

For combat missions on May 17, 18, and 19 and June 7 and 8, 1916, and related aerial reconnaissance missions in the districts of Yazlovets and Bugach. Staff Captain Pankrat'yev personally flew the IM-2 through intense enemy artillery fire and gave precise reports on the number and disposition of enemy batteries, as well as enemy positions on the banks of the Streltsa River. During a battle on May 18, 1916, he discovered the absence of enemy reserves in the area of Yazlovets as well as the area of Russilov, and he reported correctly on the reasons for the movement of enemy troops. This reconnaissance enabled us to take further action, which was crowned with success.

The dropping of bombs and machine-gun fire from the IM-2 brought losses to the enemy and forced them into a disorderly retreat. By means of direct hits, fires were ignited in the town of Yazlovets, which later was taken by Russian troops. He destroyed the roadbed west of the railway station at Bugach, which then had to be evacuated by the enemy. By means of accurate machine-gun fire, he silenced an enemy antiaircraft battery firing at his aircraft, and he drove off an enemy fighter that attempted to intercept his work. With the destruction of this battery, enemy fire was silenced. While on his mission he took photographs of enemy positions. These photographs were used by our troops during the battle around Yazlovets.

These actions by Staff Captain A.V. Pankrat'yev contributed in a significant way to the success of our troops. (The commanding officer of the Russian Seventh Army at that time was General Shcherbatov and the chief of staff was General Golovin.)

On June 24, 1916, the IM-Kievskiy of the First Combat Detachment was transferred to the western front, to a base near the town of Stan'kovo to the south of Minsk. The Murometsy were needed in this sector because of increased enemy activity in the area. After the destruction of the IM-3, there were no Murometsy active on this front. The Russian Army therefore sent this special air detachment under the command of Staff Captain I. S. Bashko, who also commanded the IM-Kievskiy.

At that time the Murometsy of the first combat detachment operated so successfully in the victorious offensive of our troops in Galicia, on the Northern Front, and below Riga that a second combat unit of EVK was put together and based at Zegevol'd. All the flying ships in this detachment were equipped exclusively with Sunbeam engines, which, as pointed out earlier, enabled the Il'ya Muromets to achieve an altitude of only 3,000 meters.

Despite this fact, the Murometsy continued to fly combat missions. There were single and group missions. For example, there was a group mission with the IM-1, the IM-6, the IM-8, and the IM-9, which was responsible for the destruction of a German hydroplane station on Lake Angern, located on the western shore of the Bay of Riga.[2]

This group flight took place on September 4, 1916, under the command of Lieutenant G. I. Lavrov, a naval pilot and commander of the IM-1. The Murometsy hit the hydroplane station with seventy-three large bombs weighing altogether 832 kilograms. Twenty-two separate hits were observed in the target area. The fire of twelve machine guns from the Murometsy suppressed the enemy antiaircraft fire and prevented the enemy fighters from taking off. Around seventeen hydroplanes were spotted. Some attempted to fly toward the Murometsy but were driven off by our machine-gun fire. Bombs dropped from the Murometsy set off fires in the enemy hangars, and columns of smoke filled the air. Several enemy hydroplanes were damaged.

None of the Murometsy suffered any damage and all four returned to their base safely. Shortly before this group flight, the IM-8, under the command of Military Pilot and Lieutenant (Cossacks) V. Lobov, flying in the

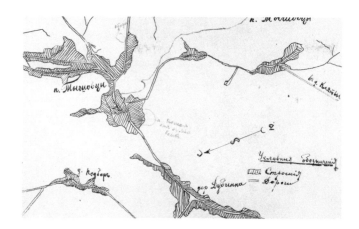

Another bombing mission by the Murometsy. This photograph and its overlay illustrate a raid by the Russians on enemy positions near the village of Dubinka. Date unknown. *Courtesy of Sergei Sikorsky*

Cockpit view of an Il'ya Muromets IX (IM-9). At the left is Igor Sikorsky. The photograph was taken in July 1916. *Courtesy of the K. N. Finne family*

district of the German hydroplane base at Lake Angern, did battle with seven hydroplanes. The attackers avoided getting too close to the Il'ya Muromets for fear of encountering the intense machine-gun fire.

Among all the memorable flights of this air detachment, the combat mission of the Il'ya Muromets X (IM-10) merits special attention.[3] Lieutenant A. M. Konstenchik commanded this flying ship. On April 26, 1916, Konstenchik and his crew received orders to destroy the huge Daudzevas railway station. This station was located near Friedrichstadt, and earlier the IM-10 had flown several missions to bomb this important railway center. On these missions bombs from the IM-10 had caused a number of fires in enemy warehouses.

Now under orders to destroy Daudzevas, the IM-10 faced the challenge of attacking a heavily fortified German position bristling with antiaircraft batteries. During its attack on Daudzevas, on the second pass, the IM-10 met intense, accurate antiaircraft fire at 2,400 meters and dropped a total of thirteen bombs. One burst of enemy shrapnel hit Lieutenant Konstenchik. As he fell from his pilot's seat, the wounded commander pulled the steering column backward, abruptly forcing the flying ship upward. The IM-10 stalled, then fell, gliding downward into a deep dive. The Germans observed the downward plunge of the IM-10 with great joy, but their elation over the downing of the Russian aircraft proved to be premature. In the midst of this dive, the deputy commander, Military Pilot Yankovius, was able to slide into the pilot's seat and with great difficulty stabilize the large aeroplane at an altitude of 1,500 meters. This was no easy task, since the IM-10 had been seriously damaged, with hits on three of its engines.

The return trip of sixty-six kilometers meant a flight of twenty-six kilometers over enemy-held territory, with a total flight time of 52 minutes. The cruising altitude of the IM-10 over the enemy trenches was about 1,000 meters. Lieutenant Yankovius flew the aeroplane to an aerodrome near

Commander of the Il'ya Muromets X (IM-10), Lieutenant A. V. Konstenchik, who was wounded in the bombing mission over Daudzevas on April 26, 1916. *Courtesy of the National Air and Space Museum*

Zegevol'd, where he made an emergency landing, damaging the wing spars on the right side. The impact of the landing almost collapsed the right wing. In addition to the damaged engines, the IM-10 had been riddled with seventy bullet holes.

In addition to Lieutenant Konstenchik, other crewmen of the IM-10 had been wounded: Lieutenant G. N. Shneur, the artillery officer, suffered wounds in the hands while holding his aerial camera, which was shattered by shrapnel.[4] The deputy commander, Lieutenant Yankovius, also received wounds.[5] Together with the volunteer Kasatkin, Lieutenant Yankovius attended to the wounds of Lieutenant Konstenchik during the flight.

During the fierce antiaircraft fire, when the Il'ya Muromets fell to an altitude of 900 meters, Marcel Pliat manned the upper machine-gun platform. Sergeant Major Pliat, half Negro and half French, saved himself from falling away from the descending Il'ya Muromets by tying his belt to the gun platform. By his own account, he was positioned on the upper platform at the moment the IM-10 began its abrupt dive. He eventually made his way to the cabin of the flying ship and commented that "he would prefer not to fall so precipitously." Pliat then climbed out of the wing to repair a damaged engine and remained there for half an hour.

For this combat mission, Lieutenant Konstenchik, the commander of the IM-10, received the Order of St. George, Fourth Degree. Lieutenant Yankovius was awarded the St. George's sword. Sergeant Major Pliat received the Cross of St. George, Third Degree. Finally, the volunteer, Sergeant Major Kasatkin, was recommended for promotion to commissioned officer status. These awards were made in October 18, 1916 (see Order of the Seventh Army, no. 770).

It was evident that the combat detachment at Riga was resented by the enemy, who attacked the aerodrome at Zegevol'd with groups of twelve or more aeroplanes at a time. Once the Germans sent a zeppelin over the base, on the night of April 28–29. The zeppelin hovered over the airfield for a while, not being able to discern our hangars in the darkness. Not all the lights were on, and the antiaircraft batteries, consisting of 75-mm navy guns attached to the aerodrome, did not open fire. After remaining over the base for a time with its engines cut off, the zeppelin then moved on to the station of Legat. When it reached Legat, it dropped large bombs, hitting a hospital.

Besides these reprisal raids, the Germans made use of their many fast fighters to intercept the Murometsy at every opportunity. They endeavored to take advantage of every blunder on our side. They gave chase to Murometsy and attacked from behind, where we were most vulnerable. From the rear our flying ships possessed no defensive fire from our two machine guns. A Russian sense of security, the tendency to be overconfident about the invulnerability of the Il'ya Muromets, contributed to these attacks. As the Russian proverb says, "If the thunder does not roar, the peasant does not make the sign of the cross."

The damaged Il'ya Muromets
X (IM-10) at the Zegevol'd
aerodrome following the April
26, 1916, combat mission.
*Courtesy of the National Air
and Space Museum*

Sergeant Major Marcel Pliat,
mechanic on the Il'ya
Muromets X (IM-10).
*Courtesy of the National Air
and Space Museum*

Igor Sikorsky (right) confers with Lieutenant D. K. Makhsheyev, commander of the Il'ya Muromets XVI (IM-16), at Pskov during the summer of 1916. Makhsheyev was killed in combat on October 8, 1916, near Molodechno. *Courtesy of the National Air and Space Museum*

An attack by an enemy fighter on the IM-6 illustrates this truth. This air battle almost ended in tragedy. On September 23, 1916, the IM-6 was returning from a combat mission. While flying over the Bay of Riga, not far from the river Aa, the crew neglected to be vigilant, thinking they were outside the range of enemy pursuit. Quite suddenly an enemy fighter appeared from behind, firing almost point-blank from a distance of ten meters.

The exploding bursts of machine-gun fire wounded several members of the crew, including Staff Captain S. N. Golovin, the commander; Captain

V. A. Ivanov, the artillery officer; and Staff Captain Loiko. All were hit, but suffered only light wounds. Also, the Vickers machine gun was damaged. Our other weapon a light machine gun, jammed after firing a few rounds. Lieutenant A. Yu. Lutts beat off the attack with the one remaining machine gun by firing ten rounds point-blank at the enemy fighter.

The enemy then fell away into a dive toward the town of Tukkum. It is possible that the enemy pilots lost their nerve and decided not to continue the attack, suffered wounds, or fell into a vortex created by the motion of the propellers of the Il'ya Muromets. The crew of the IM-6, however, could not take time to follow the descent of the enemy fighter. The situation was critical for them, since the IM-6, it was discovered later, had received 293 bullet holes. Despite all the dangers, the IM-6 landed safely at an aerodrome near Riga. As one member of the crew remarked after the mission, "The land seemed so lovely after flying over the sea."

Another air detachment of Murometsy on the western front, located near Minsk, executed their duties with considerable success during the summer and fall of 1916. This success was achieved despite the fact that all the flying ships in the detachment were equipped with Sunbeam engines, with the exception of the Argus-powered IM-Kievskiy. Among all the EVK pilots in this unit, Lieutenant Maksheyev and his crew displayed outstanding skill flying the Il'ya Muromets XVI (IM-16).[6]

During the fall of 1916, the Russians planned an offensive against the Germans in the northern sector of the Western Front, hoping to achieve a decisive breakthrough. In order to distract German attention from the northern sector, so that preparations for the Russian offensive would not be discovered prematurely, the Intelligence Section of the Headquarters Staff of the Western Front decided to make use of our aviation, as a show of force, in the areas of Smorgon' and Krevo. Accordingly, Murometsy, together with twelve light aeroplanes, were flown to the town of Myasot to launch an attack on the enemy.

The objective of our air raid was the headquarters of the German reserve division, located near the town of Boruna. On September 26, 1916, the chief of the Reconnaissance Section of the Headquarters Staff of the Western Front assumed the task of organizing the mission. For the first time Russian light and heavy aviation were to operate jointly against the enemy. Many errors, however, occurred in the planning of this unique air operation, for a number of reasons, including the novelty of the tactics and ignorance of the requirements for making it work. There was no rational explanation for the poor planning and execution.

All the participating aeroplanes took off independently one by one. Our fighters separated, then circled over the front lines. Lacking the range of small single-engine aeroplanes, they could not conduct bombing operations in the enemy rear. The Murometsy could perform such operations if they flew in formation, as they had done effectively during operations in the Riga sector and around Angern. In formation flying the Murometsy possessed strong defensive fire, but during this joint operation they were dispersed and flew singly.

The chief of the Intelligence Section flew on the IM-Kievskiy. This flying ship alone executed its assignment successfully. The IM-Kievskiy reached the target area, then located the headquarters of the German divisional staff and flew over the area for fifteen minutes, dropping bombs on the target with precision. The IM-Kievskiy then returned safely to its home base. The IM-16 was also able to penetrate deep behind the enemy front lines. During its mission it was attacked by four enemy fighters. The enemy fire was intense; a hail of explosive and incendiary bullets struck the aircraft. The fuel tank of the IM-16 exploded, and the flying ship fell to the earth in flames. The IM-16 crashed in enemy-held territory, near Lake Krevo. All the crew were killed: Lieutenant Maksheyev, the commander; Lieutenant Rakhmin, the deputy commander; Lieutenant Gaubov, the artillery officer; and the cadet Karpov. An intercepted German radio message described the event: "Finally, we have downed the huge Russian quadrimotor aeroplane, although the air battle cost us three of our fighters."

Following tradition, the Germans dropped a message from one of their aeroplanes stating that the Russian crewmen had been buried with military honors. A German newspaper later printed a photograph of the grave, which was mounted with the distinctive eight-pointed Orthodox cross. The inscription read: "Here lies the grave of four Russian airmen who died heroically in air combat on September 25, 1916 (new style)."

The Germans had placed near the cross the only remains of the famous IM-16—the wheels and the Sunbeam engine radiators. The council of St. George awarded all the crew members posthumously the Order of St. George, Fourth Degree.

And so the attempt to launch a group flight of sixteen aeroplanes, consisting of both light and heavy aircraft, ended in failure. The reasons for the failure were lack of preparation and proper organization. The price for us was one Il'ya Muromets, one Morane downed by enemy fighters, and two other small aeroplanes lost. The enemy had only one fighter unit in this area. After our abortive mission, the planned show of force was canceled.

Among all the sixteen aeroplanes, the IM-Kievskiy alone was able to fulfill its assigned task and bomb the German divisional headquarters. The overall failure of the mission cannot be ascribed to the Murometsy or to organizational inadequacies of the EVK, although many adversaries of heavy aviation, of course, gleefully blamed the Murometsy.

The failure of the mission, considered broadly, was the consequence of tactical immaturity, insufficient preparation, and too much improvisation. This kind of behaviour had characterized the use of Murometsy at the beginning of the war.

Even as Murometsy were active on all fronts—flying combat missions on the Northern, Western, and Southwestern fronts—we were busy at our base in Pskov training a new generation of flying officers for the EVK. At

Germans Down
an Il'ya Muromets Bomber
Report of Lieutenant Wolff,
Feldflieger—Detachment 45
Russia, September 1916

At seven o'clock on the sunny fall morning of September 26, 1916, a warning cry echoed through the long corridor of the officers' quarters, "The Sikorsky is coming."

On two earlier occasions, these aircraft had flown over our airport at a great height, bombing our railway station and barracks. These bombardments did not cause any significant damage, however.

Both of our single-seater fighters were already in the air, while we biplane pilots were, for the most part, still asleep.

Courtesy of the Archives, United Technologies Corporation

Most ran out onto the airfield–some rather badly dressed–to observe the giant aircraft. I dressed quickly, however, while ordering my aircraft to be prepared for flight. I believe that this was the shortest time that we ever took to become airborne. It was a beautiful morning. The air was solid, the aircraft climbed quickly. In twenty minutes we reached an altitude of 2,500 meters (about 8,200 feet) and saw over the front lines a long, thin, dark form; the "Sikorsky" which was overflying the lines at an altitude of about 3,000 meters (10,000 feet). I flew in a very wide circle around our airport, then in a shallow curve toward the Russian aircraft, by which time I had climbed to his altitude. It was imperative that I decide quickly how to attack, because the Sikorsky was a fearsome adversary; it was reported to be very heavily armed and had already damaged a number of our aircraft badly in previous encounters. We then noticed that it was escorted by a parasol-type monoplane and three or four Voisin aircraft. I let the enemy penetrate our area to a depth of three or four kilometers and took up a position parallel to him about 1,000 meters away, in order to figure out which target he had chosen this time. Judging by his direction, he was flying toward our Division Headquarters, some ten kilometers behind the front. We had moved the headquarters to another area, however, a few days earlier.

With the sun behind me I engaged the Sikorsky by moving in to his left side, aiming for the enclosed pilot's cabin, judged to be his most vulnerable point. At a distance of 300 meters [my observer] began firing. The target was big and very clear. The giant continued on his course, as if he had not noticed us. He was relatively slow, but then began to climb quite well, as he began to draw fire from our antiaircraft batteries. In a few minutes I had closed to 150 meters and was able to realize, with great satisfaction, that our opening salvo had hit, since the right outboard engine must have been damaged. The propeller was losing RPM and suddenly stopped turning. Now, only three motors were moving him forward, one on the right and two on the left. The Sikorsky began to lose altitude.

Suddenly, a hatch located in the middle of the upper wing opened, a machine gunner appeared and began to fire at us. In the meanwhile, I had closed to about a hundred meters and my observer began to fire in a nearly forward direction. I positioned my aircraft so that he could continue shooting at the main cabin between the wings. My aircraft was being thrown back and forth by the strong propwash of the giant, and I had to slow it down repeatedly to stabilize it and to keep from overtaking him, because he could then have attacked me from behind.

By this time I was about fifty meters away and could clearly see every movement of the enemy crew in the aircraft. The gunner disappeared from the upper wing, and suddenly gun ports opened at the rear of the cabin and we were immediately fired upon by two or three machine guns. The bullets rattled into my airplane, sounding as if someone was pouring dry peas onto a tabletop. As I pushed full throttle and flew over the enemy aircraft in a sort of jump, most of his fire passed below my aircraft. I immediately throttled back and dropped closer to the aircraft, so that my observer could re-open fire from a position slightly to the side and above the cabin.

I repeated this maneuver three times. The Russian aircraft was now six to ten kilometers behind our lines and slowly losing altitude. I began to hope that I could force him to make an emergency landing. We had, in the meantime, descended to about 2,500 meters (8,200 feet). Suddenly he began a turn to the left while still firing at me, probably attempting to dive to safety behind his lines. I immediately turned my aircraft and we attacked him once again, firing at his cabin. I noticed the aircraft begin to wallow, and then it suddenly dropped into a steep spiral. As the spin steepened, the outer part of the upper wing, on which the Russian insignia was painted, broke away and began to flutter down. We had probably damaged the outer portion of the main wing spar; the wing was full of bullet holes when we found it on the ground later.

I put my aircraft into a spiral dive, following the stricken machine. On the second turn, my engine stopped. All my attempts to restart it were useless. Judging by the expression on my observer's face, he was not looking forward to the landing. I set up a shallow glide toward a landing field used by a local artillery unit and made it without difficulty. During the descent from 2,400 meters (7,800 feet), I had a chance to look over my aircraft. (In the meantime, the Russian escort aircraft had been driven off by our single-seat fighters.)

On both sides, our wings were riddled with holes, one inner strut was shot away, and the propeller had two bullet holes in one blade, while gasoline and oil were sloshing across the bottom of the fuselage. After the landing, I counted more than seventy bullet holes. The combination oil and gasoline hopper tank, located directly under the engine, was completely riddled and the main fuel line was punctured. The landing gear showed many hits. We were untouched, however. One bullet "had my name on it" and would have meant a stomach wound had it not been for the fact that it lodged in the starter.

Upon landing, we were greeted by a cheering group of

soldiers who had observed the battle, which had lasted nearly ten minutes. We left immediately to look at the wreck of the giant aircraft, which had fallen about two kilometers away. The Russian crew had neglected to jettison their bombs as the combat began; some of these exploded as the aircraft impacted, tearing the machine apart. The basic structure of the aircraft could be recognized, but most of the smaller details had been destroyed in the crash. The tail section lay some thirty meters (100 feet) away from the wings, of which one half-span, that measured twenty-one paces, was still structurally intact, so the total span of the aircraft must have been between forty-four and forty-eight paces. The fuselage is very long and thin, covered in plywood. The lower half of the cabin, which is located between the wings and extending about one meter in front of and behind the leading and trailing edge of the upper wing, is made of plywood; the upper half is made of glass. There is an opening in the upper wing which allows a gunner to fire from that position, while the cabin has gun ports for protective fire. Weapons consisted of one water-cooled and two air-cooled machine guns. The motors, two on each side, mounted on the lower wings, seem to be of English manufacture and are rated at 220 horsepower each.

All four occupants were dead. The crew consisted of a pilot-captain, an artillery captain, a first lieutenant in the cavalry, and a fourth body so badly burned that no identification of any sort was possible. Probably the crew were killed before the crash, since the three officers had numerous wounds in the head and chest. The cabin was literally riddled with bullets. According to documents found in the wreckage, the giant aircraft was referred to as the "Il'ya Muromets;" two of these aircraft, plus escort fighters, form a bomber group.

On 26 September, the crew was buried with a full military honors at the Boruny cemetery.

The crash site is Bogdanov, East of Lida.

---

the Pskov aerodrome, we tested them rigorously for air combat work and leadership potential in military aviation.

At the same time, Igor Sikorsky worked tirelessly at developing the Il'ya Muromets. On September 6, 1916, he tested a new type, the Il'ya Muromets, Type Ye, for air worthiness.[7] This new flying ship could easily reach an altitude of 3,100 meters with a load of 2,457 kilograms. The cabin was more roomy than in earlier models of the Il'ya Muromets. The location of the fuel tanks was changed and the armament was augmented. The front windshield was made of a shatterproof glass and positioned in such a fashion as to give the pilot visibility, not only forward, or straight ahead, but upward, downward, and to the sides.

Il'ya Muromets, Type D (D.I.M.). This four-engine tandem version had French-made Renault engines. Photograph was taken at Pskov in the summer of 1916. *Courtesy of the National Air and Space Museum*

The Il'ya Muromets, Type Ye (Yeh), at Pskov, summer 1916. *Courtesy of the Archives, United Technologies Corporation*

Il'ya Muromets, probably a Type G-3 with a combination of Renault (outboard) and R-BVZ (inboard) engines. This late version of the Il'ya Muromets was used in 1916 and 1917. *Courtesy of the Archives, United Technologies Corporation*

A late model Il'ya Muromets, Type G-3, with two Renault and two R-BVZ engines. Note the machine gun in the side window of the fuselage. *Courtesy of the Archives, United Technologies Corporation*

The new aero engines for the Il'ya Muromets, Type Ye, were Renaults. The horsepower for the engines on this variant was increased to 740. At this point the Russo-Baltic factory was not capable of producing acceptable aero engines. The French-made Renault engines gave good results, but the result of their weight, excessive size, and high rate of fuel consumption was a less favorable weight-to-power ratio. With the Renault engines the useful load capacity and range of the Il'ya Muromets was reduced. One of these Renault-powered Murometsy was flown on May 8, 1916, by Staff Captain Alekhnovich, the commander of the IM-5. Alekhnovich flew from the town of Vinnitsa to Kishinev with a load of approximately 3,000 kilograms, in severe weather, against a strong wind of 23 meters a second and at an altitude of 1,000 meters.

At the end of September 1916, other Il'ya Muromets types (in addition to the Type Ye) were evaluated.[8] The Il'ya Muromets Type G embodied most of the characteristics of early Murometsy variants—the B (Beh) and the V (Veh) models—but differed significantly from these earlier types with its two 220-horsepower inboard Renault engines and its two R-BVZ 150-horsepower outboard engines. This particular configuration was necessitated by the fact that there was an acute shortage of aero engines in Russia. As mentioned earlier, Russia had to depend on foreign-made engines in this time of war emergency.

The Il'ya Muromets Type G, as it turned out, proved to be a better flying machine than other Murometsy equipped with Sunbeam engines. The Il'ya Muromets Type G could easily reach its altitude of 3,500 meters carrying a load in excess of 1,600 kilograms, and it could climb to an altitude of 1,000 meters in six minutes. It must be pointed out, however, that the Il'ya Muromets Type G ran out of fuel on its maiden flight, compelling the pilot, Captain R. L. Nizhevskiy, to make an emergency landing on a field thirty kilometers from base. Captain Nizhevskiy made several sharp spirals from an altitude of 200 meters to execute the emergency landing.

Besides the four-engine Murometsy, I. I. Sikorsky, at the time, also designed and built the Dvukhvostka, or S-19 aircraft, which had a twin fuselage mounted with two engines. During tests the S-19 was damaged, and no further models of it were built. The S-19 used Sunbeam aero engines in tandem.[9]

Preparation of the command staff for the Murometsy continued. By the summer of 1916 the majority of young officers assigned to the Murometsy had left Pskov for the front. They flew the Murometsy in training without complications. The only serious accident involving an Il'ya Muromets took place on May 29, 1916, an incident which involved the crash of the Il'ya Muromets XIV (IM-14), commanded by Staff Captain In'kov, who was inexperienced and died in the accident.[10] The reasons for the catastrophe were apparent. In'kov turned his flying ship without banking—that is, he executed a flat turn (commonly known among the military pilots as a "staff officer's turn"). In addition to Staff Captain In'kov's death there were sev-

This Il'ya Muromets, Type G-2, was equipped with a rear machine-gun position. The tail configuration was redesigned to reduce the vulnerability of the Il'ya Muromets to attacks from the rear by the enemy fighters. *Courtesy of the Archives, United Technologies Corporation*

eral injuries, to Staff Captain Valevachev, the mechanic Koval'chuk, and the military pilot Lieutenant Poletayev. Unfortunately, crewmen Valevachev and Koval'chuk died after a few days. A fifth crewman who was not in the cockpit of the IM-14, Volunteer Nasonov, suffered only a sprained wrist.

During the fall of 1916, the Murometsy assigned to the combat unit near Riga were recalled for new duties elsewhere. The EVK moved to the Southwestern Front, to Vinnitsa in the Podol'sk province. The squadron occupied a factory that was once owned by Germans. This factory provided excellent quarters for the squadron personnel, with an adequate airstrip nearby. The evacuation of the EVK from Pskov, including all the Murometsy from the Northern Front, caused some resentment, especially at the headquarters of the Northern Front. The move was dictated by the decision of the Stavka to launch a spring offensive on the Rumanian front in 1917.

At the beginning of 1917, our armies already possessed sufficient quantities of artillery, ammunition, and war matériel to deliver a powerful blow against the enemy—a blow that would enable us to achieve a decisive breakthrough. Everyone believed success was at hand. There was talk that the orchestra of the Guards Company was practicing a special march, "The

Igor Sikorsky's S-19 "twin-tailed" biplane with two Sunbeam engines in a tandem
configuration. This experimental aircraft was flown in the summer of 1916.
Courtesy of the Archives, United Technologies Corporation

General A. A. Brusilov inspects the EVK on the eve of the Galician campaign in
1916, the last great Russian offensive of World War I. *Courtesy of the National Air
and Space Museum*

Triumphal Entry into Constantinople." The Austrians, it is well known, awaited our offensive in anticipation of capitulation.

The detachment of Murometsy assigned to the city of Bolgrad, on the Rumanian front, represented the first harbinger of liberation for Serbia and Rumania from Austrian and German troops. The fateful events in Petrograd in March 1917 overturned everything. Instead of the sound of thunder announcing a victory, fate bequeathed shame to us; instead of our much desired state of peace, we had to endure the agony of civil war.

Notes

1. [Note by K. N. Finne.] This air detachment was also designated the first combat detachment of the EVK. The second combat detachment was stationed at Zegevol'd on the Riga front. The Murometsy assigned to the former unit were powered with Argus aero engines. The IM-2 had R-BVZ engines. After the 1917 Revolution, Staff Captain (later Colonel) A. V. Pankrat'yev was appointed first deputy commander, then commander of the EVK. In 1918 he joined the Red Army and occupied several high positions in the new Red Air Fleet. He died in an air crash in 1923 while test-flying a new aircraft.

2. [Editors' note.] The Il'ya Muromets I, Type V (Veh); the Il'ya Muromets VI, Type V (Veh); Il'ya Muromets VIII, Type V (Veh); and Il'ya Muromets IX, Type V (Veh). See appendix 6.

3. [Editors' note.] The Il'ya Muromets X, Type V (Veh).

4. [Note by K. N. Finne.] Lieutenant G. N. Shneur, a veteran of the Russo-Japanese War, joined the Russian Army in 1914 from the active reserves. Later he served at the Gatchina Military Flying School. He was arrested in Vinnitsa and executed by Ukrainian nationalists under the leadership of S. V. Petlyura (1879–1926) in November 1918.

5. [Note by K. N. Finne.] Lieutenant Yankovius was killed in 1919, while serving in an air unit in General Denikin's Army of South Russia.

6. [Editors' note.] Il'ya Muromets XVI, Type V (Veh). See appendix 6.

7. [Note by K. N. Finne.] Igor Sikorsky earlier built the Il'ya Muromets, Type D, a four-engine flying ship. This Renault-powered aircraft had its engine placed in tandem with pusher-and tractor-type propellers. This version performed well at the R-BVZ factory in Petrograd, but Sikorsky abandoned the idea of further development of it.

8. [Editors' note.] The Il'ya Muromets series G included four subtypes. Production began in December 1915 with the G or G-1. This variant differed from B (Beh) or V (Veh) types with its larger wings. The G-2 subtype incorporated a new rear gunner's position. The G-3 was designed with a fully glazed nose. The G-4, a strengthened version of the G-3, was updated with a stronger nose. See appendix 6.

9. [Editors' note.] See B. V. Shavrov, *Istoriya konstruktsii samoletov v SSSR, do 1938 g.* [The history of aircraft construction in the Soviet Union for the period up to 1938] (Moscow: Mashinostroyeniye, 1969), p. 160.

10. [Editors' note.] Il'ya Muromets XIV, Type V (Veh).

Chapter Eight

THE 1917 REVOLUTION

In earlier chapters of this narrative, I have pointed out the reasons for the slow development of the Il'ya Muromets. This pattern of delay and small production meant that few flying ships were available for combat work.

By the beginning of 1917, it should be pointed out, the EVK represented an impressive aerial squadron. At Vinnitsa, the new home base of the Murometsy, work still proceeded at full stride. At that time, the workshops of the squadron were equipped with the necessary machine tools for the ground crews to perform sophisticated tasks. The EVK remained a disciplined air unit, despite its rear-echelon status and the numerous civilian workers. This fact was acknowledged by the commander of the Southwestern Front, who had visited Vinnitsa and, to his surprise, did not discover the disorganization typical of reserve detachments on the eve of the Revolution.

The discipline that pervaded the EVK could be seen in the behavior of the lower ranks, who showed little interest in challenging authority. This relative quiet, however, was soon shattered in the course of the upheavals of 1917. The EVK, of course, fell victim in time to disintegration. In March 1917 on the day that Nicholas II issued his manifesto of abdication, one of the EVK warehouses was set on fire. The incident bore the telltale marks of arson—clearly a premeditated act, not an accident. The damage from the fire was extensive, with considerable loss of property. To the credit of the lower ranks, there was little pilfering of government property. Many soldiers took an active part in putting out the warehouse fire. Some even had to be restrained from rushing into the burning building. A number of soldiers were injured and many suffered from smoke inhalation.

One sentry who stood guard near a gasoline tank did not abandon his post even as sparks from the fire rained down near the tank. This same sentry gave the fire alarm by firing shots into the air. He summoned others, who then removed the fuel tank to a safe place.

As the revolutionary events of 1917 unfolded, the EVK eventually fell victim to the same forces of disintegration that brought collapse to the Russian Army. Those who remembered those days and had contact with the soldiers realized that the EVK was different in character from most army units. There was not a single murder, not even a single act of violence against officers, until the moment of complete disintegration of the army. From the first days of the war, of course, certain soldiers in the squadron had accepted revolutionary ideas, many becoming "conscientious" Bolsheviks.

For a better understanding of the events at Vinnitsa, it is necessary to mention certain facts. On April 13, 1917, the numerous garrison troops at Vinnitsa were ordered to appear with their weapons on the drill field of the Seventy-Third Crimean Infantry Regiment. These barracks had been occupied by an infantry regiment during peacetime but now served as a hospital and quarters for the personnel of the Fifteenth Reserve Regiment.

For this meeting, a man named Semyonov, a former member of the State Duma (second), came to speak to the soldiers. He greeted the assembled troops as "citizen soldiers" in the name of the Soviet of Soldiers and Workers Deputies. This former member of the Duma gave a speech that was typical of the time, speaking for some unknown reason about Napoleon coming to give Russia "land and freedom." Except for this curious remark I would have forgotten his speech. What Napoleon had to do with the "conquests of the Proletarians" was not comprehended by the audience, or, for that matter, by the orator. This confusion, however, did not prevent the crowd from throwing the orator into the air at the sound of the "Marseillaise." The commander of the garrison and some officers—full of awe—lifted this speaker into the air by his boots, seeing in this gesture a way to express their solidarity with the Soviets.

On May 3, 1917, military burial ceremonies took place at Vinnitsa. The funeral was for four men who had been executed by the military after a court-martial in 1916 for a number of crimes: two for spying for Austria; one for pillaging; and another, an official, for raping a seven-year-old girl. They had been buried clumsily at the edge of the precipice, only to be discovered in the spring. The discovery of these corpses gave rise to many rumors. An investigation followed, which established their true identity as the executed criminals. Yet they were buried again with great honors with the participation of the garrison. There were no other victims of the Tsarist regime.

One of first moves by the Provisional Government toward the squadron was the removal of General Shidlovskiy as commander.[1] At Stavka, General M. V. Alekseyev, the chief of staff, wrote to Shidlovskiy that Minister of War Guchkov found Shidlovskiy's role harmful and demanded his resignation. In the same letter General Alekseyev expressed his deep regret over the resignation, acknowledging with appreciation the EVK commander's highly regarded leadership and organizational work.

On April 18, General Shidlovskiy gathered together the Murometsy pilots and senior officers and informed them of Guchkov's decision and of his own resignation as well. Shidlovskiy encouraged the EVK officers to continue the struggle they had begun and not to abandon the cause for which they had given their energy. During his farewell speech General Shidlovskiy could not overcome his agitation or conceal his emotions. A man known for his strength of character, the EVK commander had been shaken and deeply moved by the events of the moment. Tears appeared in his eyes as he made his final address to the squadron. Even as General Shidlovskiy resigned, Igor Sikorsky departed from the Squadron of Flying Ships.

After the declaration of soldier's rights, "Order No. 1," and certain revolutionary steps by the new Provisional Government, effective combat work by the EVK became impossible.[2] At first, certainly, squadron life remained on the whole normal, perhaps the result of inertia even as large numbers of "warriors" defected and departed from the front. EVK units continued to fly missions despite the hostility of some "class-conscious" soldiers who believed that such action behind enemy lines would delay the peace treaty "without annexations or reparations." There were a few instances of petty sabotage on Murometsy aircraft as well as threats against officers who flew the combat missions.

Under the circumstances, combat flights against the enemy could be more aptly described as suicidal acts. Yet EVK detachments on the Rumanian front and in Galicia, near the city of Tarnopol and the Chertkov area, maintained their combat flights. On May 8, 1917, for example, Captain G. V. Klembovskiy flew the Il'ya Muromets XV (IM-15) against three German fighters in an aerial duel and downed two of them that had dared to fly too close.[3] On board the IM-15, the mechanic, Sergeant Major Golubets, was wounded slightly in the head. The flying ship was hit several times by enemy fire, with damage to the propeller blades and one engine.

The story of the IM-15's mission is as follows: The IM-15 left the town of Yagel'nitsa, near Chertkov, on the morning of May 8, 1917. The crew consisted of Captain G. V. Klembovskiy, the commander; Lieutenant Demichev-Ivanov, the deputy commander; Captain P. V. Ivanovskiy, the artillery officer; Staff Captain V. S. Federov, military pilot; and the mechanic, Sergeant Major S. Golubets. On board for the mission there were 606 kilograms of gasoline, 131 kilograms of oil, 6 16-kilogram bombs, and four machine guns, including a Vickers and a Lewis machine gun and two Madsen light machine guns. There were plenty of cartridges. The route for the mission was as follows: Yagel'nitsa, Monsterzhisko, Lipitsa Dol'na, and the farming complex of Khutsisko, where the twenty-second Turkish Division headquarters was located. While in flight, the crew of the flying ship strafed the enemy lines. Among the bombs dropped on Khutsisko, four struck some buildings and caused fires. On the return flight, at a distance of about ten kilometers from our lines, in the area of the village of Mechish-chuv, three enemy fighters of the Fokker type attacked the IM-15, approaching and firing from the rear. Return fire from the IM-15 shot down the first enemy fighter, which fell into the woods near the enemy trenches. This was clearly visible to the crew of the Il'ya Muromets. The second Fokker was shot down over our territory. Owing to the damage that the IM-15 had sustained and the injuries to the mechanic Golubets, however, the crew did not observe the second Fokker falling down. Information on the downing of the enemy fighters was provided to army headquarters by army units that were occupying positions in this area through the forty-first Army Corps headquarters. Eyewitnesses indicated that this aerial combat took place at an altitude between 1,800 and 2,400 meters.

For this combat action, the IM-15's deputy commander, Lieutenant Demichev-Ivanov, was awarded the Order of St. George, Fourth Degree. Captain P. V. Ivanovskiy and Staff Captain V. S. Federov were awarded St. George swords; Sergeant Major S. Golubets, the St. George Cross. The Commander of the IM-15, G. V. Klembovskiy, was also recommended for the award of the Order of St. George, Fourth Degree. This recommendation was sent through the headquarters of the Southwestern Front to the St. George Council in Petrograd, but subsequent revolutionary events in Petrograd prevented Captain Klembovskiy from receiving the award.

After this aerial combat, Captain Klembovskiy received the following telegram from the commander at the Southwestern Front:

> Commander in Chief requests conveyance of his deep gratitude to all the members of Il'ya Muromets XV crew for their gallant deeds in aerial combat on May 8 in the area of the village Mechishchuv.
>
> General Sukhomlinov

With reference to these missions on the Rumanian front, it is worth mentioning the flights of the Il'ya Muromets IX (IM-9), under the command of the military pilot, Captain R. L. Nizhevskiy.[4] These flights also took place in the spring of 1917. During this air action the IM-9 demonstrated its excellent combat qualities. While on one mission crossing the front lines, one of the Renault engine carburetors caught on fire, and the flames quickly spread over the lower wing surface. The crew managed to put out the fire in the face of the heavy enemy artillery fire. Sergeant Major Ivanov and the Volunteer Kapon climbed out on the wing to extinguish the flames.

After this emergency the IM-9 continued its flight, using only three

Lieutenant G. I. Lavrov and his crew were killed in the crash of the Il'ya Muromets I (IM-1) on May 11, 1917. Sabotage was suspected. Lavrov had participated with Igor Sikorsky on the flight from St. Petersburg to Kiev in 1914. *Courtesy of the National Air and Space Museum*

engines. With just three engines running it made a bombing attack and returned to base safely. While on another flight returning from a bombing mission over the Troyan station, the same flying ship was attacked by two enemy fighters. Before the sudden attack, the crew were relaxing on board, considering themselves to be safely on their way home and not having taken any precautionary measures.

The enemy fighters approached the IM-9 from the rear and opened up with a burst of machine-gun fire. Ensign Talako was wounded in the leg and Sergeant Major Yankevich was mortally wounded in the stomach. Yet the crew repelled the attack, downing one of the enemy fighters. The two inboard engine radiators had been pierced by enemy fire, forcing the crew to fly the remaining fifty-three kilometers to the aerodrome with only two engines.

Photograph of K. N. Finne (second from right) and his wife, Olga Glass (third from right), taken in September 1917. I. S. Bashko is seated on the porch with pets.
Courtesy of the K. N. Finne family

One EVK unit near Tarnopol experienced a deepening revolutionary crisis, which had tragic consequences. On May 11, 1917, near the town of Mikulinsta, the Il'ya Muromets I (IM-1) was lost, along with its entire crew.[5] While in the air, the flying ship's strut broke and collapsed. The incident was the result of deliberate sabotage. Someone had weakened the strut and its arresting cables, and the damage could have been prevented. The IM-1's regular mechanic, M. T. Shidlovskiy, who always personally inspected the flying ship thoroughly, was absent from work. Shidlovskiy claimed that he had been ill as a result of constant insults and threats received from the lower ranks of the squadron. He was put in the hospital. As a consequence, the officers of the IM-1 could have overlooked such a thing as a weakened strut or even the removal of a holding nut or locknut as they took off on their combat mission.

The entire crew were lost in the crash. The commander of the IM-1, Lieutenant G. I. Lavrov, was a naval aviator who in 1914 had flown with

Igor Sikorsky on the round-trip flight from St. Petersburg to Kiev. Lavrov at the time was the commander of the EVK Air Detachment. Other crew members who died in the tragic crash were the deputy commander, Lieutenant V. K. Vitkovskiy, Lieutenant Shokal'skiy, Captain Otreshko, Ensign Balashov, and the mechanic, Sergeant Sofronov.

Shortly after the shameful retreat of our troops from Tarnopol there was a rash of robberies and indiscriminate violence against the peaceful population of the area. These acts were justified as "revolutionary discipline." When the enemy approached, it was decided to move the EVK from Vinnitsa to the rear, deeper still into the hinterlands of Russia, but the growing anarchy and lack of transportation prevented the move.

In August 1917, an enemy aeroplane appeared over Vinnitsa. The crew, feeling free from danger, fired on the peaceful population of the town several times and dropped a few bombs on the EVK aerodrome without causing it any harm. Fragments of exploding bombs dropped near the base wounded a peasant girl and killed a pig.

Posing no threat to the enemy, the large garrison at Vinnitsa eventually fell victim to revolutionary propaganda. The idleness of those garrisoned there in turn posed a threat to the peaceful population. On October 23, 1917, armed bands of soldiers made an attempt to capture a liquor warehouse. The liquor was spilled into the Bug River, and the unusual scene for those times of soldiers and residents running to the river with their tea kettles to take their fill of this free, precious, if dirty, mix of water and spirits could be observed.

Crowds of soldiers attacking the warehouse ran away at the first sound of gunshot fired from an armored car. Nobody was injured, however. Frightened military authorities and the Vinnitsa municipal government decided to remove the Fifteenth Reserve Regiment which was stationed in the town. The regiment, however, refused to leave. When a punitive detachment of soldiers, consisting of a platoon of cadets drawn from the Second Ensign's School in the city of Zhitomir, one Cossack battery, and an armored car unit, entered Vinnitsa, the entire garrison took up arms. The armored-car unit was the same one that had attempted to defend the liquor warehouse. The Fifteenth Reserve Regiment was joined in this uprising by several units, including a machine-gun regiment, all the EVK's low-ranking troops, an antiaircraft battery, and others. The situation was rather serious. In addition to the Vinnitsa Garrison's large numbers in comparison to that of its opposition, there were the huge stockpiles of guns—more than 250 machine guns with ammunition—stored in the squadron's warehouse.

The EVK officers refused to participate in any of these "military actions." By contrast, the lower ranks of the EVK, who were confident of their victory over the Provisional Government's "counterrevolutionary" troops, declared that they could manage without the officers. These events unfolded on November 9–10, 1917, at the very time the Bolsheviks gained control in Petrograd. In the capital, "the residents were peacefully resting and did not know that one government was replacing another."

When the Vinnitsa rebel garrison refused to surrender their arms on November 9, the Cossack battery opened fire on the EVK, an attack that continued from 3:00 P.M. until 10:00 P.M. with short interruptions. Soldiers who attacked the battery were forced back in disarray. Lacking competent officers, the soldiers could not take the battery. After the first shots, the rebel soldiers returned to the barracks and remained there. Although there were some officers in the rebel garrison, there was hardly a clever leader who might have suggested to capture the battery first, which would not have been difficult to accomplish at this location, since the battery did not have any cover.

It was the "government" armored-car platoon commandant, Captain Khalil-Bekov who actually saved the situation.[6] He fired from an armored car at the door of the City Hall building, where, at that moment, the local soviet of soldiers and workers' deputies was having a meeting. He then chased the rebels out of the building. Later he, personally, in the light armored car, attacked a Bolshevik's armored car by exploding its gasoline tank. Having put the enemy on the run, Captain Khalil-Behov did not allow the initiative to fall out of his hands during the period that followed.

Later that night, the EVK surrendered, and by the evening of the next day, the 20,000-soldier garrison had surrendered their arms to their new conquerors. In Petrograd some articles appeared in the newspapers describing these confrontations in an exaggerated manner as bloody battles. The articles also described how the Murometsy were flying over the battlefield and dropping bombs. At that time in Vinnitsa, there were no Murometsy, not to mention that there were no pilots who would have wanted to fly such a mission. Most probably, a correspondent's passionate imagination mistook a Voisin flying over the area on that day—no bombs were dropped—to be an Il'ya Muromets.

During the confrontation at Vinnitsa few had been killed or wounded. In the punitive detachment, two people were killed and three cadets were wounded by machine-gun fire from members of the lower ranks of the EVK. Among the rebels, two were killed in the armored car explosion and a few others were wounded. At the plant where the EVK was located, some buildings were damaged by shells. In the city, a secondary school was damaged, as was the Orthodox Cathedral, the latter sustaining only minor damage. In spite of this victory, a detachment loyal to the Provisional Government, along with their weapons, had to retreat hastily to the city of Berdichev. This retreat was necessary because the Bolsheviks gained power in Petrograd and were expanding their power to other cities. There was little organized resistance to the Bolsheviks as they moved their power and influence into the provinces.

In this confusing political situation, the Bolsheviks were temporarily dislodged by Ukrainian nationalists of the Doroshenko regiment.[7] The

Ruined hangar at the EVK air base at Vinnitsa in 1917. A dismantled Il'ya Muromets has been abandoned. The photograph was taken by Austrian troops who occupied Vinnitsa. *Courtesy of Sergei Sikorsky*

Ukrainian movement was known as the Gaidamaki.[8] Their commissars then demobilized the "Russians" from the army and sent them home. The Gaidamaki contributed much to the thievery of EVK equipment, possessions, and stores, stealing even more than their predecessors. They stole the conditioned, dry, valuable wood for the aeroplanes, for example, in order to burn it in stoves, although there was a lot of coal and kindling wood in the area. The Gaidamaki chiefs—that is, the officers—did not prevent them from doing this, and when the soldiers were asked why they were burning this valuable material, they would respond, "but this burns better."

The officers who remained in the squadron made an attempt to save the squadron's remaining matériel. They tried to take it to the city of Berdyansk, where the Ukrainian aviation headquarters had given permission for the squadron to move. The local Ukrainian commissar endeavored to delay this transfer by not providing the trains. The situation continued until January 30, 1918, when, after a brief engagement with the Bolshevik-led Second Guards Corps under Madame Bush, the Gaidamaki departed from Vinnitsa. During this battle the EVK fell under the bombardment of the attacking Second Guards Corps artillery battery.

The Second Guards Corps retained some vestiges of its former guards status. By looking at the lapels they were wearing, one could recognize former guards skirmishers and some Lithuanians. They were marching gallantly and even brandishing old banners, although the Imperial monogram was covered with red cloth. After having entered Vinnitsa, these troops took retribution on their enemies in the form of a massive forced requisition. Horses were requisitioned, for example, with the charge that they belonged to a lord of the manor.

On February 28, 1918, these former guards troops, with the approach of the Germans, decided to depart Vinnitsa. Under fire, they retreated beyond the Dnieper.

Meanwhile, an armored train with marines and Red Guards arrived at Vinnitsa from Zhmerynka and, during the entire evening and night, kept firing on the peaceful city of Vinnitsa. On March 1, 1918 Vinnitsa was occupied by thirty soldiers of the 133rd Infantry of Saxon Landwehr regiment under the command of a noncommissioned officer and took the city without opposition.

By that time, the EVK was in disarray. Besides the railroad cars loaded with the squadron's possessions and many valuables, there was only a graveyard of Murometsy flying ships. Upon the arrival of the Germans, some of the remaining Murometsy at the aerodrome were set on fire and burned, although in reality they were in rather poor condition. Those captured flying ships that remained intact were guarded carefully by the Germans. At the former EVK aerodrome, German aeroplanes soon arrived with their black cross markings. It was difficult for Russian pilots to accept them because they had encountered these same aeroplanes earlier in aerial combat.

Shortly thereafter, the EVK became "Ukrainianized," and the officers who did not wish to take an oath to the newly proclaimed free Ukraine Republic were immediately removed from the squadron. The unit was renamed Air Ship Squadron (using the Ukrainian equivalent of EVK) and existed—in name only—as that until the fall of 1918, when the Germans withdrew and the "liberated Ukraine" ceased to exist.

In the only remaining EVK detachment on the Western Front near Minsk, where Ukrainianization was not required, the situation was difficult as well. This detachment's soldiers did not permit the officers, who were now receiving merely a soldier's salary and rations, to leave, keeping them under permanent surveillance for fear that they would fly to the Don to join the counterrevolutionaries.

This situation continued until February–March 1918, when the Germans, whose offensive had not met with any resistance, appeared forty kilometers away from the Murometsy base. On March 6, 1918, the (soldiers'?) committee requested the detachment commander, Colonel Bashko, to help resolve this situation, which threatened them with German captivity. In spite of the disintegration of the detachment, the flying ships and other equipment were still secure and in good condition, which, at that time, was remarkable. When soldiers abandoned the front, they would often sell cheaply all the government possessions they had.

At that time, a machine gun could be purchased for 25 rubles. A battery including guns, ammunition, and horses cost 800 rubles. Germans, Polish, and Rumanians got high prices selling war booty. To the credit of the lower ranks of the EVK, it is worth mentioning that at the approach of the Germans, they burned their belongings rather than allow them to be sold. Having ordered destroyed all belongings that could not be saved and advising the men of the squadron where to go to escape capture by the Germans, Colonel Bashko gave orders to prepare the Murometsy, including the IM-Kievskiy—that is, those flying ships still in good condition—for a flight out.[9] When he arrived at the aerodrome, to his surprise he saw the enlisted soldiers lining up as if under the old regime. He greeted them in the manner of former times and he received a friendly and distinct answer: "Wish you health, Your Highness."

At that time, Vinnitsa, where the EVK base and headquarters had been located, was already occupied by the Germans. Colonel Bashko therefore decided to fly to Bobruisk, which was occupied at that time by the troops of the First Polish Corps. When the IM-Kievskiy was flying over Minsk, the city was occupied by German cavalry, and there were two German aircraft flying over as well. The Germans did not attack the flying ship and it landed safely in Bobruisk.

Another view of the abandoned EVK air base at Vinnitsa in 1917. *Courtesy of Sergei Sikorsky*

Commander of the Il'ya Muromets Kievskiy, Captain I. S. Bashko. Bashko wears the Order of St. George, which was earned for bravery in destroying an Austrian train in eastern Galicia in June 1915. *Courtesy of the K. N. Finne family*

Another Il'ya Muromets flown by the volunteer Nasonov landed near Borisov and, at the approach of Germans, was burned. In May–June 1918, the Germans decided to disband the Polish Corps and to disarm it. On June 4, at two o'clock in the morning, the IM-Kievskiy took off from the aerodrome, loaded four kilometers from a railroad station then occupied by the Germans, and flew toward Moscow. The flight proceeded under very difficult conditions, with clouds as high as 3,200 meters. It was to the flying ship's advantage that it gained altitude even though it was quite rundown. The IM-Kievskiy's engines were of the Beardmore 160-horsepower type, which had earlier enabled this flying ship to attain an altitude of 4,900 meters. The flight was conducted with a compass. In addition, Colonel Bashko, tired of the constant threat of the Germans advancing to capture the aerodrome and without sleep for several nights, was falling asleep at the wheel.

After a 5½-hour flight above the clouds, when the flying ship was above Moscow, Bashko began a descent, passing through thick clouds at an altitude of 3,200 meters. When the IM-Kievskiy reached an altitude of 1,000 meters, it started to rain heavily. At an altitude of 500 meters, when the ground was not yet visible, the two left-side engines suddenly went out of order. Colonel Bashko shut off the right engines and had to glide without seeing where to land the flying ship. At an altitude of 250 meters, the crew saw a village and to the rear on the right a field for landing. Turning to the right, Bashko flew the IM-Kievskiy into a hundred-year-old fir tree. The flight had ended. Colonel Bashko later recovered when his pet bulldog, which always accompanied him in his flights, was licking his face. Fortunately, this time too Colonel Bashko and his crew received only minor injuries.

As it later became clear, the actual altitude was not 250 meters as earlier indicated by an altimeter, but 125 meters. To make a 180-degree turn while gliding at such a low altitude was impossible for an Il'ya Muromets. The IM-Kievskiy had crashed onto a church yard in a village in the Yukhnovsky region, at a distance of 106 kilometers from Moscow.

In a short while, Colonel Bashko and his crew climbed out of the debris of the flying ship and were mugged, arrested, and place under escort. They were dispatched, first to Yukhnov and later to Moscow, to the headquarters of the Cheka.[10] After his release, Colonel Bashko traveled to Petrograd, where he was appointed commander of the EVK. At that time, some former EVK officers, mainly former commanders of the IM-2, A. V. Pankrat'yev, and the IM-5, G. V. Alekhnovich, were trying to create a new EVK for the Red Air Fleet. They mobilized the existing Murometsy that remained in the R-BVZ branch plant in Petrograd. Later this squadron was renamed the Division of Murometsy.

Colonel Bashko did not take any active part in the Civil War that followed. He was under constant surveillance. By searching for new aerodromes or locations for stationing the Murometsy, Bashko was trying to delay putting the Murometsy into military action. Finally, as a result of a swift raid by General Mamontov's troops when the Murometsy were stationed in the Tambov region, he was quickly removed. He then managed to escape from Soviet Russia in 1921 and joined the new Lithuanian army, where he was appointed an aviation division commander.[11]

. . . Concerning the remaining Murometsy in Soviet Russia, there is hardly any information.

Illustration of an Il'ya Muromets with red stars. After the Bolshevik Revolution in November 1917, a number of Murometsy were mobilized for service in the Red Air Fleet. *Courtesy of the National Air and Space Museum*

Letter of Introduction
Major General Mason M. Patrick
February 17, 1919
American Expeditionary Forces
U. S. Air Services—Paris

From: Chief of Air Service, A.E.F.

To: Director of Air Service, Washington, D. C.

Subject: Introducing Mr. Sikorski.

    1. Mr. Sikorski, Russian inventor of airplanes, is proceding to the United States for the purpose of laying before the authorities there, information concerning the success of his designs.

    2. The general public at large knows little of the result of the use of airplanes on the Russian front. We have been able to collect the following brief information:

> "The Sikorski multi-motored airplanes rendered excellent service to the Russian Army as battle planes, as confirmed by official documents, and made about 400 raids over the enemy territory, representing a total distance of over 120,000 kilometers. Only one airplane, brought down by enemy fire, failed to return to its base; long distances were covered in spite of being badly damaged by shots of the enemy, several times with one and even two motors stopped at the same time."

    3. Mr. Sikorski can furnish further information and photographs concerning the results of his work. It is felt that these are interesting enough to call the matter to the attention of the Air Service in America.

/Signed/
MASON M. PATRICK
Major General, U.S.A.

Air personnel of the Red Air Fleet pose next to an Il'ya Muromets mobilized to defend the Bolshevik regime during the Civil War. Date unknown. *Courtesy of the National Air and Space Museum*

Notes

1. [Editors' note.] The Provisional Government, formed from elements in the Duma, or national parliament, became the formal successor to the Romanov dynasty. The Provisional Government existed from March to November 7, 1917, when it was toppled by the Bolsheviks under Lenin. The Bolsheviks had gained control of the Provisional Government's chief rival for power, the Petrograd Soviet of Soldiers and Workers Deputies.

2. [Editors' note.] "Order No. 1" was issued by the Petrograd Soviet of Soldiers and Workers Deputies on March 4, 1917. It called for committees of soldiers and sailors to take control of their units and resist the authority of officers. This proclamation did much to subvert the discipline of the Russian Army.

3. [Editors' note.] Il'ya Muromets XV, Type V (Veh). See appendix 6.

4. [Editors' note.] Il'ya Muromets IX, Type Ye (Yeh). See appendix 6.

5. [Editors' note.] Il'ya Muromets I, Type G-2. See appendix 6.

6 [Note by K. N. Finne.] Captain

Khalil-Bekov was killed in Ekaterinodar in 1919, during the Civil War.

7. [Editors' note.] Doroshenko was named after a seventeenth-century Ukrainian nationalist leader.

8. [Editors' note]. The Gaidamaki, named after the Ukrainians who fought for national independence in the eighteenth century, opposed the Bolsheviks during the 1918–20 Civil War in the Ukraine.

9. [Editors' note.] The Il'ya Muromets Kievskiy, Type G-2 (third). See appendix 6.

10. [Editors' note.] The Cheka was the name given to the Bolshevik secret police. The organization was set up in December 1917 and was led by Felix Dzerzinskiy. Its formal duties consisted of fighting "counterrevolution" and "sabotage," and it became an important weapon by means of which the Bolsheviks consolidated their power.

11. [Editors' note.] Bashko managed to survive the many dangers of war and revolution and to escape into exile. He took up residence in newly independent Estonia during the interwar years. When the Soviet Union occupied Estonia in 1939–40, Bashko was arrested and was later executed.

EPILOGUE

By Sergei Sikorsky

Following the October 1917 Bolshevik Revolution, Russia was thrown into chaos. To consolidate its power, the Bolsheviks started a wave of mass arrests, deportations, and executions. As the situation grew steadily worse, the chairman of the Russo-Baltic Wagon Company, M. V. Shidlovsky, asked Igor Sikorsky to leave Russia at the earliest opportunity. He took this advice seriously. In March 1918, as Russia slid deeper into revolutionary anarchy and slaughter, Sikorsky left his native land forever. After a brief stop in London, he moved to Paris. There he quickly found work, for the French government commissioned him to design and build a new four-engine bomber for the war effort. The French government ordered five of the new aircraft, but the order was canceled immediately after the Armistice that ended World War I in November 1918. In early 1919, Igor Sikorsky immigrated to the United States with $600 in his pocket and the determination that somehow he would get back into aviation.

This determination was fueled by an oddly prophetic dream my father had in 1900, when he was about eleven years of age. In his own words:

> I saw myself walking along a narrow, luxuriously decorated passageway. On both sides were walnut doors, similar to the stateroom doors of a steamer. The floor was covered with an attractive carpet. A spherical electric light from the ceiling produced a pleasant bluish illumination. Walking slowly, I felt a slight vibration under my feet and was not surprised to find that the feeling was different from that experienced on a steamer or on a railroad train. I took this for granted, because in my dream I knew that I was on board a large flying ship in

the air. Just as I reached the end of the corridor and opened a door to enter a decorated lounge, I woke up.

Everything was over. The palatial flying ship was only a beautiful creation of the imagination. At that age I had been told that man had never produced a successful flying machine and that it was considered impossible.

During the fall of 1931, after a series of extensive test flights, Sikorsky Aircraft delivered to Pan American Airways the S-40, a four-engine flying boat, which was christened the American Clipper. This plane was the first of a series of large flying clipper ships that have been used successfully for long-distance air travel to South America and which eventually started the transpacific airline and the transatlantic air route.

I did a considerable amount of flying in this plane but was usually so busy making observations, watching the instruments in the pilot's cabin, and solving various engineering problems that I had little opportunity to get an impression of the flight as a passenger. Furthermore, all the preliminary flights were made with the structure bare—that is, without any interior arrangements, trimmings, or seats. In this state the cabin was very noisy, and it was difficult to move about because the temporary floors were covered with a number of sand bags to represent the useful load. Finally, all tests were completed successfully and the ship returned to the factory for the installation of seats, tables, trimmings, carpets, and other fittings.

Upon acceptance of the plane by Pan American Airways, I was invited on a flight over New York with several members of the board of directors of that organization and a few other guests. The Pan American pilots and crew were now in charge of the ship. I had no duties on board and was able to enjoy the flight over New York, which was made partly above the clouds. We admired the scenery of the clouds against the setting sun and the city, which could be seen from time to time between the clouds.

On the way back to Bridgeport, the pilot throttled the engines and gradually brought the ship down to a lower altitude. The sun was already below the horizon, and as the ship descended, it became quite dark. The air was calm and the plane moved very slowly, with the engines running at reduced power. I was in the front cabin at the time and decided to see what was going on in the other cabins. While I was walking toward the smoking lounge, the cabin steward turned on the lights, and I stopped with a feeling of surprise. Some twenty feet ahead I saw the walnut trimmings and the elegant entrance to the smoking lounge. The bluish electric lights from the ceiling appeared bright and attractive. Usually I had been too busy to see the cabin with the lights on. Now looking at it for the first time under these conditions, I could well appreciate its fine appearance, for it was much larger than that on any other plane at the time. But I was surprised by another thought. I realized, at that very moment, that I had already seen all this a long time ago, the passageway, the bluish lights, the walnut trimmings on the walls and doors, and the feeling of smooth motion, and I tried to recall when and how I could have received such an impression, until finally I remembered the details of my dream of some thirty years before.

After several meager years, the Sikorsky Aero Engineering Corporation was officially incorporated in New York State, March 5, 1923. Working with homemade tools on a chicken farm on Long Island, using scraps of metal from a junkyard and hardware from a 5- and 10-cent store, a small group of men, with Sikorsky as the chief designer and inspiration, built a large twin-engine fourteen-passenger airliner.

This airplane, the S-29A, was completed in May 1924, thanks to a contribution of $5,000 at the last minute from the great Russian composer and pianist, Sergei Rachmaninoff. The S-29A (A for America) was barn-stormed extensively and was used on a variety of charter flights, often with Igor Sikorsky at the controls.

The S-29A was eventually sold to the colorful racing pilot Roscoe Turner, who used it for advertising and demonstration flights all around the United States. In turn, he sold it to Howard Hughes, who used it in the aviation epic, *Hell's Angels*.

After a long struggle marked by great financial difficulties and equally great disappointments, Sikorsky Aircraft scored its first important commercial success with the design of the S-38 amphibian. This aircraft, powered by two of the newly developed Pratt & Whitney Wasp engines, made its first flight on June 25, 1928. It cruised at 100 miles an hour, carrying eight passengers and a crew of two, and had a range of 600 miles. It was probably the first passenger aircraft built in the United States that could maintain altitude with a full load of passengers and fuel with one engine out. Pilots and passengers alike expressed great enthusiasm for the aircraft. Orders began to roll in for it, and after years of struggle the Sikorsky organization was at last on its way.

In 1919 Sikorsky Aircraft moved to Stratford, Connecticut, and continued production of the S-38. It was the same year that Sikorsky Aircraft became a subsidiary, later a division, of United Aircraft Corporation, which today is known as United Technologies Corporation.

The four-engine S-40s were the first of the famous line of Pan American Clippers and were used to pioneer routes to Central and South America. The S-42 was also a clipper, and like most of the other Sikorsky designs it was much advanced over other aircraft of its time. It had a top speed of 188 miles an hour, a cruising speed of 160 miles an hour, a range of 1,200 miles with a 7,000-pound payload, and a range of 3,000 miles with a 1,500-pound payload. It was designed specifically as a transoceanic airliner. All ten built were sold to Pan American and used to pioneer routes across the Atlantic and Pacific oceans.

The S-42 made another important contribution to American aviation in 1934. It was in the midst of the Great Depression and interest in aviation had waned. The National Aeronautics Association (NAA) then began a campaign urging American aircraft designers to increase the number of world records in aviation held by this country, the thought being that such activity would help restimulate interest in the industry.

On August 1, 1934, a letter arrived at Sikorsky from the NAA urging the company to help establish some new world records. At the time, the United States held nine world records, while France held sixteen. Two of the

The S-40 represented a significant step forward in transoceanic flying. Powered by four 575-horsepower Pratt & Whitney engines, this Sikorsky-designed seaplane could carry passengers across great distances in unrivaled comfort. Igor Sikorsky made a unique contribution to air travel during the interwar years through a sequence of multiengine seaplanes. *Courtesy of the K. N. Finne family*

U.S. nine had been established a few weeks earlier by the S-42; both were altitude records with payload. By the rarest but most dramatic of coincidences, Sikorsky had scheduled attempts at eight world records in August. All were successful. The S-42 proved that it could fly higher, faster, and with a heavier payload than any other flying boat in the world.

Before the end of the day, Frederick W. Neilson, president of Sikorsky, sent a letter to the NAA saying that Sikorsky was happy to report that it had complied with the request to establish world records and had, in fact captured eight new ones that day. Thus, the United States became first in world records, holding seventeen to France's sixteen.

The last fixed-wing aircraft built by Sikorsky was the S-44, a flying boat used as a navy patrol aircraft and as an airliner capable of traversing the Atlantic without refueling stops at Newfoundland or the Azores. Like its predecessors, the S-44 was a leader and pioneer in its class. The last one was built in 1942.

Having conquered the oceans for commercial aviation with his pioneering aircraft, Igor Sikorsky next turned his full attention to the design, testing, and manufacture of a new type of flying machine, the helicopter. Sikorsky had made his first attempt to construct a helicopter in 1909 as a young designer in Tsarist Russia. He built two prototypes, but for lack of powerful engines, they proved impractical. But he never gave up his dream of designing an aircraft that could take off and land vertically, hover, and fly backward and sideways as well as forward. During the ten years between 1929 and 1939 he gave as much attention as he could to the design of this novel aircraft. He applied for a patent on a helicopter in 1931 and received it in 1935.

His helicopter, the VS-300, was designed and built in 1939. It was a strange-looking machine built of tubular steel with a 75-horsepower engine. The aircraft was built so that changes in the design could be made and tested quickly. The first flight was on September 14, 1939. During the next two years hundreds of improvements were made on the aircraft. It went through four distinct configurations. A 90-horsepower engine replaced the 80-horsepower engine. Finally, a 100-horsepower engine was used. Public demonstrations were held and the helicopter attracted much attention. On May 6, 1941, the VS-300 set a world helicopter endurance record of 1 hour, 32 minutes, 26.1 seconds.

The same year, the U.S. Army awarded Sikorsky a contract for an experimental two-place helicopter, the XR-4. It was delivered in May 1942, and within a short time a new helicopter industry was born. Meanwhile, the original helicopter, the VS-300, was flown in 1943 to the Edison Institute Museum, Dearborn, Michigan, to become a permanent exhibit.

With the fundamentals established, work began on the design, development, and construction of larger and more efficient aircraft. The helicopter soon entered service and began to save lives. As technology advanced, the capabilities and performance of the helicopter improved and the variety of uses to which the machine could be put increased dramatically. These uses are limited only by the limits of the imagination. Helicopters are used by all the military forces in the United States and by those of many other governments. It has been estimated that use of the helicopter to fly wounded soldiers to medical stations has reduced deaths from certain types of wound from 80–90 percent to less than 10 percent. The Air Force's Aerospace Rescue and Recovery Service made Sikorsky helicopters famous as the Jolly Green Giants, which rescued hundreds of pilots downed in hostile territory during the Vietnam conflict.

The U.S. Navy has long used helicopters for a multitude of purposes. Sikorsky helicopters have been the primary recovery craft on all U.S. space flights. The aircraft are used to spot and track submarines and to sweep mines from the seas without the necessity of risking ships and men. Large, swift helicopters operating from ships have given the Marine Corps new, more flexible striking capability. The U.S. Army has used helicopters for everything from flying troops to battle to rescuing civilians from villages being overrun by hostile forces. During the Vietnam conflict, Army Skycranes made by Sikorsky built bridges, carried large weapons, and flew portable detachable pods to the battlefields for use as hospitals, command posts, and even chapels.

As a division of United Aircraft Corporation, Sikorsky Aircraft participated in the technological advancements of other divisions. The world records established were facilitated by the improved engines of the Pratt & Whitney Aircraft division and the controllable pitch and constant speed propellers of the Hamilton Standard division. The Sikorsky laboratories developed numerous high lift and control devices for airplanes, which were applied both to Sikorsky and Chance Vought airplanes. The Sikorsky flaps, ailerons, spoilers, and tail surfaces were incorporated on the OS2U-1 Kingfisher and the F4U-1 Corsair, as well as on the S-42, S-43, and S-44 airplanes.

Before World War II, in 1939, the two airplane divisions were combined in Stratford as Vought-Sikorsky Aircraft, providing much-needed space in East Hartford for the expanded operation of the Pratt & Whitney and Hamilton Standard divisions. The combined airplane operations made possible the development and production of the OS2U-1, F4U-1, TBU-1, S-44, VS-300, R-4, and V-173 "flying wing." The last-named aircraft proved the virtue of a low aspect ratio of 1.27 for stability and control. Continued research on low aspect ratio to the Dart shape was the forerunner of supersonic configurations and is compatible with helicopter rotor systems for future compound helicopters for very high-speed flight.

The success of the VS-300 and the production contracts for the R-4 and R-5 warranted the reestablishment in 1943 of Sikorsky Aircraft as a separate division to concentrate on helicopter developments. The operations were transferred to a plant in Bridgeport, Connecticut. In 1955 further expansion required the construction of a new factory. This plant, located on the Housatonic River at the Merritt Parkway at the north end of Stratford, is Sikorsky's main plant and headquarters.

The leadership of Igor Sikorsky was marked by several notable qualities. Foremost, of course, was his skill and ingenuity in analyzing a myriad of data to interpret the significant design and configuration. He often graciously shared credit with his associates by pointing out that he always tried to engage people who knew more about a particular problem than he did. His explanation for astute analysis noted the veracity of test results which contradicted unproven theory. The theory would then be modified to conform with these results.

The success of the Sikorsky helicopter designs was appreciated by companies in other countries around the world. License agreements were arranged with Westland in England, Aerospatiale in France, VFW-Fokker in Germany, Agusta in Italy, United Aircraft in Canada, and Mitsubishi of Japan. In England and France the license agreements provided technical assistance to permit modification of the basic helicopter or design of new

The VS-300 became the prototype of modern helicopters. Igor Sikorsky is at the controls of his VS-300 in 1940 during a series of test flights. *Courtesy of the National Air and Space Museum*

products. The Super Frelon of France, for example, was designed and constructed jointly by Sikorsky Aircraft and Aerospatiale.

Of all the many missions of the helicopter, none gave Igor Sikorsky greater satisfaction than the hundreds of thousands of lives that have been saved by helicopter. The first recorded mercy mission by helicopter was flown on January 3, 1944, when a Coast Guard R-4 flown by a pioneer helicopter pilot, Commander Frank Ericksen, braved a snowstorm and freezing rain to rush blood plasma to crewmen badly burned in an explosion aboard a United States destroyer off the coast of New Jersey. One year later, the helicopter was used to make the first wartime rescue behind Japanese lines in Burma, and this proud tradition has continued to this day.

The devastating floods of 1955 probably head the list of mass rescues by helicopter: almost 10,000 people airlifted to safety in Tampico, Mexico, of whom some 2,500 were saved by rescue hoists, and about 1,100 saved in Connecticut and 1,000 in northern California during that same flood-stricken year. During the 1960s many more were saved from floods in Japan, Germany, and the Netherlands. Probably no single organization has used helicopters more widely for rescue than the United States Coast Guard as it carries out its job of patrolling some 8,800 miles of coastline. The USAF's aerospace rescue and recovery service depends to a large degree on helicopters as it reaches around the world to save lives. The crews of the USAF's Sikorsky Jolly Green Giants and buffs have written new chapters of heroism in Southeast Asia by rescuing hundreds of downed airmen from jungles, mountaintops, and even enemy-held harbors, defying capture and death themselves on almost every flight. The crews of rescue helicopters both in Korea and Vietnam became probably the most decorated men of their time.

My father spoke to me often about his aviation career in both Russia and the United States. He believed not only in practical engineering, but also in a faculty that he called intuition, or the sixth sense. The construction of the "Grand" in 1912, for example, represented an important milestone in aircraft design. His choice of extremely high aspect-ratio wings was probably the key to his success. It made the job more difficult, but intuitively he felt that it was the only way to go.

Igor Sikorsky's life was filled with many moments of personal satisfaction, which were often important moments in the history of aviation as well. My father's eyes would light up when he spoke of the 1,600-mile round-trip flight of the Il'ya Muromets from St. Petersburg to Kiev in 1914. This memorable flight remained a vivid memory all his life.

As he built and tested the prototype VS-300 helicopter, he again designed almost as much by intuition as by technical logic. At that time, during the years 1934–40, it was the prevailing opinion among aeronautical experts that the only way to build a helicopter was to design a machine with two or more rotors rotating in opposite directions to neutralize the torque. Igor Sikorsky felt intuitively, however, that the helicopter would not really need two or more rotors; that it was possible to design and develop successfully a configuration that was considered technically to be aerodynamically unsound—that is, the single-rotor machine. Today it is interesting to note that the single-rotor configuration dominates the helicopter scene: some 95 percent of all the helicopters built throughout the world have been of the single-rotor configuration proven by Igor Sikorsky on the VS-300 prototype.

Igor Sikorsky's latter years were marked by many awards and honors. Through all this acclaim, he always remained polite, gentle, and under perfect self-control. He enjoyed meeting the military and civil air crews that had flown his aircraft; particularly daring rescue missions with helicopters would prompt his interest, and he enjoyed discussing the details of the flights with pilots and crew.

Born at a time when most scientists considered heavier-than-air flight an impossible dream, he lived to see man walk on the moon. His work both as a pilot and as an engineer helped make that dream a a reality.

He died peacefully in his sleep in October 1972, and he was buried near the factory in Stratford. Frank DeLear, author of the biography *Igor Sikorsky, His Three Careers in Aviation* and a longtime associate of Igor Sikorsky, summed it up eloquently in the conclusion to his book:

> From the ancient city of Kiev in the Russian Ukraine to a hilltop in Stratford,
> Connecticut, for Igor Sikorsky the long voyage of love, wisdom, and personal

achievement is over. But for the world there remains the priceless heritage always left by intelligent men of action, integrity, and good will—words and deeds of widespread benefit to mankind. And for others—his family, friends, and associates (and, perhaps the thousands who knew him by reputation only)—there remains the growing realization that they had been brushed by greatness and had benefited, each according to his own awareness and capacities.

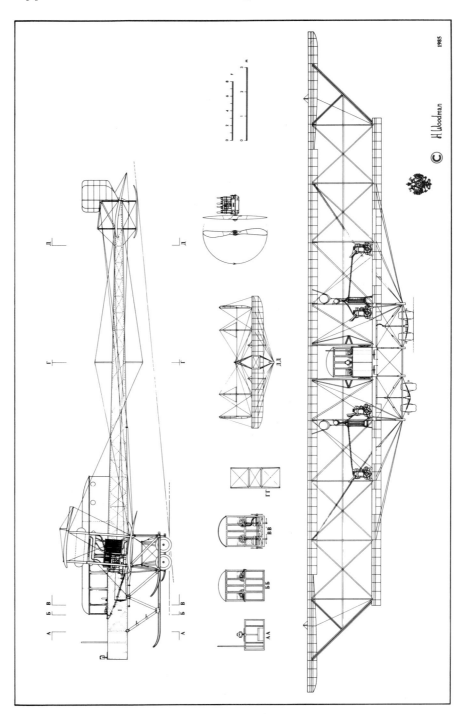

Russian Knight [Russkiy vityaz], by Harry Woodman.

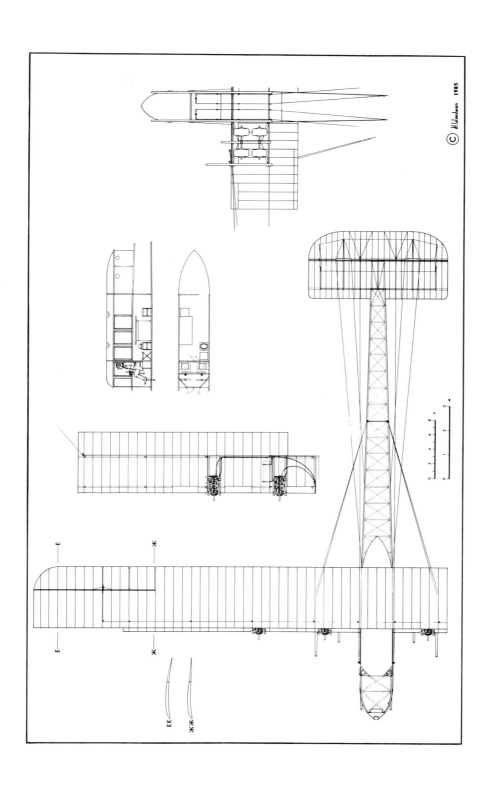

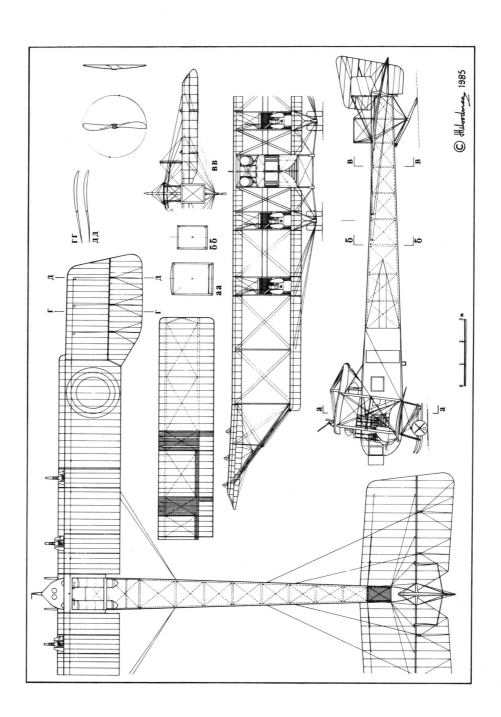

Il'ya Muromets, by Harry Woodman

Appendix 2 The Il'ya Muromets

This work provides a look at the unique and often innovative designs applied to the construction of the Il'ya Muromets. It is not my intention to cover the entire range of specifications of the Murometsy but to familiarize the reader with important details not mentioned in the book.

There has been much confusion over the different types of Il'ya Muromets that were produced. The Murometsy were built between 1913 and 1918. Each successive type was designated by a different letter. There was the type "Beh" and the type "Veh." The Russian alphabet produces a confusing situation. The Russian letter б is pronounced "Beh" while the Russian letter В is pronounced "Veh." So it was that some historians made the mistake of confusing the two production types, б and В.

The chart that appears in the appendixes is from the V. B. Shavrov book titled *History of Aircraft Design in the U.S.S.R.* It contains a great deal of information as to the types of Il'ya Muromets that were produced and the subtypes as well.

The first production of the Murometsy that were built were the type B "Beh." This was a six-strut biplane with very large wings. The wings were constructed in separate parts. Only the top wings had ailerons. The fuselage framework was made of wood that was wire braced and fabric covered. Only the cabin was plywood covered. The four engines were accessible in flight via a plywood path on the lower wing. Each of the engines could be controlled individually as well as together. The fuel was gravity fed from cylindrical tanks that were slung under the upper wing over each engine. There were three rudders, one main one in the middle at the end of the fuselage and two smaller ones at the sides on top of the stabilizer. The under carriage consisted of pairs of N shaped struts attached to skids and wheels which utilized a simple and effective shock absorber system. The eight wheels were encased as pairs covered with leather sheaths. One model had a gunners platform mounted approximately one meter below the nose between the center skids, with passage to the platform through a hatch. It is interesting to note that during the winter large skis were installed to land successfully on snow and ice. Since the early Il'ya Muromets were flying test beds, special adaptations were required for naval use. Three large plywood and ash floats were added, with the two main floats attached below the inboard engines and the third float at the tail.

Then the type V "Veh" were produced and these were smaller in size and weighed less than the type B "Beh." The type V "Veh" were specifically designed for military use where the type B "Beh" were merely adapted for this purpose. The type V "Veh" were faster and able to reach higher altitudes. The crew consisted of four. The bulbous nose of the type B "Beh" was replaced on the type V "Veh" first by a sharp pointed nose, later a flat front polyhedral. Both of these nose designs were constructed of metal framing and glass from top to bottom providing the pilot with better visibility. The fuel tanks were moved on the type V "Veh" to a safer placement under the center section of the top wing to prevent leaking onto the engines in case of puncture. The external wing rim was made of metal pipe instead of wood as with the type B "Beh." On the type V "Veh" a machine gun was installed in the center section providing top cover. This installation was accomplished by removing a few ribs and fabric between the spars of the center section of the upper wing. Machine gun positions were installed at the doors and/or in the windows as well as a hatch on top of the fuselage aft of the wings on some Il'ya Muromets. Included in the type V "Veh" series there was a training version with only two engines, used either in a tractor mode or as pushers.

After the type V "Veh" came the type G variants which were the G-1, G-2, G-3, and G-4. These were more advanced military designs of the Murometsy. They differed from the type V "Veh" in that they had larger upper and lower wings. The G-2, with its strengthened wing structure, was an improved version of the G-1. More machine guns were added for greater fighting efficiency, with up to six of them installed. The G-2 had a position for a tailgunner. To get to this position a trolley was installed. It ran on a pair of angular rails to the rear through the fuselage. By pulling on the cross wire bracing the crew member pulled the trolley to the rear or forward to the main cabin. With the addition of a tailgun the central vertical tailplane was first removed, then later a small fixed fin was placed behind the gunner. The two enlarged rudders were placed closer to the end of the stabilizer. Some of the G types had construction of welded tube with fabric covering. The aerodynamics and armaments were further improved in the G-3 and G-4 variants.

Next came the D (D.I.M.) series which was an attempt to produce an aeroplane with four engines in tandem. When the tandem pairs proved unsuccessful the engines were moved forward with all four engines in a tractor style. The high cabin was fully glazed for better visibility and the fuel tanks were enclosed on top of the fuselage. This design was lighter and smaller than any of the other Il'ya Muromets.

Finally the E "Ye" type variants were built. These were designed to defend themselves from the ever-increasing faster and better armed German and Austro-Hungarian aeroplanes. They had provisions for up to eight machine guns. They were the largest and most advanced of all the Murometsy. The nose was fully glazed and the fuel tanks were enclosed as in the type D. The first of the type E "Ye" was not fitted with a tailgun but rather a platform that was lowered from the fuselage floor aft of the wings. From this position the gunner lying on the platform could fire towards the rear.

The crew size also increased with the change in types from a four or five man crew up to as many as eight on the larger type E "Ye."

Various machine guns were made available to the E.V.K. Maxim, Vickers, Colt, Lewis, and Madsens found their way onto Murometsy. The advent of the nose gun did not appear until the production of the later D and the E "Ye" which were designed to accommodate a machine gun in this position.

The instrumentation that was used on the Murometsy reflect the limits of technology of the time. For example, a bank indicator was composed of two glass V-shaped tubes and a ball. The idea was for the ball to remain in the center of the instrument during horizontal flight. Other instruments included four tachometers, one for each engine, a compass, an altimeter, an airspeed indicator, and a drift indicator that was used as an aid for bombing.

The national marking used on the Il'ya Muromets was the cockade. It was taken from the French design in late 1914 by the Imperial Russian Air Service. The color order was red for the outer ring, blue for the middle ring, and white for the center. In late 1915 the proportions of the cockade changed several times but the color pattern remained the same. A large red, blue, and white triangular pennon was used on the fuselage for added identification.

The engines available to the Il'ya Muromets varied from year to year. The engines that were used were Argus 100 h.p. in-line 4 cylinder, Argus 115 h.p. in-line 4 cylinder, Argus 125 h.p. in-line 6 cylinder, Argus 140 h.p. in-line 6 cylinder, Salmson 135 h.p. radial 9 cylinder, Salmson 200 h.p. radial 14 cylinder, Sunbeam 150 h.p. vee 8 cylinder, Sunbeam 160 h.p. vee 8 cylinder, Sunbeam 225 h.p. vee 12 cylinder,

Russo-Baltic Wagon Works 150 h.p. in-line 6 cylinder, Renault 200 h.p. vee 12 cylinder, Renault 220 h.p. vee 12 cylinder, and Beardmore 160 h.p. in-line 6 cylinder. It is probable that Hall-Scott 150 h.p. in-line 6 cylinder engines from the U.S.A. and possibly Fiat 150 h.p. vee 6 cylinder engines from Italy were used. Murometsy with four Russo-Baltic Wagon Works engines were named "Russobalt." The term "Renaultbalt" was used when powered by a pair of Renault engines and a pair of Russo-Baltic Wagon Works engines.

The bombs and the bombing devices used were limited since at that time there was little research and development in this area. Since the Murometsy were so large many bombs were carried inside. Types up to 10 kg. were placed on the floor of the Il'ya Muromets and were dropped by hand. Whereas 16 to 32 kg. bombs were stored in special containers with the ability to release them individually or in groups. Large bombs of 82, 164, and 246 kilograms were carried outside the fuselage. Bombs were released by a lever or by hand. Aiming devices varied from a simple type, designed by I. I. Sikorsky, to more complex systems. One such device, developed by Captain V. A. Ivanov, through a series of sightings and consulting of ballistic tables enabled accurate bombing. These tables were developed by Professor Botezat to aid in high altitude bombing. Another device involving triangular calculations of the speed of the aeroplane, wind, and the resulting ground speed which for any approach to the target could be taken with high percentage of direct hits was developed by Staff Captain A. N. Zhuravchenko, an artillery officer assigned to the E.V.K., and Staff Captain G. V. Alekhnovich, Commander of Il'ya Muromets V.

Aside from offensive missions, the Murometsy were also designed to carry out photoreconnaissance. The Ulyanin camera supplied with a Zeiss/Tessar f4.5 lens had a unique system that enabled the simultaneous recording of the time and altitude on the same plate negative of the photographed area for reference.

Some interesting experiments were developed in an attempt to ensure safety for the crew and aeroplane. Armor plate up to 10 mm. thick, made from pressed metal chips, was installed on the floor of the cockpit and behind the pilot seat to protect the pilot in the cabin. Other developments such as the covering of the fuel tanks with rubber, thick felt, and heavy material treated with boric acid were used. This provided protection against fuel leakage in case of shrapnel or bullets hitting the tanks.

As can be seen from these brief descriptions, the Murometsy were unique. The role they played in the development of aviation directly and indirectly can be seen.

The numbering system is another point often confused. The Il'ya Muromets had three numbers. The first was the Russo-Baltic Wagon Works serial number. The second number was the class number which consisted of the type and series. The third was the E.V.K. number which was always in Roman numerals. For example, the Il'ya Muromets flown by Staff Captain A. V. Pankrat'yev had three numbers:

1) Factory—No. 167.
2) Class—IM B-21 (this meant it was the twenty-first Il'ya Muromets built and was a type V "Veh").
3) E.V.K. Ship (Korabley) No. II.

Reports (submitted by the pilot Rudnev) Concerning the Il'ya Muromets I (IM-1B)

Telegram from Belostok, dated October 21, 1914

"Today, at the start of our mission, two engine carburetors froze over. It was −5 degrees C. The engines on the Il'ya Muromets I produced only 900 rpms. Our landing was smooth, the flying ship touching the ground smoothly, but the chassis broke as we taxied across the frozen and undulating airstrip. The chassis broke on the right side with damage to 20 wing ribs. The repairs will take 3–5 days. I am requesting, if possible, two additional small aeroplanes."

Report on the Il'ya Muromets I (IM-1B), dated January 10, 1915, City of Lvov

The flight from Petrograd to Belostok took a long time—a flight of 23 days and in four stages with flight times in the following stages: 5 hours, 31 minutes; 3 hours, 25 minutes; 2 hours, 51 minutes; and 2 hours, 5 minutes. It took 13 hours and 52 minutes to cover a distance of 912 km. Depending on the wind, the cruising speeds varied from 27 to 102 kph, and our cruising altitude ranged from 900 to 1,300 meters. The last segment of the flight was made with the fuel tanks half-filled.

During these flights it became apparent that the IM-1B was not capable of maintaining proper altitude with one engine shut off. With one engine off, I was forced to land at Ol'keniki. This situation makes the Il'ya Muromets type aeroplane less reliable than regular types because it is more difficult to handle four engines than just one. Moreover, there is the higher risk of an engine failure on an Il'ya Muromets. The unreliability of the engines was reported, and, as a consequence, the senior mechanic of the Russo-Baltic factory was sent to adjust them on September 28.

At Belostok we received orders from the Headquarters Staff of the Northwestern Front to conduct extensive aerial reconnaissance operations. Accordingly, I have made several reconnaissance flights with loads of 1600–1800 kg, but the results have been unsatisfactory. The flying ship lifted off poorly, and the engines did not function properly, especially in this cold weather when carburetors would freeze even on the ground. A mechanic who participated in the flights confirmed my conclusion that IM-1B could not attain high altitude.

After several attempts were made to adjust the engines, we dismantled the least efficient of them. This inspection revealed the following problems: the valves were not properly set; large dents were discovered on the push rods and cams of the driveshaft; and there were cracks in the crankcase. All these difficulties indicated an inadequate engine design. All the engines for the IM-1B were reassembled and remounted.

On November 7, Igor Sikorsky arrived in Belostok, where he advised us not to carry aloft a load of 1600–1800 kg. He also recommended the following: 1) the maximum load should be 1800 kg; 2) the normal load should be around 1300 kg, however, 1150 kg is better for this would allow the aeroplane to remain aloft with just three engines functioning; 3) the best take-off angle is 10 degrees; 4) climbing time should take twenty minutes to reach 1,000 meters and about one hour to reach an altitude of 2,000 meters.

In general, Sikorsky recommended that the load distribution should be as follows:

four-man crew	328 kg
machine-gun, light machine-gun, and armor	164 kg
gasoline—four hours (normally 460 kg)	655 kg

Total: 1147 kg

During the last flight from Belostok to Lvov, my assistant and I noticed that the aeroplane could only reach an altitude of 1,375 meters.
The following loads were on board at that time:

gasoline and oil (unused)	344 kg
five-man crew	394 kg
bombing apparatus	6 kg
one machine-gun with ammunition	36 kg
one pistol (Mauser) and binoculars	3 kg
miscellaneous small items	33 kg
armor	42 kg
supplementary electrical and signal equipment	9 kg
accumulator (battery)	4 kg

At Lvov, I removed the two extra tanks with a total weight of 107 kg. This action complied with the directive of your Imperial Highness to lighten the Il'ya Muromets I.
During an experimental flight to attain a certain altitude, I decided to depart from the official Sikorsky data, that is to exceed a total load limit of 1,150 kg. If you take into consideration that at Belostok, the front area had been removed, weighing 113 kg, and at Lvov, two extra tanks with a total weight of 107 kg, had also been removed, the actual weight was less than Sikorsky's requirement. . . .
During the flight, the angle of attack was at all times 10 degrees (according to the Sikorsky data, the optimum angle), whereas the speed remained constant. The aeroplane rate of climb was as follows:

250	meters in 6 minutes
500	meters in 16 minutes
750	meters in 26 minutes
1000	meters in 43 minutes
1250	meters in 1 hour 6 minutes
1350	meters in 1 hour 20 minutes

At the end of the flight, the rate of climb was very slow; to reach the last 75 meters took 14 minutes. . . . During the flight from Belostok to Lvov, it was impossible to attain a greater altitude. Owing to better performance of the engines, the rate of climb during the test flight was effective: for example, at an altitude of 1,300 meters, the flying ship could climb another 75 meters in 14 minutes, a fact which, in accordance with barogram (flight curve) readings, indicated the approximate ceiling of the Il'ya Muromets.

This slow, steady climb rate is impaired by another obstacle: the aeroplane carries enough gasoline for a three hour flight (in one tank enough fuel for $1^1/_2$ hours) in order to attain an altitude of 1,300 meters. This requires about half the flight time. After that, there is the mission over an enemy fortress which we assume to take twenty minutes or perhaps half an hour. Moreover, one must consider the required time for the return flight. Even if we neglected all these deliberations and supposed that the aeroplane were attaining its altitude while maintaining its rate of climb of 75 meters each 14 minutes, then at the end of three hours, that is, when the fuel is consumed, the aeroplane would be able to gain an altitude of 1,775 meters. In reality this altitude could not be attained, that is, the rate of climb speed was all the time steadily decreasing.

Regular aeroplanes have a combat altitude of not less than 1,700 meters. Our missions over enemy fortresses where the guns are capable of firing in different directions, as illustrated in the Brest-Litovsk experience, the combat altitude should not be less than 2,200 meters. For an aeroplane such as Il'ya Muromets, whose surface is as large as 200 square meters instead of the usual 15–50 square meters, it is better to fly at an altitude of 2,200 meters, but under present conditions this operational altitude is not attainable. It should be noted that the engines of the Il'ya Muromets could not be improved even with the efforts of the best mechanic available working from September 15 to November 27. During these 67 days the engines of the Il'ya Muromets were completely dismantled, reassembled, and adjusted. . . .

Yesterday, I made another attempt to climb as high as possible with a required load on board in order to complete my mission over the fortress. On board, there was a mechanic from the Russo-Baltic factory, who was checking the instrument readings during the flight. Up to an altitude of 1,000 meters, I maintained a 10 degree angle for my ascent. After reaching an altitude of 1,000 meters, my assistant, in order to maintain a required speed, assumed a new angle of 9 degrees. Minimum speed was maintained from the moment of take-off. We did not reduce the speed because the flying ship would become unsteady with a loss of speed. During the flight, the speed remained constant. . . . The total load carrying capacity was up to 1150 kg., but in order to account for the removed platform and tanks, it totaled 926 kg. In spite of the fact that I tried to maintain precisely the required speed and climbing angle, the Il'ya Muromets leveled off at an altitude of 800 meters and remained at this altitude for a period of time, flying against the wind. After reaching an altitude of 1,200 meters, no further climb was possible.

The above report was signed by the Field Inspector General of Aviation and accompanied by the following note:

"To His Supreme Excellency:

Enclosed you will find the report by the command pilot of the Il'ya Muromets I, an outstanding military pilot, who did his best to bring the Il'ya Muromets to combat readiness, to enable the aircraft to fly at minimum altitude for air operations.

His report concluded that the Il'ya Muromets did not achieve the required performance standard. However, we hope that in the future new Il'ya Muromets types will be built and they will meet the military requirements. I regret that the delays in the construction of the Il'ya Muromets aeroplanes prevented the mobilization of a group of outstanding pilots now posted at Petrograd. These men could have been assigned to the front where there is shortage of experienced military pilots."

Earlier the Field Inspector General of Aviation sent the following telegram to the Chief of Staff, Stavka:

"Despite all possible efforts to adapt the Il'ya Muromets I to meet military requirements, the flying ship could not reach an altitude above 1,350 meters. I consider this aeroplane useless for air operations at the front. In view of this fact, I am requesting the appointment of the squadron commander, Staff-Captain Rudnev, to the command of a squadron formed by the Army of the Southwest Front. One Il'ya Muromets will be retained in this squadron for further testing."

Early Sikorsky Aeroplanes

Designer: Sikorsky, Igor Ivanovich
Manufacturer: Sikorsky

Year: 1909	Aeroplane type: Helicopter
Model: S-1	H.P.: 25
Engine(s) type: Anzani	Span m.: 4.6/5.0 Area m.2: 2.0
Length m.:	Wt.fuel/oil kg.: 15
Wt.empty kg.: 162	Wt.flying kg.: 250
Wt.load kg.: ±90	Power kg/hp: 10.0
Wing kg/m.2:	Speed km/h.:

Notes: Two two bladed rotors, tested but unsuccessful

Designer: Sikorsky, Igor Ivanovich
Manufacturer: Sikorsky

Year: 1910	Aeroplane type: Helicopter
Model: S-2	H.P.: 25
Engine(s) type: Anzani	Span m.: Area m.2:
Length m.:	Wt.fuel/oil kg.: 15
Wt.empty kg.: 182	Wt.flying kg.: 270
Wt.load kg.: ±90	Power kg/hp: 10.8
Wing kg/m.2:	Speed km/h.:

Notes: Two three bladed rotors, tested but unsuccessful

Designer: Sikorsky, I.I., Bylinkin, F.I., Iordan, V.V.
Manufacturer: Sikorsky, Bylinkin, Iordan

Year: 1910	Aeroplane type: Biplane
Model: BIS No.1	H.P.: 15
Engine(s) type: Anzani	Span m.: 8.0 Area m.2: 24.0
Length m.: 8.0	Wt.fuel/oil kg.: 10
Wt.empty kg.: 180	Wt.flying kg.: 250
Wt.load kg.: 70	Power kg/hp: 16.0
Wing kg/m.2: 10.4	Speed km/h.:

Notes: Single pusher prop, tested but taxied only

Designer: Sikorsky, I.I., Bylinkin, F.I., Iordan, V.V.
Manufacturer: Sikorsky, Bylinkin, Iordan

Year: 1910	Aeroplane type: Biplane
Model: BIS No.2	H.P.: 25
Engine(s) type: Anzani	Span m.: 8.0 Area m.2: 24.0
Length m.: 8.0	Wt.fuel/oil kg.: 10

Wt.empty kg.: 190　　　　　　Wt.flying kg.: 260
Wt.load kg.: 70　　　　　　　Power kg/hp: 10.2
Wing kg/m.2: 10.8　　　　　　Speed km/h.:
Notes: Single tractor prop, third Russian aeroplane to fly June 11, 1910 (O.C.)

Designer: Sikorsky, Igor Ivanovich
Manufacturer: Sikorsky

Year: 1910　　　　　　　　　Aeroplane type: Biplane
Model: S-3　　　　　　　　　H.P.: 35
Engine(s) type: Anzani　　　　Span m.: 8.0　Area m.2: 24.0
Length m.: 8.0　　　　　　　Wt.fuel/oil kg.: 20
Wt.empty kg.: 220　　　　　　Wt.flying kg.: 310
Wt.load kg.: 90　　　　　　　Power kg/hp: 8.9
Wing kg/m.2: 13.0　　　　　　Speed km/h.:
Notes: Single tractor prop, successful flight

Designer: Sikorsky, Igor Ivanovich
Manufacturer: Sikorsky

Year: 1910　　　　　　　　　Aeroplane type: Biplane
Model: S-4　　　　　　　　　H.P.: 50
Engine(s) type: Anzani　　　　Span m.: 9.0　Area m.2: 28.0
Length m.: 8.0　　　　　　　Wt.fuel/oil kg.: 30
Wt.empty kg.: 260　　　　　　Wt.flying kg.: 360
Wt.load kg.: 100　　　　　　　Power kg/hp: 7.2
Wing kg/m.2: 12.9　　　　　　Speed km/h.:
Notes: Single tractor prop, successful flight

Designer: Sikorsky, Igor Ivanovich
Manufacturer: Sikorsky

Year: 1911　　　　　　　　　Aeroplane type: Biplane
Model: S-5　　　　　　　　　H.P.: 50
Engine(s) type: Argus　　　　　Span m.: 12.0/9.0　Area m.2: 33.0
Length m.: 8.5　　　　　　　Wt.fuel/oil kg.: 40
Wt.empty kg.: 320　　　　　　Wt.flying kg.: 440
Wt.load kg.: 120　　　　　　　Power kg/hp: 8.8
Wing kg/m.2: 13.3　　　　　　Speed km/h.:
Notes: Single tractor prop, successful flight

Designer: Sikorsky, Igor Ivanovich
Manufacturer: Sikorsky

Year: 1912　　　　　　　　　Aeroplane type: Biplane (seaplane)
Model: S-5A　　　　　　　　H.P.: 60/80
Engine(s) type: Gnome/Gnome　Span m.: 12.0/8.5　Area m.2: 30.0
Length m.: 8.0　　　　　　　Wt.fuel/oil kg.:
Wt.empty kg.:　　　　　　　Wt.flying kg.:
Wt.load kg.:　　　　　　　　Power kg/hp:
Wing kg/m.2:　　　　　　　　Speed km/h.:
Notes: Single tractor prop, successful flight

Designer: Sikorsky, Igor Ivanovich
Manufacturer: Sikorsky

Year: 1911   Aeroplane type: Biplane
Model: S-6   H.P.: 100
Engine(s) type: Argus   Span m.: 11.8   Area m.2: 35.4
Length m.: 8.8   Wt.fuel/oil kg.: 60
Wt.empty kg.: 650   Wt.flying kg.: 850/990
Wt.load kg.: 200/340   Power kg/hp: 8.5
Wing kg/m.2: 24.0   Speed km/h.:
Notes: Single tractor prop, successful flight

Designer: Sikorsky, Igor Ivanovich
Manufacturer: Sikorsky

Year: 1912   Aeroplane type: Biplane
Model: S-6A   H.P.: 100
Engine(s) type: Argus   Span m.: 14.5/11.7   Area m.2: 39.0
Length m.: 9.2   Wt.fuel/oil kg.: 60
Wt.empty kg.: 650   Wt.flying kg.: 900/1100
Wt.load kg.: 250/450   Power kg/hp: 9.0
Wing kg/m.2: 23.0   Speed km/h.:
Notes: Single tractor prop, successful flight

Designer: Sikorsky, Ergant, Klimikseyev, Serebrennikov, Kudashev, & Adler
Manufacturer: R-BVZ

Year: 1912   Aeroplane type: Biplane
Model: S-6B   H.P.: 100
Engine(s) type: Argus   Span m.: 14.9/10.9   Area m.2: 37.5
Length m.: 8.5   Wt.fuel/oil kg.:
Wt.empty kg.: 590   Wt.flying kg.: 917
Wt.load kg.: 327   Power kg/hp: 9.2
Wing kg/m.2: 24.4   Speed km/h.: 113
Notes: Single tractor prop, successful flight

Designer: Sikorsky, Ergant, Klimikseyev, Serebrennikov, Kudashev, & Adler
Manufacturer: R-BVZ

Year: 1912   Aeroplane type: Monoplane
Model: S-7   H.P.: 70
Engine(s) type: Gnome   Span m.: 10.0   Area m.2: 20.0
Length m.: 8.2   Wt.fuel/oil kg.:
Wt.empty kg.: 449   Wt.flying kg.: 776
Wt.load kg.: 327   Power kg/hp: 11.0
Wing kg/m.2: 39.0   Speed km/h.: 108
Notes: Single tractor prop, successful flight

Designer: Sikorsky, Ergant, Klimikseyev, Serebrennikov, Kudashev, & Adler
Manufacturer: R-BVZ

Year: 1912
Model: S-8
Engine(s) type: Gnome
Length m.: 7.5
Wt.empty kg.:
Wt.load kg.:
Wing kg/m.2:

Aeroplane type: Biplane
H.P.: 50
Span m.: 12.0/8.0   Area m.2: 27.0
Wt.fuel/oil kg.:
Wt.flying kg.:
Power kg/hp:
Speed km/h.:

Notes: Single tractor prop, successful flight

Designer: Sikorsky, Ergant, Klimikseyev, Serebrennikov, Kudashev, & Adler
Manufacturer: R-BVZ

Year: 1913
Model: S-9
Engine(s) type: Gnome Monosoupape
Length m.:
Wt.empty kg.: 690
Wt.load kg.: 300
Wing kg/m.2: 33.0

Aeroplane type: Monoplane
H.P.: 100
Span m.: 12.0   Area m.2: 30.0
Wt.fuel/oil kg.:
Wt.flying kg.: 990
Power kg/hp: 10.0
Speed km/h.: 30

Notes: Single tractor prop, successful flight

Designer: Sikorsky, Ergant, Klimikseyev, Serebrennikov, Kudashev, & Adler
Manufacturer: R-BVZ

Year: 1913
Model: S-10 competition
Engine(s) type: Gnome
Length m.: 8.0
Wt.empty kg.: 567
Wt.load kg.: 444
Wing kg/m.2: 22.0

Aeroplane type: Biplane
H.P.: 80
Span m.: 16.9/12.0   Area m.2: 46.0
Wt.fuel/oil kg.:
Wt.flying kg.: 1011
Power kg/hp: 12.7
Speed km/h.: 99

Notes: Single tractor prop, successful flight

Designer: Sikorsky, Ergant, Klimikseyev, Serebrennikov, Kudashev, & Adler
Manufacturer: R-BVZ

Year: 1913
Model: S-10A
Engine(s) type: Anzani
Length m.:
Wt.empty kg.:
Wt.load kg.:
Wing kg/m.2:

Aeroplane type: Biplane
H.P.: 125
Span m.: 13.7/8.8   Area m.2: 35.5
Wt.fuel/oil kg.: 120/20
Wt.flying kg.:
Power kg/hp:
Speed km/h.:

Notes: Single tractor prop, successful flight

Designer: Sikorsky, Ergant, Klimikseyev, Serebrennikov, Kudashev, & Adler
Manufacturer: R-BVZ

Year: 1914
Model: S-10A Gidro (Hydro)
Engine(s) type: Gnome Monosoupape
Length m.:
Wt.empty kg.: 565
Wt.load kg.: 310
Wing kg/m.2: 24.7

Aeroplane type: Biplane (seaplane)
H.P.: 100
Span m.: 13.7/8.8   Area m.2: 35.5
Wt.fuel/oil kg.: 160
Wt.flying kg.: 875
Power kg/hp: 8.7
Speed km/h.:

Notes: Single tractor prop, successful flight

Designer: Sikorsky, Ergant, Klimikseyev, Serebrennikov, Kudashev, & Adler
Manufacturer: R-BVZ

Year: 1913
Model: S-10 Gidro (Hydro)
Engine(s) type: Argus
Length m.:
Wt.empty kg.: 700
Wt.load kg.: 380
Wing kg/m.2: 31.0

Aeroplane type: Biplane (seaplane)
H.P.: 100
Span m.: 13.7/8.8   Area m.2: 35.5
Wt.fuel/oil kg.:
Wt.flying kg.: 1080
Power kg/hp: 10.8
Speed km/h.:

Notes: Single tractor prop, successful flight

Designer: Sikorsky, Ergant, Klimikseyev, Serebrennikov, Kudashev, & Adler
Manufacturer: R-BVZ

Year: 1913
Model: S-10
Engine(s) type: Argus
Length m.:
Wt.empty kg.: 550
Wt.load kg.: 300
Wing kg/m.2: 24.3

Aeroplane type: Biplane
H.P.: 100
Span m.: 13.7/8.8   Area m.2: 35.5
Wt.fuel/oil kg.:
Wt.flying kg.: 850
Power kg/hp: 8.5
Speed km/h.:

Notes: Single tractor prop, successful flight

Designer: Sikorsky, Ergant, Klimikseyev, Serebrennikov, Kudashev, & Adler
Manufacturer: R-BVZ

Year: 1913
Model: S-11
Engine(s) type: Gnome Monosoupape
Length m.: 7.6
Wt.empty kg.: 578
Wt.load kg.: 427
Wing kg/m.2: 38.6

Aeroplane type: Monoplane
H.P.: 100
Span m.: 11.6   Area m.2: 26.0
Wt.fuel/oil kg.:
Wt.flying kg.: 1005
Power kg/hp: 10.0
Speed km/h.: 102

Notes: Single tractor prop, successful flight

Designer: Sikorsky, Ergant, Klimikseyev, Serebrennikov, Kudashev, & Adler
Manufacturer: R-BVZ

Year: 1913   Aeroplane type: Monoplane
Model: S-12   H.P.: 80
Engine(s) type: Gnome   Span m.:   Area m.2: 19.7
Length m.:   Wt.fuel/oil kg.: 72/24
Wt.empty kg.: 419   Wt.flying kg.: 681
Wt.load kg.: 262   Power kg/hp: 8.5
Wing kg/m.2: 34.5   Speed km/h.:
Notes: Single tractor prop, successful flight

1913 Bolshoi Baltiskiy Great Baltic: Grand

Engines	
number	2
type	Argus
power	100
Length (m)	20.0
Wing span	
upper	27.0
lower	20.0
Wing Area (m2)	120.0
Weights (kg)	
empty	3000
fuel/oil	150
full load	400
flying	3400
Unit load	
wing (kg/m2)	28.5
power (kg/h.p.)	18.0
Load Ratio (in %)	12
Max. Speed (km/h) (sea level)	80
Landing Speed (km/h)	65
Time to Height (in min)	
1000m	—
2000m	—
3000m	—
Practical Ceiling (m)	100
Duration (hours)	2.0
Range (km)	150
Take-off Run (m)	650
Landing Run (m)	150

1913 Bolshoi Baltiskiy (Great Baltic; Grand) (4 Engines)

Engines	
number	4
type	Argus
power	100
Length (m)	20.0
Wing span	
upper	27.0
lower	20.0
Wing Area (m2)	120.0
Weights (kg)	
empty	3400
fuel/oil	250
full load	600
flying	4000
Unit Load	
wing (kg/m2)	33.0
power (kg/h.p.)	11.0
Load Ratio (in %)	15
Max. Speed (km/h) (sea level)	90
Landing Speed (km/h)	70
Time to Height (in min)	
1000m	—
2000m	—
3000m	—
Practical Ceiling (m)	500
Duration (hours)	2.0
Range (km)	170
Take-off Run (m)	400
Landing Run (m)	200

1913 Russkiy vityaz
(Russian Knight; Grand)

Engines	
number	4
type	Argus
power	100
Length (m)	20.0
Wing span	
upper	27.0
lower	20.0
Wing Area (m2)	120.0
Weights (kg)	
empty	3500
fuel/oil	250
full load	700
flying	4200
Unit Load	
wing (kg/m2)	35.0
power (kg/h.p.)	11.5
Load Ratio (in %)	17
Max. Speed (km/h) (sea level)	90
landing Speed (km/h)	70
Time to Height (in min)	
1000m	—
2000m	—
3000m	—
Practical Ceiling (m)	600
Duration (hours)	2.0
Range (km)	170
Take-off Run (m)	350
Landing Run (m)	200

Il'ya Muromets
No. 107 with additional wing

Engines	
number	4
type	Argus
power	100
Length (m)	22.0
Wing span	
upper	32.0
lower	22.0
additional wing	210.0
Wing Area (m2)	210.0
Weights (kg)	
empty	4000

fuel/oil	384
full load	1500
flying	5500
Unit Load	
wing (kg/m2)	26.0
power (kg/h.p.)	14.8
Load Ratio (in %)	27
Max. Speed (km/h) (sea level)	85
Landing Speed (km/h)	70
Time to Height (in min)	
1000m	—
2000m	—
3000m	—
Practical Ceiling (m)	500
Duration (hours)	3.0
Range (km)	250
Take-off Run (m)	400
Landing Run (m)	200

1913 Il'ya Muromets
No. 107

Engines	
number	4
type	Argus
power	100
Length (m)	22.0
Wing span	
upper	32.0
lower	22.0
Wing Area (m2)	182.0
Weights (kg)	
empty	2800
fuel/oil	384
full load	1300
flying	5100
Unit Load	
wing (kg/m2)	28.0
power (kg/h.p.)	13.8
Load Ratio (in %)	25
Max. Speed (km/h) (sea level)	95
Landing Speed (km/h)	75
Time to Height (in min)	
1000m	25
2000m	—
3000m	—
Practical Ceiling	1500
Duration (hours)	3.0
Range (km)	270
Take-off Run (m)	300
Landing Run (m)	200

1914 Il'ya Muromets No. 107 floatplane

Engines

number	2	2
type	Salmson	Argus
power	200	115

Length (m)	23.5

Wing span

upper	32.0
lower	22.0
Wing Area (m2)	182.0

Weights (kg)

empty	4800
fuel/oil	900
full load	1500
flying	6300

Unit Load

wing (kg/m2)	34.5
power (kg/h.p.)	10.0
Load Ratio (in %)	24
Max. Speed (km/h) (sea level)	90
Landing Speed (km/h)	75

Time to Height (in min)

1000m	20
2000m	60
3000m	—
Practical Ceiling (m)	2000
Duration (hours)	6.0
Range (km)	550
Take-off Run (m)	500
Landing Run (m)	180

1914 Il'ya Muromets Kievskiy No. 128

Engines

number	2	1
type	Argus	Argus
power	140	125

Length (m)	19.0

Wing span

upper	30.95
lower	22.45
Wing Area (m2)	150.0

Weights (kg)

empty	3040
fuel/oil	700
full load	1610
flying	4650

Unit Load

wing (kg/m2)	31.0
power (kg/h.p.)	8.6
Load Ratio (in %)	34
Max. Speed (km/h) (sea level)	100
Landing Speed (km/h)	75

Time to Height (in min)

1000m	15
2000m	35
3000m	70
Practical Ceiling (m)	3000
Duration (hours)	5.0
Range (km)	500
Take-off Run (m)	—
Landing Run (m)	—

1914 Il'ya Muromets No. 135 (type B "Beh")

Engines

number	4
type	Argus
power	130
Length (m)	19.0

Wing span

upper	30.95
lower	22.45
Wing Area (m2)	150.0

Weights (kg)

empty	3100
fuel/oil	700
full load	1500
flying	4600

Unit Load

wing (kg/m2)	30.7
power (kg/h.p.)	8.3
Load Ratio (in %)	33
Max. Speed (km/h) (sea level)	105
Landing Speed (km/h)	75

Time to Height (in min)

1000m	13
2000m	30
3000m	—
Practical Ceiling (m)	3000
Duration (hours)	5.0
Range (km)	520
Take-off Run (m)	—
Landing Run (m)	—

1914 Il'ya Muromets
No. 136–139 (type B "Beh")

Engines		
number	2	2
type	Salmson	Salmson
power	200	135
Length (m)		19.0

Wing span

upper		30.95
lower		22.45
Wing Area (m2)		150.0

Weights (kg)

empty		3600
fuel/oil		700
fuel load		1200
flying		4800

Unit Load

wing (kg/m2)		32.0
power (kg/h.p.)		7.2
Load Ratio (in %)		26
Max. Speed (km/h) (sea level)		96
Landing Speed (km/h)		75

Time to Height (in min)

1000m	20
2000m	70
3000m	—
Practical Ceiling (m)	2000
Duration (hours)	4.0
Range (km)	380
Take-off Run (m)	—
Landing Run (m)	—

1914 Il'ya Muromets
No. 143 Korabley Kievskiy
(1st) (type V "Veh")

Engines		
number	2	2
type	Argus	Argus
power	140	125
Length (m)		17.1

Wing span

upper		29.8
lower		21.0
Wing Area (m2)		125.0

Weights (kg)

empty		2900
fuel/oil		550

full load	1500
flying	4400

Unit load

wing (kg/m2)	35.3
power (kg/h.p.)	8.3
LOAD RATIO (IN %)	34
Max. Speed (km/h) (sea level)	120
Landing Speed (km-h)	75

Time to Height (in min)

1000m	12
2000m	25
3000m	55
Practical Ceiling (m)	3500
Duration (hours)	5.0
Range (km)	630
Take-off Run (m)	250 (17 secs)
Landing Run (m)	200

1915 Il'ya Muromets
No. 151 (type V "Veh")

Engines	
number	4
type	Argus
power	140
Length (m)	17.1

Wing span

upper	29.8
lower	21.0
Wing Area (m2)	125.0

Weights (kg)

empty	2950
fuel/oil	550
full load	1500
flying	4450

Unit load

wing (kg/m2)	35.5
power (kg/h.p.)	8.1
Load Ratio (in %)	34
Max. Speed (km/h) (sea level)	125
Landing Speed (km/h)	75

Time to Height (in min)

1000m	11
2000m	25
3000m	—
Practical Ceiling (m)	3700
Duration (hours)	5.3
Range (km)	650
Take-off Run (m)	220 (17 secs)
Landing Run (m)	200

1915 Il'ya Muromets
No. 150, 157 (type V "Veh")

Engines
number	2
type	Salmson
power	200
Length (m)	17.1

Wing span
upper	28.0
lower	19.2
Wing Area (m2)	120.0

Weights (kg)
empty	2700
fuel/oil	400
full load	800
flying	3500

Unit load
wing (kg/m2)	29.0
power (kg/h.p.)	8.8
Load Ratio (in %)	23
Max. Speed (km/h) (sea level)	100
Landing Speed (km/h)	70

Time to Height (in min)
1000m	—
2000m	—
3000m	—
Practical Ceiling (m)	—
Duration (hours)	—
Range (km)	—
Take-off Run (m)	—
Landing Run (m)	—

1915 Il'ya Muromets
No. 159, 161 (type V "Veh")

Engines
number	2
type	Sunbeam
power	225
Length (m)	17.1

Wing span
upper	20.0
lower	19.2
Wing Area (m2)	120.0

Weights (kg)
empty	2800
fuel/oil	400
full load	800

flying	3600

Unit load
wing (kg/m2)	30.0
power (kg/h.p.)	8.0
Load Ratio (in %)	22
Max. Speed (km/h) (sea level)	105
Landing Speed (km/h)	70

Time to Height (in min)
1000m	—
2000m	—
3000m	—
Practical Ceiling (m)	—
Duration (hours)	—
Range (km)	—
Take-off Run (m)	—
Landing Run (m)	—

1915 Il'ya Muromets Military,
narrow wings (type V "Veh")

Engines
number	4
type	Sunbeam
power	150
Length (m)	17.5

Wing span
upper	29.8
lower	21.0
Wing Area (m2)	125.0

Weights (kg)
empty	3150
fuel/oil	600
full load	1450
flying	4600

Unit load
wing (kg/m2)	36.8
power (kg/h.p.)	7.7
Load Ratio (in %)	—
Max. Speed (km/h) (sea level)	110
Landing Speed (km/h)	73

Time to Height (in min)
1000m	16
2000m	40
3000m	—
Practical Ceiling (m)	2900
Duration (hours)	4.0
Range (km)	440
Take-off Run (m)	400
Landing Run (m)	220

1915 Il'ya Muromets training (type V "Veh")

Engines	
number	2
type	Sunbeam
power	150
Length (m)	17.1
Wing span	
upper	28.0
lower	19.2
Wing Area (m2)	120.0
Weights (kg)	
empty	2500
fuel/oil	300
full load	700
flying	3200
Unit load	
wing (kg/m2)	27.0
power (kg/h.p.)	10.7
Load Ratio (in %)	22
Max. Speed (km/h) (sea level)	90
Landing Speed (km/h)	70
Time to Height (in min)	
1000m	—
2000m	—
3000m	—
Practical Ceiling (m)	—
Duration (hours)	—
Range (km)	—
Take-off Run (m)1	400
Landing Run (m)	180

1915 Il'ya Muromets No. 167 (type V "Veh")

Engines	
number	4
type	R-BVZ-6
power	150
Length (m)	17.5
Wing span	
upper	29.8
lower	21.0
Wing Area (m2)	125.0
Weights (kg)	
empty	3500
fuel/oil	600
full load	1500
flying	5000
Unit load	
wing (kg/m2)	40.0
power (kg/h.p.)	8.3
Load Ratio (in %)	30
Max. Speed (km/h) (sea level)	120
Landing Speed (km/h)	75
Time to Height (in min)	
1000m	9
2000m	20
3000m	45
Practical Ceiling (m)	2500
Duration (hours)	4.5
Range (km)	—
Take-off Fun (m)	—
Landing Run (m)	—

1915 Il'ya Muromets No. 179 broad wings (type V "Veh")

Engines	
number	4
type	Sunbeam
power	150
Length (m)	17.1
Wing Span	
upper	30.87
lower	22.0
Wing Area (m2)	148.0
Weights (kg)	
empty	3800
fuel/oil	600
full load	1300
flying	5100
Unit load	
wing (kg/m2)	34.5
power (kg/h.p.)	8.5
Load Ratio (in %)	25
Max. Speed (km/h) (sea level)	110
Landing Speed (km/h)	75
Time to Height (in min)	
1000m	—
2000m	—
3000m	—
Practical Ceiling (m)	—
Duration (hours)	—
Range (km)	—
Take-off Fun (m)	—
Landing Run (m)	—

1915 Il'ya Muromets
No. 183 (type G-1)

Engines	
number	4
type	Sunbeam
power	150
Length (m)	17.1
Wing span	
upper	30.87
lower	22.0
Wing Area (m2)	148.0
Weights (kg)	
empty	3800
fuel/oil	600
full load	1300
flying	6100
Unit load	
wing (kg/m2)	34.5
power (kg/h.p.)	8.5
Load Ratio (in %)	25
Max. Speed (km/h) (sea level)	110
Landing Speed (km/h)	75
Time to Height (in min)	
1000m	—
2000m	—
3000m	—
Practical Ceiling (m)	—
Duration (hours)	4.0
Range (km)	440
Take-off Run (m)	450
Landing Run (m)	250

1916 Il'ya Muromets
No. 187 (type G-1)

Engines	
number	4
type	Argus
power	125
Length (m)	17.1
Wing span	
upper	30.87
lower	22.0
Wing Area (m2)	148.0
Weights (kg)	
empty	3700
fuel/oil	500
full load	1500

flying	5200
Unit load	
wing (kg/m2)	35.1
power (kg/h.p.)	10.4
Load Ratio (in %)	29
Max. Speed (km/h) (sea level)	120
Landing Speed (km/h)	75
Time to Height (in min)	
1000m	—
2000m	—
3000m	—
Practical Ceiling (m)	—
Duration (hours)	—
Range (km)	—
Take-off Run (m)	—
Landing Run (m)	250

1916 Il'ya Muromets
No. 190, G-44 (type G-1)

Engines	
number	4
type	Argus
power	140
Length (m)	17.1
Wing Span	
upper	30.87
lower	22.0
Wing Area (m2)	148.0
Weights (kg)	
empty	3750
fuel/oil	500
full load	1600
flying	5350
Unit load	
wing (kg/m2)	36.2
power (kg/h.p.)	9.6
Load Ratio (in %)	30
Max. Speed (km/h) (sea level)	125
Landing Speed (km/h)	75
Time to Height (in min)	
1000m	—
2000m	—
3000m	—
Practical Ceiling (m)	—
Duration (hours)	—
Range (km)	—
Take-off Run (m)	—
Landing Run (m)	—

1916 Il'ya Muromets (type G-1)

Engines	
number	4
type	Sunbeam
power	160
Length (m)	17.1
Wing span	
upper	30.87
lower	22.0
Wing Area (m2)	148.0
Weights (kg)	
empty	3800
fuel/oil	650
full load	1560
flying	5400
Unit load	
wing (kg/m2)	36.5
power (kg/h.p.)	8.4
Load Ratio (in %)	28
Max. Speed (km/h) (sea level)	135
Landing Speed (km/h)	75
Time to Height (in min)	
1000m	8
2000m	18
3000m	35
Practical Ceiling (m)	4000
Duration (hours)	4.0
Range (km)	500
Take-off Run (m)	—
Landing Run (m)	300

1916 Il'ya Muromets "Russobalt" (type G-2)

Engines	
number	4
type	R-BVZ-6
power	150
Length (m)	17.1
Wing span	
upper	30.87
lower	22.0
Wing Area (m2)	159.6
Weights (kg)	
empty	3800
fuel/oil	600

full load	1500
flying	5300
Unit load	
wing (kg/m2)	33.2
power (kg/h.p.)	8.8
Load Ratio (in %)	28
Max. Speed (km/h) (sea level)	115
Landing Speed (km/h)	75
Time to Height (in min)	
1000m	—
2000m	—
3000m	—
Practical Ceiling (m)	—
Duration (hours)	4.0
Range (km)	460
Take-off Run (m)	—
Landing Run (m)	—

1916 Il'ya Muromets (type G-2)

Engines		
number	2	2
type	Renault	R-BVZ-6
power	220	150
Length (m)		17.1
Wing span		
upper		30.87
lower		22.0
Wing Area (m2)		159.6
Weights (kg)		
empty		3800
fuel/oil		740
full load		1700
flying		5500
Unit load		
wing (kg/m2)		34.5
power (kg/h.p.)		7.4
Load Ratio (in %)		31
Max. Speed (km/h) (sea level)		120
Landing Speed (km/h)		75
Time to Height (in min)		
1000m		9
2000m		20
3000m		40
Practical Ceiling (m)		3500
Duration (hours)		4.0
Range (km)		480
Take-off Run (m)		—
Landing Run (m)		—

1916 Il'ya Muromets "Korabley Kievskiy" (3rd) (type G-2)

Engines	
number	4
type	Beardmore
power	160
Length (m)	17.1
Wing span	
upper	30.87
lower	22.0
Wing Area (m2)	159.6
Weights (kg)	
empty	3800
fuel/oil	686 + 57
full load	1700
flying	5500
Unit load	
wing (kg/m2)	34.5
power (kg/h.p.)	8.6
Load Ratio (in %)	31
Max. Speed (km/h) (sea level)	137
Landing Speed (km/h)	78
Time to Height (in min)	
1000m	6
2000m	14
3000m	35
Practical Ceiling (m)	4600
Duration (hours)	4.0
Range (km)	540
Take-off Run (m)	350
Landing Run (m)	250

1916 Il'ya Muromets (type G-2)

Engines		
number	2	2
type	Sunbeam	R-BVZ-6
power	150	150
Length (m)		17.1
Wing span		
upper		30.87
lower		22.0
Wing Area (m2)		159.6
Weights (kg)		
empty		3800
fuel/oil		600

(continued)

full load	1470
flying	5300
Unit load	
wing (kg/m2)	33.0
power (kg/h.p.)	8.8
Load Ratio (in %)	27.5
Max. Speed (km/h) (sea level)	115
Landing Speed (km/h)	78
Time to Height (in min)	
1000m	10.0
2000m	22
3000m	48
Practical Ceiling (m)	3200
Duration (hours)	4.0
Range (km)	460
Take-off Run (m)	—
Landing Run (m)	—

1916 Il'ya Muromets "Renobalt" (type G-3)

Engines		
number	2	2
type	Renault	R-BVZ-6
power	220	150
Length (m)		17.1
Wing span		
upper		30.87
lower		22.0
Wing Area (m2)		159.6
Weights (kg)		
empty		3800
fuel/oil		880
full load		1600
flying		5400
Unit load		
wing (kg/m2)		33.8
power (kg/h.p.)		7.3
Load Ratio (in %)		29.6
Max. Speed (km/h) (sea level)		115
Landing Speed (km/h)		80
Time to Height (in min)		
1000m		7.3
2000m		17
3000m		44
Practical Ceiling (m)		3400
Duration (hours)		4.5
Range (km)		570
Take-off Run (m)		220
Landing Run (m)		250

1916 Il'ya Muromets (type G-3)

Engines		
number	2	2
type	Renault	Sunbeam
power	220	150
Length (m)		17.1

Wing span

upper		30.87
lower		22.0
Wing Area (m2)		159.6

Weights (kg)

empty		3800
fuel/oil		880
full load		1500
flying		5300

Unit load

wing (kg/m2)		33.1
power (kg/h.p.)		7.2
Load Ratio (in %)		28.3
Max. Speed (km/h) (sea level)		115
Landing Speed (km/h)		78

Time to Height (in min)

1000m		12.0
2000m		29
3000m		—
Practical Ceiling (m)		2700
Duration (hours)		4.0
Range (km)		460
Take-off Run (m)		—
Landing Run (m)		—

1917 Il'ya Muromets "Renobalt" strengthened (type G-3)

Engines		
number	2	2
type	Renault	R-BVZ-6
power	220	150
Length (m)		17.1

Wing span

upper		30.87
lower		22.0
Wing Area (m2)		159.6

Weights (kg)

empty		4070
fuel/oil		686 + 57

full load	1530
flying	5600

Unit load

wing (kg/m2)	35.0
power (kg/h.p.)	7.6
Load Ratio (in %)	27.3
Max. Speed (km/h) (sea level)	115
Landing Speed (km/h)	80

Time to Height (in min)

1000m	11.0
2000m	27
3000m	—
Practical Ceiling (m)	2800
Duration (hours)	4.0
Range (km)	460
Take-off Run (m)	—
Landing Run (m)	—

1917 Il'ya Muromets strengthened (type G-2)

Engines		
number	2	2
type	Renault	R-BVZ-6
power	220	150
Length (m)		17.1

Wing span

upper		30.87
lower		22.0
Wing Area (m2)		159.6

Weights (kg)

empty		3800
fuel/oil		686 + 57
full load		1500
flying		5300

Unit load

wing (kg/m2)		33.2
power (kg/h.p.)		7.1
Load Ratio (in %)		28.3
Max. Speed (km/h) (sea level)		120
Landing Speed (km/h)		78

Time to Height (in min)

1000m		9.0
2000m		20
3000m		40
Practical Ceiling (m)		3500
Duration (hours)		4.0
Range (km)		480
Take-off Run (m)		—
Landing Run (m)		—

1917 Il'ya Muromets strengthened (type G-4)

Engines		
number	2	2
type	Renault	R-BVZ
power	220	150
Length (m)		17.1

Wing span	
upper	30.87
lower	22.0
Wing Area (m2)	159.6

Weights (kg)	
empty	3900
fuel/oil	686 + 57
full load	1500
flying	5400

Unit load	
wing (kg/m2)	33.8
power (kg/h.p.)	7.3
Load Ratio (in %)	28.0
Max. Speed (km/h) (sea level)	128
Landing Speed (km/h)	78

Time to Height (in min)	
1000m	10.0
2000m	25
3000m	78
Practical Ceiling (m)	3300
Duration (hours)	4.0
Range (km)	500
Take-off Run (m)	—
Landing Run (m)	—

1916 Il'ya Muromets DIM (type D-1)

Engines	
number	4
type	Sunbeam
power	150
Length (m)	15.5

Wing span	
upper	24.9
lower	17.6
Wing Area (m2)	132.0

Weights (kg)	
empty	3150
fuel/oil	690
full load	1250
flying	4400

Unit load	
wing (kg/m2)	33.2
power (kg/h.p.)	7.3
Load Ratio (in %)	28.4
Max. Speed (km/h) (sea level)	120
Landing Speed (km/h)	80

Time to Height (in min)	
1000m	—
2000m	—
3000m	—
Practical Ceiling (m)	200
Duration (hours)	4.0
Range (km)	480
Take-off Run (m)	700
Landing Run (m)	350

1916 Il'ya Muromets (type D-2)

Engines	
number	4
type	Sunbeam
power	150
Length (m)	17.0

Wing span	
upper	29.7
Wing Area (m2)	148.0

Weights (kg)	
empty	3800
fuel/oil	540 + 160
full load	1400
flying	5200

Unit Load	
wing (kg/m2)	35.5
power (kg/h.p.)	8.5
Load Ratio (in %)	27.0
Max. Speed (km/h) (sea level)	110
Landing Speed (km/h)	75

Time to Height (in min)	
1000m	16.0
2000m	40
3000m	—
Practical Ceiling (m)	2900
Duration (hours)	4.8
Range (km)	520
Take-off Run (m)	—
Landing Run (m)	—

1916 Il'ya Muromets (type E "Yeh") experimental

Engines

number	4
type	Renault
power	220
Length (m)	17.1

Wing span

upper	33.0
lower	27.0
Wing Area (m2)	190.0

Weights (kg)

empty	4620
fuel/oil	540 + 160
full load	2000
flying	6620

Unit load

wing (kg/m2)	32.6
power (kg/h.p.)	7.0
Load Ratio (in %)	32.2
Max. Speed (km/h) (sea level)	130
Landing Speed (km/h)	80

Time to Height (in min)

1000m	10.1
2000m	25
3000m	75
Practical Ceiling (m)	3000
Duration (hours)	4.8
Range (km)	620
Take-off Run (m)	350
Landing Run (m)	—

1916 Il'ya Muromets (type E "Yeh"-1)

Engines

number	4
type	Renault
power	220
Length (m)	18.2

Wing span

upper	31.35
lower	24.0
Wing Area (m2)	200.0

Weights (kg)

empty	4800
fuel/oil	920 + 130
full load	2200
flying	7000

Unit load

wing (kg/m2)	35.0
power (kg/h.p.)	8.0
Load Ratio (in %)	29.0
Max. Speed (km/h) (sea level)	130
Landing Speed (km/h)	80

Time to Height (in min)

1000m	9.0
2000m	25
3000m	74
Practical Ceiling (m)	3000
Duration (hours)	4.4
Range (km)	560
Take-off Run (m)	400
Landing Run (m)	300

1917 Il'ya Muromets (type E "Yeh"-2)

Engines

number	4
type	Renault
power	220
Length (m)	18.8

Wing span

upper	34.5
lower	26.6
Wing Area (m2)	220.0

Weights (kg)

empty	5000
fuel/oil	920 + 130
full load	2460
flying	7460

Unit load

wing (kg/m2)	34.2
power (kg/h.p.)	8.5
Load Ratio (in %)	33.0
Max. Speed (km/h) (sea level)	130
Landing Speed (km/h)	80

Time to Height (in min)

1000m	9.4
2000m	26
3000m	68
Practical Ceiling (m)	3200
Duration (hours)	4.4
Range (km)	560
Take-off Run (m)	450
Landing Run (m)	300

1918 Il'ya Muromets
(type E "Yeh")

Engines

number	4
type	Renault
power	220
Length (m)	18.5

Wing span

upper	30.4
lower	24.4
Wing Area (m2)	190.0

Weights (kg)

empty	4200
fuel/oil	—
full load	1900
flying	6100

Unit load

wing (kg/m2)	32.0
power (kg/h.p.)	6.9
Load Ratio (in %)	31.2
Max. Speed (km/h) (sea level)	137
Landing Speed (km/h)	93

Time to Height (in min)

1000m	10.0
2000m	25
3000m	48
Practical Ceiling (m)	4000
Duration (hours)	4.0
Range (km)	540
Take-off Run (m)	350
Landing Run (m)	300

This listing is not inclusive or adjusted for uniform transliteration.

Name: Adler, G.P.
Rank:
Assignment: Engineer at R-BVZ
Il'ya Muromets:
Source: Shavrov
Decorations:
Notes: Worked with I. I. Sikorsky on early designs
Fate:

Name: Alekhnovich, Gleb Vasilievich
Rank: Lieut & Staff Capt
Assignment: Commander
Il'ya Muromets: V
Source: Finne & Kolyankovskiy & Shavrov
Decorations:
Notes: Test pilot at R-BVZ
Fate: K.I.A. 11/17/18 while serving with the Bolsheviks

Name: Andreiev,
Rank: Warrant Officer
Assignment: Mechanic
Il'ya Muromets: Korabley Kievskiy 1
Source: Finne & Kolyankovskiy
Decorations:
Notes:
Fate:

Name: Arai,
Rank:
Assignment: Mechanic at R-BVZ
Il'ya Muromets:
Source: Finne
Decorations:
Notes: Wounded during air raid at EVK
Fate:

Name: Balashov,
Rank: Warrant Officer
Assignment: Mechanic
Il'ya Muromets: I
Source: Finne & Kolyankovskiy

Decorations:
Notes:
Fate: K.I.A. 5/11/17 in crash of IM-1

Name: Bashko, I.S.
Rank: Lieut & Staff Capt & Colonel
Assignment: Deputy Commander; Commander 1, 2, 3,
Il'ya Muromets: Korabley Kievskiy 1; 2; 3;
Source: Finne & Kolyankovskiy
Decorations: Order of St. George 4th Degree and Sword of St. George
Notes: W.I.A. 7/19/15 in IM-Kievskiy 1, C-in-C Estonian AF,
Fate: Executed in 1940 by the Soviets after the occupation of Estonia

Name: Bazanov,
Rank: Lieut
Assignment: Commander
Il'ya Muromets: XI
Source: Kolyankovskiy
Decorations:
Notes:
Fate:

Name: Bazilevich, Leonid Vasilievich
Rank:
Assignment: Service Shop Chief
Il'ya Muromets:
Source: Finne
Decorations:
Notes:
Fate:

Name: Belyakov,
Rank: Staff Capt
Assignment: Commander
Il'ya Muromets: XVII
Source: Kolyankovskiy
Decorations:
Notes:
Fate:

Name: Berkhi, V. M.
Rank: Ensign
Assignment:
Il'ya Muromets:
Source: Finne
Decorations:
Notes:
Fate:

Name: Boie,
Rank: Staff Capt
Assignment:
Il'ya Muromets: Korabley Kievskiy 3
Source: Kolyankovskiy
Decorations:
Notes: Crew member 7.5 hr flight April
1917 in IM-Kievskiy
Fate:

Name: Boye, Y. G.
Rank: Lieut
Assignment: Artillery Officer
Il'ya Muromets: Korabley Kievskiy 1
Source: Finne
Decorations:
Notes:
Fate:

Name: Brodovich, V. M.
Rank: Staff Capt
Assignment: Commander
Il'ya Muromets: III
Source: Finne & Kolyankovskiy
Decorations: Sword of St. George
Notes: Transferred out of EVK May
1915
Fate:

Name: Bukoiavorin,
Rank: Lieut (Field Artillery)
Assignment: Pilot
Il'ya Muromets:
Source: Finne
Decorations:
Notes:
Fate:

Name: Burobin,
Rank: Sgt Major
Assignment:
Il'ya Muromets: Korabley Kievskiy 3
Source: Kolyankovskiy
Decorations:

Notes: Crew member 7.5 hr flight April
1917 in IM-Kievskiy
Fate:

Name: Chechulin,
Rank: Staff Capt
Assignment:
Il'ya Muromets:
Source: Finne
Decorations:
Notes:
Fate:

Name: Colon,
Rank:
Assignment: Artillery Officer
Il'ya Muromets: III
Source: Kolyankovskiy
Decorations:
Notes:
Fate: K.I.A. 11/15/15 in crash of IM-3

Name: Datskevich,
Rank: Staff Capt
Assignment: Commander
Il'ya Muromets: IV
Source: Kolyankovskiy
Decorations:
Notes:
Fate:

Name: Demidchev-Ivanov,
Rank: Lieut & Capt
Assignment: Deputy Commander XV;
Commander XV
Il'ya Muromets: XV
Source: Finne & Kolyankovskiy
Decorations: Order of St. George 4th
Degree
Notes:
Fate:

Name: Desilos,
Rank: Lieut
Assignment:
Il'ya Muromets:
Source: Finne
Decorations:
Notes:
Fate:

Name: Ergant, K. K.
Rank:

Assignment: Engineer at R-BVZ
Il'ya Muromets:
Source: Shavrov
Decorations:
Notes: Worked with I. I. Sikorsky on early designs
Fate:

Name: Federov, V. S.
Rank: Lieut & Staff Capt
Assignment: Military pilot
Il'ya Muromets: II & XV
Source: Finne & Kolyankovskiy
Decorations: Sword of St. George
Notes: W.I.A. 4/1/16 in IM-2
Fate:

Name: Fimov, K.
Rank: Capt
Assignment:
Il'ya Muromets:
Source: Finne
Decorations:
Notes:
Fate:

Name: Finne, K. N.
Rank:
Assignment: Senior Physician of EVK
Il'ya Muromets:
Source: Finne & Kolyankovskiy & Shavrov
Decorations:
Notes:
Fate: Emigrated to Yugoslavia at the time of the revolution, then to U.S.A.

Name: Fiodorov,
Rank: Junior Officer
Assignment:
Il'ya Muromets:
Source: Finne
Decorations:
Notes:
Fate:

Name: Firsov, B. N.
Rank: Lieut & Staff Capt
Assignment: Deputy Commander II; Commander VI
Il'ya Muromets: II; VI
Source: Finne & Kolyankovskiy
Decorations:

Notes: W.I.A. 4/1/16 in IM-2
Fate:

Name: Fogt,
Rank: Sgt Major
Assignment: Mechanic
Il'ya Muromets: III
Source: Finne & Kolyankovskiy
Decorations:
Notes: Improved Sikorsky's bombing (aiming) device
Fate: K.I.A. 11/15/15 in crash of IM-3

Name: Gague,
Rank: Lieut
Assignment: Artillery Officer
Il'ya Muromets: III
Source: Finne & Kolyankovskiy
Decorations:
Notes: Improved Sikorsky's bombing (aiming) device
Fate: K.I.A. 1916 Gatchina Flying School accident

Name: Gelvig, P. A.
Rank: Lieut-Colonel
Assignment:
Il'ya Muromets:
Source: Shavrov
Decorations:
Notes: Worked on development of recoiless gun
Fate:

Name: Golovin, S. N.
Rank: Staff Capt
Assignment: Commander
Il'ya Muromets: VI
Source: Finne & Kolyankovskiy
Decorations:
Notes: W.I.A. 9/23/16 in IM-6
Fate:

Name: Golubets,
Rank: Sgt Major
Assignment: Mechanic
Il'ya Muromets: XV
Source: Finne
Decorations: Order of St. George Cross
Notes: W.I.A. 5/8/17 in IM-15
Fate:

Name: Gorodetskiy,
Rank: Staff Capt
Assignment: Commander
Il'ya Muromets: XII
Source: Kolyankovskiy
Decorations:
Notes:
Fate:

Name: Gorshkov, Georgiy
Georgiyevich
Rank: Capt & Colonel
Assignment: Commander, C-in-C of
EVK (after Shidlovskiy)
Il'ya Muromets: Korabley Kievskiy 1
Source: Finne & Kolyankovskiy
Decorations: Sword of St. George
Notes: Deputy Commandant of
Gatchina Flying School
Fate: Executed by the Bolsheviks at the
time of the revolution

Name: Grek,
Rank: Lieut
Assignment: Commander
Il'ya Muromets: XIX
Source: Kolyankovskiy
Decorations:
Notes:
Fate:

Name: Gribov,
Rank: Lieut
Assignment: Artillery Officer
Il'ya Muromets: XVI
Source: Finne & Kolyankovskiy
Decorations: Order of St. George 4th
Degree
Notes:
Fate: K.I.C. 10/8/16 in the crash of
IM-16

Name: Gromov,
Rank: Senior Junior Officer
Assignment:
Il'ya Muromets:
Source: Finne
Decorations:
Notes:
Fate:

Name: In'kov,
Rank: Staff Capt

Assignment: Commander
Il'ya Muromets: XIV
Source: Finne & Kolyankovskiy
Decorations:
Notes:
Fate: K.I.A. 5/29/16 in crash of IM-14

Name: Ivanov,
Rank: Sgt Major
Assignment: Mechanic
Il'ya Muromets: IX
Source: Finne & Kolyankovskiy
Decorations:
Notes:
Fate:

Name: Ivanov, V. A.
Rank: Staff Capt & Lieut-Colonel
Assignment: Artillery Officer
Il'ya Muromets: V; VI
Source: Finne & Kolyankovskiy
Decorations: Sword of St. George
Notes: W.I.A. 9/23/16 in IM-6;
improved Sikorsky bombing (aiming)
device
Fate:

Name: Ivanovskiy, P. V.
Rank: Lieut & Capt & Lieut-Colonel
Assignment: Artillery Officer
Il'ya Muromets: XV
Source: Finne & Kolyankovskiy
Decorations: Sword of St. George
Notes:
Fate:

Name: Kammachokovskiy, A. M.
Rank: Staff Capt
Assignments:
Il'ya Muromets:
Source: Finne
Decorations:
Notes:
Fate:

Name: Kananch,
Rank: Senior Junior Officer
Assignment:
Il'ya Muromets:
Source: Finne
Decorations:
Notes:
Fate:

Name: Kapon,
Rank: Sgt Major
Assignment: Mechanic
Il'ya Muromets: IX
Source: Finne & Kolyankovskiy
Decorations:
Notes:
Fate:

Name: Karpov,
Rank: Jnr Lieut
Assignment:
Il'ya Muromets: XVI
Source: Finne & Kolyankovskiy
Decorations: Order of St. George 4th
Degree
Notes:
Fate: K.I.C. 10/8/16 in crash of IM-16

Name: Kasatkin,
Rank: Sgt Major
Assignment:
Il'ya Muromets: X
Source: Finne
Decorations:
Notes:
Fate:

Name: Khoietesov, Mikhail Kuzmich
Rank: Lieut
Assignment: Quartermaster of EVK
Il'ya Muromets:
Source: Finne
Decorations:
Notes:
Fate:

Name: Kireiev,
Rank:
Assignment: Engineer at R-BVZ
Il'ya Muromets:
Source: Finne & Kolyankovskiy
Decorations:
Notes: Designed R-BVZ 6 engine
Fate:

Name: Kirillovich,
Rank: Warrent Officer
Assignment: Mechanic
Il'ya Muromets: V
Source: Finne
Decorations:

Name: Kiriviev,
Rank: Ensign
Assignment:
Il'ya Muromets: II
Source: Finne
Decorations:
Notes:
Fate:

Name: Kirsynovich,
Rank: Volunteer
Assignment:
Il'ya Muromets:
Source: Finne
Decorations:
Notes:
Fate:

Name: Kisel,
Rank: Official
Assignment: Mechanic
Il'ya Muromets: V
Source: Finne
Decorations:
Notes:
Fate:

Name: Klembovskiy, G. V.
Rank: Staff Capt & Lieut-Colonel
Assignment: Commander
Il'ya Muromets: XV
Source: Finne & Kolyankovskiy
Decorations: Sword of St. George
Notes:
Fate:

Name: Klimikseyev, M. F.
Rank:
Assignment: Engineer at R-BVZ
Il'ya Muromets:
Source: Shavrov
Decorations:
Notes: Worked with I. I. Sikorsky on
early designs
Fate:

Name: Klytov,
Rank: Ensign
Assignment:

Il'ya Muromets:
Source: Finne
Decorations:
Notes:
Fate:

Name: Kolotov
Rank: Warrant Officer
Assignment: Aerodrome duty
Il'ya Muromets:
Source: Kolyankovskiy
Decorations:
Notes: Designed portable hangers for Murometsy
Fate:

Name: Kolyankovskiy, Arsenii Mikhailovich
Rank: Staff Capt
Assignment: Aerodrome duty
Il'ya Muromets:
Source: Finne
Decorations:
Notes:
Fate:

Name: Komarov,
Rank: Volunteer
Assignment:
Il'ya Muromets:
Source: Finne
Decorations:
Notes:
Fate:

Name: Kostenchik, A. V.
Rank: Lieut & Capt
Assignment: Deputy Commander V; Commander X
Il'ya Muromets: V; X
Source: Finne & Kolyankovskiy
Decorations: Order of St. George 4th Degree
Notes: W.I.A. 4/26/16 in IM-10
Fate:

Name: Kotiekonov,
Rank: Ensign
Assignment:
Il'ya Muromets:
Source: Finne
Decorations:
Notes:
Fate:

Name: Kovalchuk,
Rank:
Assignment: Mechanic
Il'ya Muromets: XIV
Source: Finne
Decorations:
Notes: W.I.A. 5/29/16 in crash of IM-14
Fate:

Name: Kovanko, A. A.
Rank: Lieut
Assignment: Deputy Commander V
Il'ya Muromets: V
Source: Finne
Decorations:
Notes:
Fate:

Name: Koz'min,
Rank: Staff Capt
Assignment: Commander
Il'ya Muromets: XV
Source: Finne
Decorations:
Notes:
Fate: K.I.A. 6/4/16 in crash of a Farman 16 near Pskov's Kresty aerodrome

Name: Kozielin,
Rank: Staff Capt
Assignment:
Il'ya Muromets:
Source: Finne
Decorations:
Notes:
Fate:

Name: Krotkov,
Rank: Lieut
Assignment: Pilot
Il'ya Muromets:
Source: Finne
Decorations:
Notes:
Fate:

Name: Krzhichkovskiy,
Rank: Lieut
Assignment:
Il'ya Muromets:
Source: Finne

Decorations:
Notes:
Fate:

Name: Kudashev, A. S.
Rank:
Assignment: Engineer at R-BVZ
Il'ya Muromets:
Source: Shavrov
Decorations:
Notes: Worked with I. I. Sikorsky on
early designs
Fate:

Name: Lavrov, A. M.
Rank: Sgt Major & Warrant Officer &
Lieut
Assignment: Mechanic
Il'ya Muromets: Korabley Kievskiy 1
Source: Finne & Kolyankovskiy
Decorations: Order of St. George Cross
2nd Degree
Notes: W.I.A. 7/19/15 in IM-Kievskiy 1
Fate:

Name: Lavrov, G. I.
Rank: Lieut Commander
Assignment: Commander
Il'ya Muromets: I
Source: Finne & Kolyankovskiy
Decorations: Gold Medal Imp. Russian
Fire Soc.
Notes: Naval Pilot, Flight with I. I.
Sikorsky St. Petersburg-Kiev
Fate: K.I.A. 5/11/17 in crash of IM-1

Name: Lobov, V.
Rank: Capt of Cossacks
Assignment: Commander
Il'ya Muromets: VIII
Source: Finne & Kolyankovskiy
Decorations:
Notes:
Fate:

Name: Loiko,
Rank: Lieut & Staff Capt
Assignment: Deputy Commander
Il'ya Muromets: VI
Source: Finne
Decorations:
Notes: W.I.A. 9/23/16 in IM-6
Fate:

Name: Lukinskiy,
Rank: Lieut
Assignment: Pilot
Il'ya Muromets:
Source: Finne
Decorations:
Notes:
Fate:

Name: Luts, A. Y.
Rank: Jnr Lieut
Assignment:
Il'ya Muromets: VI
Source: Finne
Decorations:
Notes:
Fate:

Name: Makhsheyev, D. K.
Rank: Lieut
Assignment: Commander
Il'ya Muromets: XVI
Source: Finne & Kolyankovskiy
Decorations: Order of St. George 4th
Degree
Notes:
Fate: K.I.C. 10/8/16 in the crash of
IM-16

Name: Modrakh,
Rank: Lieut
Assignment: Commander
Il'ya Muromets: IV
Source: Kolyankovskiy
Decorations:
Notes:
Fate:

Name: Naidenov, V. F.
Rank: Colonel
Assignment: Deputy Commander of
EVK
Il'ya Muromets:
Source: Finne & Kolyankovskiy
Decorations:
Notes: Professor at Nicholas Military
and Engineering Academy
Fate: Died in 1924 in USSR

Name: Nasonov,
Rank:
Assignment:
Il'ya Muromets: XIV

Source: Finne
Decorations:
Notes: W.I.A. 5/29/16 in crash of
IM-14
Fate:

Name: Naumov, Aleksandar A.
Rank: Staff Capt & Colonel
Assignment: Artillery Officer
Il'ya Muromets: Korabley Kievskiy 1
Source: Finne & Kolyankovskiy
Decorations: Order of St. George 4th
Degree and Sword of St. George
Notes: Improved Sikorsky's bombing
(aiming) device
Fate:

Name: Nekrasov,
Rank: Capt
Assignment: Artillery Officer
Il'ya Muromets:
Source: Finne
Decorations:
Notes:
Fate:

Name: Nikolskiy, M. N.
Rank: Lieut
Assignment: Mechanic, Senior
Engineer
Il'ya Muromets:
Source: Kolyankovskiy, Shavrov
Decorations:
Notes:
Fate: Died in USSR in the 1960s

Name: Nikolskiy, S. N.
Rank: Staff Capt of Guards
Assignment: Deputy Commander II;
Commander XIV
Il'ya Muromets: II; XIV
Source: Finne & Kolyankovskiy
Decorations:
Notes:
Fate: Emigrated to France at the time
of the revolution

Name: Nizhevskiy, R. L.
Rank: Capt & Colonel
Assignment: Commander, C-in-C of
EVK (after Pankratiev)
Il'ya Muromets: IX

Source: Finne & Kolyankovskiy
Decorations: Sword of St. George
Notes: Staff member at the School of
Aeronautics before joining EVK
Fate: Emigrated to France at the time
of the revolution

Name: Oranovsky,
Rank: Capt & Colonel
Assignment:
Il'ya Muromets:
Source: Shavrov
Decorations:
Notes: Worked on development of
recoiless gun, designer of aerial bombs
for EVK
Fate:

Name: Otreshkov,
Rank: Staff Capt of Calvary
Assignment: Gunner
Il'ya Muromets: I
Source: Finne & Kolyankovskiy
Decorations:
Notes:
Fate: K.I.A. 5/11/17 in crash of IM-1

Name: Ozerskiy, D. A.
Rank: Lieut & Staff Capt
Assignment: Commander
Il'ya Muromets: III
Source: Finne & Kolyankovskiy
Decorations: Sword of St. George
Notes: Instructor at Gatchina Flying
School before joining EVK
Fate: K.I.A. 11/15/15 in crash of IM-3

Name: Panasiuk, Vladimir S.
Rank:
Assignment: Mechanic
Il'ya Muromets:
Source: Finne
Decorations: Silver Medal Imp.
Russian Fire Soc.
Notes: Mechanic at R-BVZ, Flight with
I. I. Sikorsky St. Petersburg-Kiev, 1914
Fate:

Name: Pankrat'yev, Aleksei Vasilievich
Rank: Staff Capt & Colonel
Assignment: Commander, C-in-C of
EVK (after Gorshkov)
Il'ya Muromets: II

Source: Finne & Kolyankovskiy
Decorations: Order of St. George 4th
Degree
Notes: Deputy Commandant of EVK
after the 1917 revolution then
Commandant
Fate: Died in test flight crash in USSR
1923

Name: Pavlov,
Rank: Lieut
Assignment: Pilot
Il'ya Muromets: II
Source: Finne
Decorations:
Notes:
Fate:

Name: Pleshkov,
Rank: Lieut
Assignment: Commander
Il'ya Muromets: XX
Source: Kolyankovskiy
Decorations:
Notes:
Fate:

Name: Pliat, Marcel
Rank: Sgt Major
Assignment: Mechanic
Il'ya Muromets: X
Source: Finne
Decorations: Order of St. George Cross
3rd Degree
Notes:
Fate:

Name: Plotnikov,
Rank: Lieut
Assignment:
Il'ya Muromets:
Source: Finne
Decorations:
Notes:
Fate:

Name: Poletaiev,
Rank: Lieut
Assignment:
Il'ya Muromets: XIV
Source: Finne
Decorations:

Notes:
Fate: K.I.A. 5/29/16 in crash of IM-14

Name: Popov, Ivan Vasilievich
Rank: Capt of Cossack
Assignment: Staff Aide at EVK
Il'ya Muromets:
Source: Kolyankovskiy & Finne
Decorations:
Notes:
Fate:

Name: Poshekhonov,
Rank: Lieut
Assignment:
Il'ya Muromets: IX
Source: Kolyankovskiy
Decorations:
Notes:
Fate:

Name: Potikhonov,
Rank: Ensign
Assignment: Pilot
Il'ya Muromets:
Source: Finne
Decorations:
Notes:
Fate:

Name: Prussis, Kh. F.
Rank: Staff Capt
Assignment: Gatchina Aviation School
Instructor
Il'ya Muromets:
Source: Finne
Decorations:
Notes: Flight with I. I. Sikorsky St.
Petersburg–Kiev 6/30/14
Fate: K.I.A. at Gatchina flying school

Name: Rakhmin,
Rank: Lieut
Assignment: Deputy Commander XVI
Il'ya Muromets: XVI
Source: Finne & Kolyankovskiy
Decorations: Order of St. George 4th
Degree
Notes:
Fate: K.I.C. 10/8/16 in the crash of
IM-16

Name: Romanov,
Rank: Lieut
Assignment: Commander
Il'ya Muromets: II
Source: Kolyankovskiy
Decorations:
Notes:
Fate:

Name: Rudnyev, E. V.
Rank: Staff Capt
Assignment: Commander
Il'ya Muromets: I
Source: Finne & Kolyankovskiy
Decorations:
Notes: Transferred to XXXI Army
Corps Aviation Detachment
Fate: Emigrated to France at the time
of the revolution

Name: Rykachev, Mikhail
Mikhailovich
Rank: Jnr Lieut
Assignment: Head of Meteorological
unit in EVK
Il'ya Muromets:
Source: Finne
Decorations:
Notes:
Fate:

Name: Sashardukov,
Rank: Ensign
Assignment:
Il'ya Muromets:
Source: Finne
Decorations:
Notes:
Fate:

Name: Serebrennikov, A. A.
Rank:
Assignment: Engineer at R-BVZ
Il'ya Muromets:
Source: Finne & Shavrov
Decorations:
Notes: Worked with I. I. Sikorsky on
early design
Fate:

Name: Serednitskiy, A. V.
Rank: Staff Capt of Cavalry
Assignment: Deputy Commander

Kievskiy 1; Commander XVIII
Il'ya Muromets: Korabley Kievskiy 1;
XVIII
Source: Finne & Kolyankovskiy
Decorations:
Notes:
Fate: Died in airplane crash in 1926
serving with Polish AF

Name: Seversky-Prokofiev, Nicolai
Georgevich
Rank: Lieut
Assignment: Pilot
Il'ya Muromets:
Source: Finne
Decorations:
Notes: Father of Alexander and George
S-P, the latter of Republic Aircraft
Fate: Family left Russia via
Constantinople after the Revolution

Name: Sharov, Ia.
Rank: Lieut & Capt
Assignment: Commander, C-in-C EVK
(after Nizhevskiy)
Il'ya Muromets: IV
Source: Finne & Kolyankovskiy
Decorations:
Notes:
Fate:

Name: Shebarshin,
Rank: Lieut
Assignment:
Il'ya Muromets:
Source: Finne
Decorations:
Notes:
Fate:

Name: Shestov,
Rank: Lieut
Assignment: Junior Officer
Il'ya Muromets: V
Source: Finne
Decorations:
Notes:
Fate:

Name: Shidlovskiy, M
Rank:
Assignment: Mechanic
Il'ya Muromets: I

Source: Finne
Decorations:
Notes:
Fate:

Name: Shidlovskiy, Mikhail
Vladimirovich
Rank: Major General
Assignment: C-in-C EVK
Il'ya Muromets:
Source: Finne & Kolyankovskiy
Decorations: Order of St. Vladimir 2nd
Degree
Notes: Chairman of R-BVZ
Fate: Executed by Bolsheviks in 1919

Name: Shkudov,
Rank: Sgt Major
Assignment: Mechanic
Il'ya Muromets: Korabley Kievskiy 1
Source: Finne & Kolyankovskiy
Decorations: Order of St. George Cross
Notes:
Fate:

Name: Shneur, G. N.
Rank: Lieut & Capt
Assignment: Artillery Officer
Il'ya Muromets: VI & X
Source: Finne & Kolyankovskiy
Decorations:
Notes: W.I.A. 4/26/16 in IM-10
Fate: Executed in Russia 1918

Name: Shokalskiy,
Rank: Lieut
Assignment: Artillery Officer
Il'ya Muromets: I
Source: Finne & Kolyankovskiy
Decorations:
Notes:
Fate: K.I.A. 5/11/17 in crash of IM-1

Name: Sirotin, N. V.
Rank:
Assignment: Mechanic
Il'ya Muromets:
Source: Finne
Decorations:
Notes:
Fate:

Name: Smirnov, M. V.
Rank: Lieut & Capt
Assignment: Deputy Commander IV &
Kievskiy 1; Commander VIII
Il'ya Muromets: IV & Korabley
Kievskiy 1; VIII
Source: Finne & Kolyankovskiy
Decorations: Sword of St. George
Notes: W.I.A. 7/19/15 in IM-Kievskiy 1
Fate:

Name: Sofronov,
Rank: Sgt Major
Assignment: Gunner
Il'ya Muromets: I
Source: Finne & Kolyankovskiy
Decorations:
Notes:
Fate: K.I.A. 5/11/17 in crash of IM-1

Name: Soloviyev, V. A.
Rank: Staff Capt
Assignment: Commander
Il'ya Muromets: XIII
Source: Finne & Kolyankovskiy
Decorations:
Notes:
Fate:

Name: Spasov, M. P.
Rank: Lieut & Lieut-Colonel
Assignment: Deputy Commander III
Il'ya Muromets: III
Source: Finne & Kolyankovskiy
Decorations: Sword of St. George
Notes: W.I.A. 11/15/15 in crash of IM-3
Fate: Emigrated to Serbia at the time of
the revolution

Name: Speranskiy,
Rank: Ensign
Assignment:
Il'ya Muromets:
Source: Finne
Decorations:
Notes:
Fate:

Name: Stepanov,
Rank: Capt
Assignment: General Staff
Il'ya Muromets:
Source: Finne

Decorations:
Notes:
Fate:

Name: Strogonov, V. I.
Rank:
Assignment: Engineer at R-BVZ
Il'ya Muromets:
Source: Finne
Decorations:
Notes:
Fate:

Name: Talaka,
Rank: Warrant Officer
Assignment:
Il'ya Muromets: IX
Source: Kolyankovskiy
Decorations:
Notes: W.I.A. spring of 1917 in IM-9
Fate:

Name: Ulyanin, S. A.
Rank: Lieut-Colonel & Colonel
Assignment: Commandant Gatchina
Flying School
Il'ya Muromets:
Source: Finne & Kolyankovskiy &
Shavrov
Decorations:
Notes: Designed aerial camera,
Organized first IM detachment
Fate: Emigrated to England at the time
of the revolution

Name: Ushakov,
Rank: Sgt Major
Assignment: Mechanic
Il'ya Muromets: II
Source: Kolyankovskiy
Decorations:
Notes:
Fate: K.I.C. 4/1/16 in IM-2

Name: Valevachev,
Rank: Staff Capt
Assignment:
Il'ya Muromets: XIV
Source: Finne
Decorations:
Notes:
Fate: K.I.A. 5/29/16 in crash of IM-14

Name: Vebel,
Rank: Lt. Colonel
Assignment:
Il'ya Muromets: V
Source: Finne
Decorations:
Notes:
Fate:

Name: Vedeneyev,
Rank: Staff Capt of Guards
Assignment:
Il'ya Muromets: Korabley Kievskiy 3
Source: Kolyankovskiy
Decorations:
Notes: Crew member 7.5 hr flight April
1917 in IM-Kievskiy
Fate:

Name: Vitkovskiy, K. K.
Rank: Staff Capt & Lieut Colonel
Assignment: Section Operations Staff
Chief EVK
Il'ya Muromets:
Source: Finne & Kolyankovskiy
Decorations:
Notes: Member General Headquarters
Staff
Fate:

Name: Vitkovskiy, V. K.
Rank: Lieut
Assignment: Deputy Commander I
Il'ya Muromets: I
Source: Finne & Kolyankovskiy
Decorations:
Notes:
Fate: K.I.A. 5/11/17 in crash of IM-1

Name: Voinilovich, G. M.
Rank: Colonel
Assignment: Deputy commander of
EVK
Il'ya Muromets:
Source: Kolyankovskiy
Decorations:
Notes: Resigned from EVK along with
General Shidlovskiy
Fate:

Name: Von-Goerts, A. A.
Rank: Capt
Assignment: 1st Army General H.Q.

Il'ya Muromets:
Source: Finne
Decorations:
Notes:
Fate:

Name: Yankevich,
Rank: Sgt Major
Assignment:
Il'ya Muromets: IX
Source: Finne & Kolyankovskiy
Decorations: Order of St. George Cross
Notes:
Fate: K.I.C. spring 1917 in IM-19

Name: Yankevius,
Rank: Lieut
Assignment: Deputy Commander X
Il'ya Muromets: X
Source: Finne & Kolyankovskiy
Decorations: Order of St. George 4th
Degree and Sword of St. George
Notes:
Fate: K.I.A. serving with White
Russians (Donsky AF) 1919

Name: Yankovskiy, Georgii
Viktorovich
Rank: Lieut & Capt
Assignment: Commander
Il'ya Muromets: III
Source: Finne & Kolyankovskiy
Decorations:
Notes: Test pilot at R-BVZ
Fate: Emigrated to Serbia at the time of
the revolution

Name: Yetrikhovtsy,
Rank:
Assignment:
Il'ya Muromets:
Source: Finne

Decorations:
Notes:
Fate:

Name: Zagurskiy, K.
Rank: Staff Capt
Assignment:
Il'ya Muromets:
Source: Finne
Decorations:
Notes:
Fate:

Name: Zhagalov, K.
Rank: Capt
Assignment: Pilot
Il'ya Muromets:
Source: Finne
Decorations:
Notes:
Fate:

Name: Zhuravchenko, A. M.
Rank: Staff Capt
Assignment: Artillery Officer
Il'ya Muromets: V
Source: Finne & Shavrov
Decorations:
Notes: Developed aiming device for
bombing
Fate: Died in USSR in 1964

Name: Zvegintsev,
Rank: Lieut-Colonel
Assignment: Staff 3rd Army
Il'ya Muromets: III
Source: Finne & Kolyankovskiy
Decorations:
Notes: Member of the State Duma
Fate: K.I.A. 11/15/15 in crash of IM-3

This listing is not inclusive or adjusted for uniform transliteration.

Ship No: Grand; Bolshoi Baltiskiy
Type: A
IM Class No:
R-BVZ No:
Engines: 2 × 100 Argus
Commander: I.I. Sikorsky

Ship No: Grand; Bolshoi Baltiskiy
Type: A
IM Class No:
R-BVZ No:
Engines: 4 × 100 Argus
Commander: I. I. Sikorsky

Ship No: Grand; Russkiy vityaz
Type: A
IM Class No:
R-BVZ No:
Engines: 4 × 100 Argus
Commander: I.I. Sikorsky

Ship No: Il'ya Muromets
Type: B
IM Class No:
R-BVZ No: 107
Engines: 4 × 100 Argus
Commander: I.I. Sikorsky

Ship No: Il'ya Muromets Hydroplane
Type: B
IM Class No:
R-BVZ No: 107
Engines: 2 × 200 Salmson
+ 2 × 115 Argus
Commander: Lieut. Commander
Lavrov

Ship No: Kievskiy
Type: B
IM Class No:
R-BVZ No: 128
Engines: 2 × 140 Argus
+ 2 × 125 Argus
Commander: I.I. Sikorsky

Ship No: 1
Type: B
IM Class No:
R-BVZ No: 135
Engines: 4 × 140 Argus
Commander: St.Capt. Rudnyev

Ship No: 2
Type: B
IM Class No:
R-BVZ No: 136-139
Engines: 2 × 200 Salmson
+ 2 × 135 Salmson
Commander: Lieut. Pankratiyev

Ship No: 3
Type: B
IM Class No:
R-BVZ No: 136-139
Engines: 2 × 200 Salmson
+ 2 × 135 Salmson
Commander: St. Capt. Brodovich

Ship No: 4
Type: B
IM Class No:
R-BVZ No: 136-139
Engines: 2 × 200 Salmson
+ 2 × 135 Salmson
Commander: Lieut. Modrakh

Ship No: 5
Type: B
IM Class No:
R-BVZ No: 136-139
Engines: 2 × 200 Salmson
+ 2 × 135 Salmson
Commander: Lieut. Alekhnovich

Ship No: 6
Type: B
IM Class No:
R-BVZ No:
Engines: 2 × 200 Salmson
+ 2 × 135 Salmson
Commander: Lieut. Firsov

Ship No: Korabley Kievskiy 1st
Type: V
IM Class No:
R-BVZ No:
Engines: 2 × 140 Argus
+ 2 × 125 Argus
Commander: Capt. Gorskov,
Lieut. Bashko

Ship No: 1
Type: V
IM Class No:
R-BVZ No:
Engines: 4 × 150 Sunbeam
Commander: Lieut. Commander
Lavrov

Ship No: 2
Type: V
IM Class No: V-21
R-BVZ No: 167
Engines: 4 × 150 R-BVZ
Commander: St.Capt. Pankratiyev,
Lieut. Romanov

Ship No: 3
Type: V
IM Class No:
R-BVZ No:
Engines: 4 × 140 Argus
Commander: St.Capt. Brodovich,
Lieut. Ozerskiy

Ship No: 4
Type: V
IM Class No:
R-BVZ No:
Engines: 4 × 150 Sunbeam
Commander: St.Capt. Datskevich

Ship No: 5
Type: V
IM Class No:
R-BVZ No:
Engines: 4 × 150 Sunbeam
Commander: Lieut. Alekhnovich

Ship No: 6
Type: V
IM Class No:
R-BVZ No:
Engines: 4 × 150 Sunbeam
Commander: Lieut. Firsov, St.Capt.
Golovin

Ship No: 8
Type: V
IM Class No:
R-BVZ No:
Engines: 4 × 150 Sunbeam
Commander: Lieut. Smirnov

Ship No: 9
Type: V
IM Class No:
R-BVZ No:
Engines: 4 × 150 Sunbeam
Commander: Capt. Nizhevskiy

Ship No: 10
Type: V
IM Class No:
R-BVZ No:
Engines: 4 × 150 Sunbeam
Commander: Lieut. Konstenchik

Ship No: 11
Type: V
IM Class No:
R-BVZ No:
Engines: 4 × 150 Sunbeam
Commander: Lieut. Bazanov

Ship No: 12
Type: V
IM Class No:
R-BVZ No:
Engines: 4 × 150
Commander: St.Capt. Gorodetskiy

Ship No: 15
Type: V
IM Class No:
R-BVZ No:
Engines: 4 × 150 Sunbeam
Commander: St.Capt. Klembovskiy,
Lieut. Demidchev-Ivanov

Ship No: 16
Type: V
IM Class No:
R-BVZ No:
Engines: 4 × 150 Sunbeam
Commander: Lieut. Maksheyev

Ship No: 17
Type: V
IM Class No:
R-BVZ No:
Engines: 4 × 150 Sunbeam
Commander: St.Capt. Belyakov

Ship No: Korabley Kievskiy 2nd
Type: G
IM Class No:
R-BVZ No:
Engines: 4 × 140 Argus
Commander: St.Capt. Bashko

Ship No: 1
Type: G
IM Class No:
R-BVZ No:
Engines: 2 × 220 Renault
+ 2 × 150 R-BVZ
Commander: Lieut. Commander
Lavrov

Ship No: 3
Type: G
IM Class No:
R-BVZ No:
Engines: 2 × 220 Renault
+ 2 × 150 R-BVZ
Commander: Lieut. Yankovskiy

Ship No: 4
Type: G
IM Class No:
R-BVZ No:
Engines: 2 × 220 Renault
+ 2 × Argus
Commander: Lieut. Sharov

Ship No: 8
Type: G
IM Class No:
R-BVZ No:
Engines: 2 × 220 Renault
+ 2 × 150 Hall-Scott
Commander: Lieut. Lobov

Ship No: 13
Type: G
IM Class No:
R-BVZ No:
Engines: 2 × 140 Argus
+ 2 × 125 Argus
Commander: St.Capt. Solovyev

Ship No: 14
Type: G
IM Class No:
R-BVZ No:
Engines: 4 × 150 R-BVZ
Commander: St.Capt. Nikolskiy

Ship No: 18
Type: G
IM Class No:
R-BVZ No:
Engines: 2 × 220 Renault
+ 2 × 150 Hall-Scott
Commander: Cavalry St.Capt.
Serednitskiy

Ship No: 19
Type: G
IM Class No:
R-BVZ No:
Engines: 2 × 220 Renault
+ 2 × Argus
Commander: Lieut. Grek

Ship No: 20
Type: G
IM Class No:
R-BVZ No:
Engines: 2 × 220 Renault
+ 2 × 150 R-BVZ
Commander: Lieut. Pleshkov

Ship No: 5
Type: E
IM Class No:
R-BVZ No:
Engines: 4 × 220 Renault
Commander: St.Capt. Alekhnovich

Ship No: Korabley Kievskiy 3rd
Type: E
IM Class No:
R-BVZ No:
Engines: 4 × 160 Beardmore
Commander: Col. Bashko

Ship No: 9
Type: E
IM Class No:
R-BVZ No:
Engines: 4 × 220 Renault
Commander: Capt. Nizhevskiy

BIBLIOGRAPHY

Published works dealing with the history of early Russian aeronautics exist in both English and Russian. They fall into three categories: a small number of English-language titles; Russian-language titles published before the 1917 Revolution or by Russian émigrés; and books and articles published in the Soviet Union since 1917. These materials are uneven in quality, and, in comparison to the larger corpus of Soviet aviation titles, they are few in number.

One valuable bibliographical reference which includes Tsarist and Soviet titles is A. A. Zhabrov's *Annotirovannyy ukazatel' literatury na russkom yazyke po aviatsii i vozdukhoplavaniya za 50 let, 1881–1931* [Annotated guide to Russian-language literature on aviation and aeronautics for fifty years, 1881–1931] (Moscow, 1931). A more recent source of aviation-related materials is *Istoriya SSSR, Ukazatel' sovetskoy literatury za 1917–1967 gg.* [History of the USSR, guide to Soviet literature for the years 1917–1967] (Moscow: Nauka, 1977). In addition, there are numerous Soviet and Western histories of World War I, but in general they provide little coverage of or detail on the air war in the east between 1914 and 1918. This is true as well of the numerous histories of the Russian Revolution and the Civil War, covering the period 1917–1921.

Below is a selected bibliography of works in English and Russian that refer to early Russian aviation or to the career of Igor I. Sikorsky. At the end of the bibliography there is a short list of Russian periodicals, old and modern, that refer to the theme of aviation.

Books and Articles

Baldwin, S. *Vozdukhoplavatel'nyye dvigateli* [Aero engines]. St. Petersburg, 1909.

Barsh, G. V. *Vozdukhoplavaniye v yevo proshlom i nastoyashchem* [Aeronautics past and present]. St. Petersburg, 1903.

Belizhev, A. A. *40 let sovetskoi aviatsii* [Forty years of Soviet aviation]. Moscow: Znaniye, 1958.

Bobrow, Carl. "Early Aviation in Russia." *W. W.1 Aero* no. 114 (April 1987), p. 18.

Boreyko, D. A. *Ukhod za aeroplanami i gidroplanami* [The maintenance of airplanes and seaplanes]. Petrograd: A. N. Lavrov, 1916.

———. *Osnovy aviatsii* [Foundations of aviation]. Petrograd: A. N. Lavrov, 1917.

Borozdin, N. *Zavoyevaniye i letaniye, Russkiye letuny* [Aeronautics and flight: Russian aviators]. St. Petersburg: Tipographiya A. S. Suvorina, 1911.

Boyd, Alexander. *The Soviet Air Force since 1918.* London: Macdonald and Janes, 1977.

Burche, Ye. F. "Nesterov" (Part of a series on the lives of famous people). Molodaya gvardiya, 1955.

Cain, Claude W. "Flying for the Czar. Alexander Riaboff. Imperial Russian Air Service. A Photo Essay." *Cross and Cockade* vol. 11, no. 4 (Winter 1970), pp. 305–32.

Cheremnykh, N., and I. Shipilov. *A. F. Mozhaiskiy—sozdatel' pervogo v mire samoleta* [A. F. Mozhaiskiy: Creator of the first airplane]. Moscow: Voyenizdat, 1955.

Delear, Frank J. *Igor Sikorsky: His Three Careers in Aviation.* New York: Dodd, Mead & Company, 1969.

Duz', P. D. *Istoriya vozdukhoplavaniya i aviatsii v SSSR, Period 1914–1918* [A history of aeronautics and aviation in the USSR for the period 1914–1918]. Moscow: Oborongiz, 1944, 1960, and 1979).

Ferber, F. *Aviatsiya, yeye nachaloi razvitiye* [Aviation, its beginnings and development]. Kiev, 1910.

Frank, M. L. *Istoriya vozdukhoplavaniya i yego sovremennoye sostoyaniye* [The history of aeronautics and its current situation]. St. Petersburg: Izdatel'stvo Vozdukhoplavaniye, 1910.

Glagolev, N. *K zvezdam Istoriya vozdukhoplavaniya, Kn.1* [To the stars: History of aeronautics, book 1]. St. Petersburg, 1912.

———. *Vozdushnyy flot, Istoriya i organizatisya voyennogo vozdukhoplavaniya* [The air fleet: a history and organization of military aeronautics]. Petrograd: "Viktoriya," 1915.

Glavneyshiye dannyye razlichnykh samoletov (po 15 avgusta 1917 g.) Samolety, primenyayemyye na fronte (tablitsy). [Certain data on various aircraft (up to 15 August 1917), with tables on aircraft at the front. Petrograd: Uvoflot, 1917.

Golubev, V. V. *Sergei Alekseyevich Chaplygin* [Sergei Alekseyevich Chaplygin]. Moscow: TsAGI, 1947.

Hardesty, Von. *Red Phoenix: The Rise of Soviet Air Power, 1941–1945*. Washington, D.C.: Smithsonian Institution Press, 1982.

———. "Aeronautics Comes to Russia, the Early Years, 1908–1918." *Research Report 1985*, National Air and Space Museum. Washington, D.C.: Smithsonian Institution Press, pp. 23–44.

Ivanov, N. I. *Aeroplanovedeniye* [Data on airplanes]. Moscow: MOV, 1915 and 1916.

Iz neopublikovannoi perepiski N. E. Zhukovskogo [From unpublished notes of N. E. Zhukovskiy]. Moscow: TsAGI, 1957.

Jackson, Robert. *Red Falcons Soviet Airmen in Action, 1919–1969*. New York: International Publications Service, 1970.

Jones, David R. "The Birth of the Russian Air Weapon." *Aerospace Historian,* vol. 21, no. 3 (Fall 1974), pp. 169–71.

Kilmarx, Robert A. *History of Soviet Air Power*. New York: Frederick A. Praeger, 1962.

———. "The Russian Imperial Air Forces of World War I." *Airpower Historian,* vol. X, no. 3 (July 1963), pp. 90–95.

Kritskiy, P. *Podvigi russkikh aviatorov* [Heroic deeds of Russian aviators]. Yaroslav: n.p., 1915.

Kryl'ya rodiny: Sbornik [Wings of the motherland: A collection]. Moscow: DOSAAF, 1983.

Lelase, L, and R. Mark. *Problema vozdukhoplavaniya* [Problems of aeronautics]. St. Petersburg, 1910.

N. E. Zhukovskiy—Bibliografiya pechatnykh trudov [N. E. Zhukovskiy: A bibliography of printed works]. Moscow: TsAGI, 1968.

Naidenov, V. F. *Aviatsiya v 1909 godu* [Aviation in the year 1909. St. Petersburg: Tipografiya Usmanova, 1910.

———. *Zapiski po aviatsii* [Notes on Aviation]. St. Petersburg, 1911–12.

———. *Aeroplany* [Airplanes]. St. Petersburg, 1911–12.

———. ed. *Vozdukhoplavaniye, ego proshloye i nastoyashcheye* [Aeronautics: Its past and its contemporary status]. St. Petersburg, 1911.

Novarra, H. J., and G. R. Duval, eds. *Russian Civil and Military Aircraft 1884–1969*. London: Fountain Press, 1971.

Pamyati Professora Nikolaya Yegorovicha Zhukovskogo [Recollections of Professor Nikolai Yegorovich Zhukovskiy]. Moscow, 1922.

Popov, V. A., ed. *Vozdukhoplavaniye i aviatsii v Rossii do 1907 g. Sbornmik dokumentov i materialov* [Aeronautics and aviation in Russia up to 1907: A collection of documents and materials]. Moscow: Oborongiz, 1956.

Prepodavaniye vozdukhoplavaniya v institute Putey soobshcheniya imperatora Aleksandra I [Teaching of aeronautics in the Alexander I Institute of Transportation]. St. Petersburg, 1911.

Riaboff, Alexander. *Gatchina Days: Reminiscences of a Russian Pilot*. Edited by Von Hardesty. Washington, D.C.: Smithsonian Institution Press, 1985.

Rodnykh, A. A. *Istoriya vozdukhoplavaniya i letaniya v Rossii* [History of aeronautics and flying in Russia]. 2 vols. St. Petersburg: Gramotnost', 1911.

————. *Voyna v vozdukhe v byloye vremya i teper'* [The war in the air, past and present]. Petrograd: Delo, 1915.

Roustem-Bek, B. *Aerial Russia.* London: John Lane, 1916.

Russkiy morskoi i vozdushnyy flot, sooruzhennyy na dobrovol'nyye pozhertvovaniya [The Russian Naval and Air Fleet: Building through voluntary support]. St. Petersburg, 1913.

Russkoye vozdukhoplavaniye Istoriya i uspekhi [Russian aeronautics: History and successes]. St. Petersburg, 1911.

Rynin, N. A., and Naidenov, eds., V. F. *Russkoye vozdukhoplavaniye. Istoriya i uspekhi* [Russian aeronautics: Its history and successes]. St. Petersburg, 1911–13.

S. A. Chaplygin—Bibliografiya pechatnykh trudov [S. A. Chaplygin: A bibliography of printed works]. Moscow: TsAGI, 1968.

Shavrov, V. B., *Istoriya konstruktsii samoletov v SSSR do 1938 g.* [A History of aircraft design in the USSR for the period before 1938]. Moscow: Mashinostroyeniye, 1969; 3d ed., 1985.

Sher, A. S. *Kul'turno-istoricheskoye znacheniye vozdukhoplavaniya* [Cultural and historical significance of aeronautics]. St. Petersburg, 1912.

Shipilov, I. F. *Vydayushchiisya russikiy voyennyy letchik P. N. Nesterov* [Peter Nesterov: Outstanding Russian military pilot]. Moscow, 1951.

Sikorsky, Igor I. *The Story of the Winged-S: An Autobiography.* New York: Dodd, Mead & Company, 1938.

Strizhevsky, S. *Nikolai Zhukovsky, Founder of Aeronautics.* Moscow: Foreign Language Publishing House, 1957.

Tiraspol'skiy, G. L. *Vozdukhoplavaniye i vozdukholetaniye* [Aeronautics and flight]. St. Petersburg, 1910.

Trunov, K. I. *Petr Nesterov* [Peter Nesterov]. Moscow: Sovetskaya Rossiya, 1971.

Uteshev, N. I. *Zapiski po istorii voyennogo vozdukhoplavaniya* [Notes on the history of military aeronautics]. St. Petersburg, 1912.

Veygelin, K. Ye. *10–15 iyulya 1911 g. perelet S. Peterburg–Moskva* [Flight from St. Petersburg to Moscow]. St. Petersburg, 1911.

————. *Azbuka vozdukhoplavaniya* [ABCs of aeronautics]. St. Petersburg, 1912.

————. *Zavoyevaniye vozdushnago okeana, Istoriya i sovremennoye sostoyanye vozdukhoplavaniya* [Conquest of the air, ocean history, and contemporary state of aeronautics]. St. Petersburg: Knigoizdatel'stvo P. P. Soikina, 1912.

————. *Vozdushnyy spravochnik. Yezhegodnik Imp. vseross. aerokluba* [Air directory: Annual publication of the Imperial All-Russian Aero Club]. St. Petersburg: P. P. Soikin, 1912–16.

————. *Put' letchika Nesterova* [Path of the flier Nesterov]. Moscow and Leningrad, 1939.

————. *Ocherki po istorii letnogo dela* [Reflections on the history of flight]. Moscow: Oborongiz, 1940.

Vladimirov, L. *Sovremennoye vozdukhoplavaniye i yego istoriya* [Contemporary aeronautics and its history]. Kiev: n.p., 1909.

Vozdukhoplavaniye i letaniye, Russkiye letuny [Aeronautics and flight—Russian aviators]. St. Petersburg: Tipographiya A. S. Suvorina, 1911.

Yankevich, P. *Aerofotographiya Rukovodstvo vozdushnoi fotographii* [Aerial photography]. Petrograd: A. N. Lavrov, 1917.

Woodman, Harry. "Les Bombardiers geants d'Igor Sikorsky." *Le Fanatique de l'aviation* no. 150 (May 1982), p. 10; no. 151 (June 1982, p. 16.

———. "Le Sikorsky S.29.A." *Le Fanatique de l'aviation* no. 174 (May 1984), p. 28.

———. "Il'ya Muromets type 'B' of WW 1." *Airfix Magazine,* May 1985, p. 351.

Zaustinskiy, M. V. *Vozdukhoplavatel'nyye dvigateli* [Aero engines]. St. Petersburg, 1910.

Periodicals

Avtomobil' i vozdukhoplavaniye, 1911–1912.
Avtomobil'naya zhizn' i aviatsiya, 1913–1914.
Aero, 1909–1910.
Aero-i-avtomobil'naya zhizn', 1910–1914.
Aeromobil', 1912.
Biblioteka vozdukhoplavaniya, 1909–1910.
Byulleten' Moskovskogo obshchestva vozdukhoplavaniya, 1910.
Vestnik vozdukhoplavaniya, 1910–1913.
Vestnik vozdukhoplavaniya i sporta, 1913.
Vestnik vozdushnogo flota, 1918–1938.
Vestnik letchikov i aviatsionnykh motoristov svobodnoi Rossii, 1917.
Voyenno-vozdushnyy flot, 1914.
Voyennyy letchik, zhurnal Sevastopol'skoi aviatsionnoi shkoly, 1917.
Voyennyy mir, 1912–1914.
Voyennyy shornik, 1911–1914.
Vozdukhoplavaniye i sport, 1910.
Vozdukhoplavaniye, nauka i sport, 1910.
Vozdukhoplavatel', 1903–1916.
Vozdushnyy put', 1911.
K'sport!, 1911–1917.
Letaniye, 1910.
Sevastopol'skiy aviatsionnyy illustrirovannyy zhurnal, 1910–.

See also these contemporary periodicals which on occasion publish historical articles on early Russian or Soviet aviation: *Aviatsiya i kosmonavtika; Istoriya SSSR; Krasnaya zvezda; Kryl'ya rodiny; Morskoy sbornik; Vestnik PVO;* and *Voprosy istorii.*

INDEX

Sikorsky, Igor Ivanovich: Russian background, 17–18, 27; early "S" series, 28–33; early work at R-BVZ, 27, 33–34; flight to Kiev, 47–53 *passim;* as Il'ya Muromets flight instructor, 61; development of Murometsy, 40–45 *passim;* 54, 61, 138–41, 144n 7; development of S-19, 141; Russian Revolution, 147; emigration, 158, 161; work on S-29A, 162–63; "S" series flying boats, 161–64; development of helicopter, 28, 165–66; on intuitive thought, 168

Smirnov, M. V.: receives Order of St. George sword, 92; commander of IM-4, 106

Soloviyev, V. A.: commander of IM-13, 125

Spasov, M. P.: survives crash of IM-3, 100–101

Yankovskiy, G. V.: work at R-BVZ, 33

Zvegintsev, Alexander: death, 100